A HISTORY OF JAPAN

A History of Japan

From Stone Age to Superpower

Kenneth G. Henshall
Professor of Japanese Studies
University of Waikato
New Zealand

First published 1999 by
MACMILLAN PRESS LTD
Houndmills, Basingstoke, Hampshire RG21 6XS
and London
Companies and representatives
throughout the world

ISBN 0–333–74479–9 hardcover
ISBN 0–333–74940–5 paperback

A catalogue record for this book is available
from the British Library.

This book is printed on paper suitable for recycling and
made from fully managed and sustained forest sources.

10 9 8 7 6 5 4 3 2 1
08 07 06 05 04 03 02 01 00 99

Printed and bound in Great Britain by
Antony Rowe Ltd, Chippenham, Wiltshire

 Published in the United States of America by
ST. MARTIN'S PRESS, INC.,
Scholarly and Reference Division
175 Fifth Avenue, New York, N.Y. 10010

ISBN 0–312–21986–5

Contents

Contents

List of Tables

Preface

AIMS AND SOURCES

The main aim of this book is to tell the story of Japan. The story needs to be told from the beginning. It needs to be told in a balanced and comprehensive way but without becoming cluttered, and in a way that makes Japan's history accessible and understandable without becoming simplistic or superficial. Many books on Japan's history are encyclopaedic in nature and have so much detail it becomes difficult to see overall trends. Others tend to focus narrowly on a theme and omit background important for a balanced perspective. Still others tend to start Japan's story in modern times, omitting important earlier background.

Such books all have their merits, but they do tend to daunt the non-specialist. In this day and age, when so many people are interested in Japan and particularly its rise to superpower status, this seems a pity. General readers, students, and scholars in other specialist fields should all have easier access to Japan's fascinating and instructive history.

Accessibility, therefore, has been a major consideration in the writing of this book. A related consideration has been to encourage readers to follow up particular points that interest them. For these reasons I have deliberately confined my sources to those in the English language, and I have deliberately and very frequently given references with a view to readers following these up if they wish. They will not have to read Japanese to do so.

My own knowledge of Japan's history has been built up over many years from both Japanese and English sources, but not everyone can afford to spend ten years or so learning to read Japanese. When I started studying Japanese, some thirty years ago, an inability to read the script was a major barrier to acquiring any sort of authoritative knowledge of the country. This is no longer so. Nowadays there is a vast amount of material available in English, not only works written originally in English but translations of just about every major Japanese work. As a result, it is perfectly possible for the English-language reader to gain a very informed understanding of even detailed matters about Japan. Part of my aim in this book is to draw the attention of a wider reading public to this wealth of available material. In fact, there is so much available that I simply cannot touch upon all of it.

Japan's story is a fascinating one. It has elements of adventure, of mystery and intrigue, and of controversy, and I include these in the story in these pages. It is important for all readers, even if they are not academics, to know what areas and events in Japan's history are still unclear and uncertain.

Many readers will be particularly interested in how Japan became a superpower. Japan's achievements are the result of both circumstance itself and Japan's response to circumstance, a response-pattern often based on deep-rooted values and practices. I do not let these values and practices dominate my account of Japan's history, but I do highlight them and list them in the review at the end of each part, as well as writing my conclusion around them.

The periodic reviews are intended to help accessibility. Japan's history is so long and rich that it is important to stop from time to time and look back, to try to pick out major trends and events. The more we can digest of Japan's history, the greater our reward, for it is a history well worth knowing.

Romanisation

Long 'o' and 'u' are indicated by macrons except where they are initial letters.

The independent 'n' is usually rendered as 'm' when directly followed by 'b', 'm', or 'p', but this tends to be case-by-case. This should be borne in mind when following up references. Thus, for example, 'Temmu' may be 'Tenmu' in some texts.

Acknowledgements

I am particularly indebted to Ken Coates, Professor of History at the University of New Brunswick, for his insightful comments and valuable suggestions about the book as a whole. A number of other scholars and individuals around the world have commented on drafts of various sections of this book or advised on specific points, and I am grateful to them for their advice. They include Laurie Barber, Gina Barnes, Steven Lim, Derek Massarella, Tsutomu Nishigaki, Yoshio Okamoto, Ian Pool, Ray Richards, Eric Thompson, Tadashi Uda, and Brian Whitley. The shortcomings of the final product are in no way a reflection of their advice. Nor are any conclusions drawn or views asserted necessarily a reflection of their own positions.

I am also grateful to the staff at Macmillan, especially Tim Farmiloe and Vicki Johnson, for their guidance and support; to the University of Waikato for funding various overseas study trips, allowing me leave, and for buying so many books for me; and to my family and colleagues for their understanding.

Introduction: Japan and History

The impact Japan has had on the modern world is enormous. It occupies less than one three-hundredth of the planet's land area, yet wields one-sixth of the planet's economic might. There would be few homes and offices that do not rely on at least some Japanese technology. Japanese cars rule the roads. Despite recent problems with so-called 'Japanese-style management', many western and Asian managers still try to do things 'the Japanese way'. Japanese foreign aid props up many a developing country's economy. Project developers around the world seek Japanese investment. Tourist operators target the large numbers of wealthy Japanese who now travel overseas. Japan itself features as one of the most popular of all 'places I would like to visit' in western surveys. The list goes on.

A leading player on the world scene, Japan's absence from any major international forum would be unthinkable. No modern history of the world could fail to give it very considerable space.

And yet, of all the nations on the planet, Japan has come closest to annihilation. It is the only nation ever to have suffered nuclear attack. Many among its enemies in World War Two genuinely believed the extermination of the Japanese race was necessary for the safety of humankind. Even humanitarians like Franklin Roosevelt seemed to think 'ethnic cleansing' might be beneficial all round.

In the end, the Japanese survived. Far from being annihilated, Japan is one of the most powerful nations on earth. Far from being forced into inter-ethnic breeding, the Japanese remain ethnically the most homogeneous of all populations.

Japan's arrival in the world arena has been dramatic. From a quaint and obscure land of paddy fields and feudal despots just 150 years ago, it rapidly became a major contender among the imperialist powers, a military threat to the world order, and then, its crisis passed, an economic superpower. For many westerners, exotic and patronising nineteenth-century images of coolie-hatted rice farmers, doll-like geisha and funny little men trying to look civilised gave way to brutal warlords and fanatical samurai soldiers mindlessly loyal to an evil emperor. After the war the images changed again to slave-like workers controlled by ruthless capitalists out to dominate the world—and who succeeded in doing so. For many Asians, especially Chinese and Koreans, the one-time 'land of dwarfs' ceased to be a backward pupil. The pupil became a harsh master, and a vicious and exploitative one at that. Though they respect Japan's inspirational economic achievements, most Asians have still not forgiven Japan for its prewar and wartime behaviour in their lands.

Not all images have been negative. Among westerners, at the start of the twentieth century Japan was respected for its military victories over China and Russia and was considered an ally by some powers. After its defeat in World War Two, it was admired for the way it set about the task of rebuilding the nation. The 'economic miracle' that soon followed was an object for analysis, and would-be imitators looked for the key to success in its educational system, its political organisation, and particularly its management practices. Among Asians, alongside the wartime images of rape and pillage and murder there is also a grudging recognition that Japan has at least put Asia on the map in terms of world respect, and overturned western condescension. Many Asian nations are openly trying to model their economies on Japan's, despite a few pitfalls. Some, notably Malaysia, positively sing its praises.

Even though Japan in the 1990s has fallen from grace a little as a result of its economic recession and holes in its management practices, it is still clear that the current prevailing image of Japan, and its impact on the world, is largely economic in nature. In fact, Japan's focus on economic growth at the expense of quality of life and other matters has been one of the major criticisms levelled at it. At least an image of economic obsession is better than one of military fanaticism.

To understand the makings of an economic superpower it is not enough just to examine its economic development. Certainly this is important, and is dealt with in some detail in these pages. However, Japan's postwar drive to achieve economic supremacy cannot be separated from its prewar drive to achieve military supremacy—nor from its nineteenth-century drive to modernise and become a world imperialist power, or even from its grand ambitions of the seventh century to be taken seriously as a civilised nation. It is vital to consider the historical progress of the nation in broad terms.

The progression through history of any nation owes much to chance and circumstance. In Japan's case, it was largely a matter of luck that the ancient Chinese and Koreans did not take Japan seriously enough to make a concerted effort to occupy it, or that the Mongols did not do a better job of their botched invasions in the thirteenth century. The Japanese were fortunate again that in the sixteenth century the European powers of the day were more interested in exploiting the New World than Japan, thanks to a chance discovery by Columbus. Similarly, western powers of the nineteenth century were more interested in carving up China than bothering about Japan. And if America had decided to be more punitive and less constructive after the war, Japan would have been powerless to prevent it. At any of these turning-points fortune could have turned against Japan instead of for it, and produced a different history.

But a nation's historical development also owes much to the way in which it responds to circumstance—how it makes the most of opportunities and in a sense makes its own luck. These patterns of response, at least in Japan's case, are based on values and practices that often have deep roots in its history. It is impossible to understand fully Japan's emergence as a modern superpower without some understanding of these. It is important to start at the beginning, tracing Japan's development, and noting these continuities as they emerge and recur.

Along the way lie a number of probable surprises. For example, Japan has the oldest pottery vessels yet discovered anywhere in the world. On the other hand, despite its association with rice, it was the latest of all Asian nations to cultivate it. The medieval samurai was typically nothing like his modern idealised image of a loyal warrior who fought to the death for his lord. In the eighteenth century Japan had the world's largest city, and the world's most literate population. In the nineteenth century, Japan was not just following the west, as popularly believed, but busily resurrecting practices from its ancient past. In the twentieth century, Pearl Harbor was not the first Japanese strike in the Pacific War, nor was America the first victim. And for all his massive impact during the Occupation, it was not really MacArthur who designed postwar Japan but little-known planners in Washington's State Department, particularly Hugh Borton. Who?

There are also mysteries and controversies. Who exactly were the Yayoi invaders of more than 2,000 years ago? Where did they come from? How many came? Why did they come? Who was the mysterious Queen Himiko of the third century, and where was her realm of Yamatai located? Was it the same as the later Yamato, from which modern-day Japan derives? Why did the Japanese furiously adopt firearms after they were introduced by the Portuguese in the sixteenth century, but seemingly show no interest when the Mongols introduced gunpowder-based weapons three centuries earlier? In more recent times, just how much of a surprise was Japan's attack on Pearl Harbor?

How close was Japan to developing its own atom bomb? How guilty was Hirohito?

Japan's history is many things. It is an adventure story, fascinating reading even just as a simple chronicle of events. It is a mystery story, with intriguing questions yet to be fully answered. And it is a textbook, with many lessons—both dos and don'ts—for the Japanese themselves and for the world at large.

Part One

From the Stone Age to Statehood: Myths, Prehistory, and Ancient History (to 710)

1.1 MAKING GODS OF EMPERORS: ANCIENT HISTORY ACCORDING TO JAPAN'S MYTHS

In Takamagahara (the Plain of High Heaven) a number of deities have come into existence. Below lies a swirling mass of liquid. Two of the deities, Izanagi ('He Who Invites') and Izanami ('She Who Invites'), are sent to turn this liquid into land. Izanagi dips his spear into the liquid and the drops that fall coagulate into the island of Onogoro ('Self-Curdling' Island). The two deities descend to populate it.

Numerous divine offspring are produced, not only by vaginal birth but from other bodily parts and even from bodily waste. The God of Fire, alas, is one deity born vaginally, and Izanami is burned to death as she gives birth.

Her distraught husband Izanagi travels to Yomi, the Land of the Dead, to try to bring her back to the Land of the Living. However, she is shamed and angered when he sees her maggot-riddled body, and she chases him out of Yomi. As he bathes himself in a river to wash away the pollution of death, deities emerge from his clothes and eyes and nose. They include the Sun Goddess Amaterasu ('Light of Heaven') and the Storm/Sea God Susano-o ('Wild Male').

Izanagi sends Amaterasu to Takamagahara to rule over the heavens, while Susano-o is given the sea to rule. The wayward Susano-o, however, disobeys his father, who banishes him.

Before heading into exile Susano-o visits his sister Amaterasu in Takamagahara. At his suggestion they produce a number of children, but quarrel over his motives. Susano-o then torments his sister. He destroys the ridges between her rice-paddies, smears excrement on the

1

walls of her palace, and throws a flayed pony through the roof of her weaving-shed. Amaterasu retreats into a cave, plunging the universe into darkness. The other deities try to lure her back out. They hang a mirror and jewelled necklace in a tree. One goddess then performs a lewd dance, exposing herself and making all the other deities laugh uproariously. Intrigued by the laughter Amaterasu peeps out from the cave, sees the jewels and mirror, and comes out to inspect them. The deities seize her and block up the entrance to the cave with a boulder. Susano-o has his banishment enforced.

He goes to Izumo (Shimane Prefecture), where he has various adventures. On one occasion he slays a monster that has been devouring children. In one of its eight tails he finds a sword, which he later presents to his sister Amaterasu as a token of remorse.

The sword, mirror, and jewels still form the imperial regalia of Japan.

Susano-o's son, Okuninushi, is credited with pacifying the wild land. A hero, he becomes the victim of numerous treacherous acts by his jealous brothers and even by his father Susano-o. They murder him several times, but he is restored to life each time.

Okuninushi's sons agree to a request from Amaterasu to let her descendants rule the land. Her great-great-grandson, Jimmu, becomes the first ruler of Japan.

Japan's ancient myths were first recorded in the late seventh century, eventually appearing as the *Kojiki* (Record of Ancient Things) in 712 and the *Nihongi* or *Nihon Shoki* (Chronicle[s] of Japan) in 720. They were initiated by Emperor Temmu (r. 673–86), who wanted to legitimise the supremacy of the imperial family by giving it divine origins.

Given this aim, it is curious that no real distinction is made between deity and mortal, either behaviourally, morally, or in terms of creation. Apart from a few unexplained references to mysterious aboriginals,[1] the people of the myths seem to be earth-born descendants of gods or demigods, meaning that almost all Japanese could claim divine descent. At least the imperial family could claim descent from the *supreme* deity, Amaterasu, and not the fallen deity Susano-o.

The chronicles are obviously unreliable as records of historical fact.[2] Nevertheless, to the cautious observer they still provide a valuable means of understanding Japan's ancient past.

In broad terms, they reveal a clash between the imperial family (represented by Amaterasu's line) and a rival family based in Izumo (represented by Susano-o's line), which ended with the supremacy of the imperial family being 'agreed to'. This is almost certainly a reflection of real events. However, the political slant of the accounts downplays the importance of Izumo. A dramatic hint of its actual threat as a rival power-base was revealed in 1984 with the discovery there of a cache of 358 bronze swords dating back around 2,000 years. This was more than the total number of ancient swords found anywhere else in Japan.

The unusual and specific nature of many of the events in the myths, such as the incident with the flayed pony, also strongly suggests actual persons and occurrences. Such incidents provide an interesting commentary on life in ancient Japan—a world of violence and sudden death, a world where brutality and raw emotion prevail over finer feelings, and where parents kill or abandon their children and brother slays brother.

Cruelty seems to have been commonplace. On one occasion Okuninushi's brothers split open a tree, keep it open with a wedge, force him into the opening, and then remove the wedge, crushing him to death. Out of sheer malice the same brothers also trick a live skinned rabbit into bathing in saltwater and then lying in the wind, to suffer torment when its body blisters. Another episode describes a prince killing his elder brother—in the sneakiest of ways, when his victim is in the toilet— and then pulling off his limbs and throwing them away.[3]

Such cruel acts are not unknown in myths and early histories elsewhere in the world. But what is quite distinctive about the Japanese myths is an avoidance of moral judgement as to good and evil. Certain acts bring censure and punishment, but no moral sermonising. For example, Susano-o is simply removed as disruptive rather than condemned as evil. Gods and their earth-born descendants are as good and as bad as each other. Behaviour is accepted or rejected depending on the situation, not according to any obvious set of universal principles. This is exactly what many commentators remark upon in present-day Japanese behaviour. The roots of such behaviour clearly run deep.

1.2 THE EARLIEST INHABITANTS (TO CA 13,000 BC)

No one is quite sure when the first humans appeared in Japan. Claims have been made for a date as far back as 500,000 years, and some even expect a history of a million years to be proven in due course. The general agreement at present allows for around 200,000 years, though the earliest definite human fossil remains are only about 30,000 years old.[4]

Until the end of the last glacial period, around 15,000 years ago, Japan was joined to the Asian mainland by a number of land bridges.

These were through Sakhalin to the north, Tsushima to the west, and the Ryūkyū Islands to the south. In other words, migration into the area was not difficult. Immigrants arrived in waves, particularly from east and southeast Asia some 30,000 years ago, followed by people from northeast Asia about 14,000 years ago.[5]

It is hard to paint a picture of Palaeolithic (Old Stone Age) life with any certainty. One major difficulty is that much of the coastline of that time is now deep under water. There may have been far more coastal activity than the surviving inland sites suggest.

The picture emerging so far is basically one of small and seasonally mobile groups of hunter-gatherers. The hunters targeted not only boar and deer but also big game such as elephant and bison, though these were becoming scarcer in the last Palaeolithic phase due to climatic warming and increased hunting by a growing population. Gatherers searched for a variety of berries and nuts such as hazel.

Palaeolithic groups were made up of a small number of extended families, and totalled between 20 and 150 individuals. Extended families were important for the rearing of children, since many parents were dead before their thirties, and there were many orphaned children needing the protection of the longer-lived among the adults.[6] Although the population was growing it probably never exceeded 20,000.

As nomadic hunter-gatherers most groups had only temporary seasonal bases. However, there was some—but limited—stable settlement towards the end of the period. There was also a degree of specialisation, which led to trading. As early as 20,000 years ago obsidian (volcanic glass valued for tool-making) was traded over at least 150 km. This was almost certainly carried by water, indicating that watercraft were in use from very early times.

Stone Age people are popularly portrayed as cave dwellers. However, at least in the case of Japan, caves seem only rarely to have been used as sites of significant permanent occupation—though quite a large number of caves were used as temporary shelters. The preference for open-space sites suggests the widespread use of artificial shelter, though the nature of this is unclear.

Important Palaeolithic sites include Babadan and Takamori in Miyagi Prefecture, Hoshino in Tochigi Prefecture, Fukui Cave in Nagasaki Prefecture, Nogawa near Chōfu in Tōkyō Prefecture, Iwajuku in Gunma Prefecture, and Minatogawa in Okinawa. Judging by a 155 cm male skeleton excavated at Minatogawa and estimated to be around 17,000 years old, Palaeolithic people in Japan appear to have been small by modern standards but similar to other Palaeolithic peoples elsewhere in east Asia.

Knowledge of Japan's prehistoric past was hampered till after World War Two by the tendency of Japanese archaeologists to interpret their finds in line with the pseudo-historical accounts in early chronicles such as the *Kojiki* and *Nihon Shoki*.[7] Knowledge of the period is now increasing but much still remains to be discovered. It is still not even clear whether the first inhabitants were *homo sapiens* or the earlier *homo erectus*.

1.3 STONE-AGE HUNTERS AND GATHERERS: THE JŌMON PERIOD (CA 13,000 BC–CA 300 BC)

Around 13,000 BC pottery vessels appeared in Japan. They are the oldest in the world.[8] They also mark the beginning of the Jōmon period, named after the *jōmon* (cord-pattern) found impressed on much of that pottery.

Pottery vessels might suggest a settled lifestyle. Settlement did increase during the period, especially from around 5,000 BC. Groups also expanded into larger tribal communities. The largest Jōmon village yet discovered, at Sannai-Maruyama in Aomori Prefecture, thrived for about 1,500 years between 3,500 BC and 2,000 BC. It covered almost 100 acres and may have had as many as 500 inhabitants at its peak. It is even seen by some as suggesting that Japan could have been a cradle of early civilisation.[9]

Settlement is also associated with agriculture. Primitive slash-and-burn agriculture may have been practised in the west of the country as early as 5,700 BC, but this remains to be confirmed.[10] Also awaiting confirmation are the remains of what appears to be a prehistoric farming community, unearthed very recently at Bibi in Hokkaidō.[11] Dating back to around 4,000 BC, if confirmed this would be the oldest evidence of real farming in Japan. Rice was introduced into the southwest of the country from the continent towards the end of the period, around 1,000 BC,[12] along with millet and barley, but was not widely grown. When it was, it was in dry-fields or marshes rather than paddies. Prior to these introduced plants the most important cultivated plants were probably the beefsteak herb and barnyard grass.

However, despite the pottery and the occasional evidence of farming, the life of the Jōmon people was for the most part one of hunting and gathering, particularly on the coast. Settlements were typically of a semi-permanent nature, in the form of a base camp in a given area, and had around a dozen dwellings. These dwellings were usually pit-houses with thatched roofs reaching down to the ground.

Inland Jōmon people, using the bow and arrow that appeared around the same time as pottery, mostly hunted boar and deer. At times they also ate a variety of creatures from frogs to badgers to wolves to the Siberian lion—in fact, seemingly the entire range of Japan's rich fauna. The dog was the only domesticated animal during the period.

Many if not most Jōmon people dwelt on the coast, and became particularly adept at using marine resources, from shellfish to oceanic fish. So well did they adapt to this life that Jōmon skeletons, particularly of the latter half of the period, show development of bony protection for the ear mechanisms, strongly suggesting regular and frequent diving.[13] The reason for this coastal preference was that the warming of the climate around 15,000 years ago, which cut off the land bridges, also meant a warming of the seas and an increase in marine resources. Shellfish in particular became a major food source for thousands of years, as evidenced by huge shell mounds such as at Natsushima near Tōkyō Bay.

The climate started to cool again around 5,000 years ago, and sea-levels receded. Greater use was then made of inland resources. However, many Jōmon people returned to the coast within a thousand years or so, despite the still cooling climate. This suggests their preference for the life of coastal foragers and fishers was persistent.

The introduction of rice around 3,000 years ago was probably from China through Korea, where rice cultivation slightly predates that in Japan, though opinion is divided as to the route.[14] Many present-day Japanese make much of the nation's association with rice and assume it has been grown there from time immemorial, but in fact Japan was the last of the Asian nations to adopt rice cultivation.

It can be misleading to think of the Jōmon period as a single fixed entity, for it contained significant variety, both in terms of region and time.[15] Regional variety clearly reflected local conditions, producing for example subcultures such as that centred on deep-sea fishing on the northeast coast. Variety over time reflected not only the warming and cooling of the climate, but the development of new technology. For example, hempcloth was produced from around 5,000 BC, and lacquerware from around 4,000 BC.

The population also seems to have varied over time, often for reasons that are not clear. Though estimates vary and are really only 'best guesses', it was probably around 20,000 at the start of the period, rose to around 100,000 by about 5,000 BC, leapt up to more than twice that by around 3,000 BC (despite the cooling of the climate), then fell back again to about 100,000 by the end of the period. Moreover, again for reasons that are unclear, by this stage the population was gathered largely in the north and northeast.[16]

Other broad changes over time include a progressive increase in awareness of the supernatural. This brought increased shamanism and ritualism, new burial practices, mysterious stone circles in northern Japan, and figurines that seem to have a supernatural significance. Representations of snakes in some locations suggest snake worship.[17]

The increased importance of religious ritual brought about a need for specialised knowledge of procedure. This in turn would have helped lead to differentiation in levels of status within society. Tribal chiefs too, along with the more capable hunters and producers, obviously enjoyed a higher status than most. However, it remains a contested issue as to whether Jōmon society was mainly hierarchical or egalitarian.[18]

It is highly likely that over such a long span of time as the Jōmon period, sundry groups would have migrated into Japan from various points, adding a certain degree of ethnic diversity.[19] The disappearance of the land bridges would not have meant a total severing of links with the mainland. Somebody, for example, introduced rice. The number of these immigrants is open to question, but they were perhaps not very numerous, or at least not very different physically, for there seems to have been a recognisable 'Jōmon type'.

Jōmon people as a whole are invariably described as short-statured. There are confusing differences in the heights given by experts, but in general Jōmon males towards the end of the period seem to have been around 157 cm and females 148 cm.[20] These heights contrast with those of the subsequent Yayoi immigrants who arrived around 300 BC and marked a new era. The Yayoi were some 3 or 4 cm taller and little different from their modern Japanese descendants at the start of the twentieth century.[21]

As well as being relatively short in stature, the Jōmon people typically had a stocky muscular appearance. They had heavy skeletons, flattened leg bones, and wide, square faces.

In fact, the Jōmon people bore considerable similarity to the present-day Ainu of Hokkaidō. This is not surprising, for studies by physical anthropologists confirm that the Ainu are unmistakably descended from Jōmon people.[22] This sets them apart from modern Japanese in the other main islands, who show greater descent from the Yayoi. It is unclear when exactly they arrived in the country, or even exactly where from,[23] but Ainu certainly have a very great antiquity as inhabitants of Japan.

The Ainu are in effect the original Japanese. For many centuries the Yayoi-derived modern Japanese (known in this context as Yamato

Japanese) were to deny this, and to marginalise or even ignore the Ainu. It was not until 1997 that there was official recognition of the Ainu's true status as indigenous Japanese.[24]

We see in the Ainu the Jōmon origins of Japan, but Jōmon Japan was still far from being a nation. The following Yayoi period was to contribute far more to the emergence of Japan as we know it today.

1.4   NEW BEGINNINGS: THE YAYOI PERIOD (CA 300 BC–CA AD 300)

Around 300 BC Japan was effectively invaded. Immigrants arrived in number from the continent, immigrants different in appearance and culture from the Jōmon people. They were lighter and taller, with narrower faces. Their culture included technology such as bronze and iron, and was also more rice-based than that in Japan.

There is great diversity of opinion over the nature and scale of this immigration, and even the motives and origins of the immigrants.[25] The picture is confused, but what is clear is that newcomers arrived and were to change Jōmon Japan forever.

The period when this change started takes its name from the Yayoi district in Tōkyō, where in 1884 a new, plain, reddish type of pottery was first found and recognised as different from Jōmon. The name does not convey the dynamism of the period, for at the time this was not realised.

The period has always been strongly associated with rice. At first it was thought that rice had been brought by the immigrants, but this is now known to be an over-simplification. Rice had been introduced almost a thousand years earlier. However, it was during the Yayoi period that rice cultivation first became established on any significant scale,[26] particularly in paddies and particularly in the south and west of the country, and this clearly reflected the cultural preferences of the newcomers. It was to become a cultural foundation for subsequent Japanese through to the present.

The spread of rice cultivation, like the spread of bronze and iron, reflected the probable movement of the immigrants. From the southwest it moved fairly quickly to the middle of Honshū by about the first century AD, but was slower to extend further north. Although rice, bronze, and iron were present here from an early stage, they were not adopted on any significant scale, and northern Japan was effectively to remain in a 'Continuing Jōmon' phase till around the eighth century or even later. In other words, there was a substantial cultural gap between north and south—one still symbolised today by the Ainu presence in Hokkaidō.[27]

Japan has limited metal ore of its own, so metal implements tended to be associated with high status. However, the possession of metal 'status goods' was not the only factor in the increasing social stratification that forms a major characteristic of the period. As with most agricultural development, rice cultivation brought about a narrowing of the resource base within a community, making it easier for it to be controlled by social elites. It also brought about far more permanent settlement, giving rise to greater territorial identification and—particularly as the population grew to around 2 million—the need to defend and expand boundaries. This led in turn to increased fighting, in which those who possessed metal weapons—in addition to the ability to muster warrior forces—had their status further strengthened. And of course, increasing warfare between tribes led to inter-tribal ranking in terms of winners and losers.

In this increasingly ranked world, slavery was not uncommon. Lower-ranking persons who met a superior on the road stepped aside and bowed as the superior passed—a practice that continued right through to the nineteenth century. Rank was differentiated by a range of titles, and men of high status had four or five wives, as opposed to the two or three wives of lower-ranking men.[28]

Another factor adding to the stratification was wealth, particularly as a result of trade. Some tribes were lucky enough to have some of Japan's scant metal resources in their own territory. Others benefited from new technological developments, such as that of silk, which was produced in Kyūshū from around the first century AD. There were also developments in glass technology and metallurgy. This increased diversity of products led to increased trade, both with the continent and within Japan, and each district had a marketplace. One such exchange centre, Asahi in Aichi Prefecture, is the largest Yayoi settlement yet found, covering almost 200 acres as opposed to the 5–70 acres of the typical settlement.

The combination of inter-tribal warfare, the emergence of elites, and competition for control of resources led to increasing politicisation. Many chiefdoms entered into strategic tribal allegiances with neighbours, leading to the formation of numerous small kingdoms.[29]

Much of our knowledge of these kingdoms, as indeed of life in general in Yayoi Japan, is gleaned from Chinese documents. The first written mention of the country is found in the *Han Shu* (History of Han), a

Chinese history completed around AD 82. It referred to the land of Wa—then meaning 'The Land of Dwarfs'[30]—as comprising 100 kingdoms, whose envoys regularly brought tribute to the Chinese base at Lo-lang in Korea.[31] A far more detailed description is given in the *Wei Chih* (History of Wei, one of the three kingdoms of China at the time) of AD 297, in a section on 'eastern barbarians' that also includes various peoples of Korea and Manchuria.[32]

The *Wei Chih* recounts a visit to Wa in 240 by Wei Chinese. In particular it describes the strongest of the 100 kingdoms, Hsieh-ma-t'ai, usually rendered in Japanese as 'Yamatai'. Yamatai was ruled by an unmarried shaman-queen called Himiko. She was a rather mysterious figure who achieved power after many years of warfare, and 'occupied herself with magic and sorcery, bewitching the people'.[33] Living permanently within a fortress she was guarded by 100 men, and served by 1,000 women and a single male attendant. It was through this male attendant that she communicated with the outside world. She concerned herself with spiritual matters, and left the administrative aspects of ruling to her younger brother.

In 238 Himiko sent a tributary delegation to the Chinese emperor, following a practice observed since at least AD 57 by some of the rulers of other kingdoms in Wa.[34] As a result, like those other rulers, she had her regal status officially recognised by China. However, unlike the others, she seems to have been recognised as sovereign of the whole land of Wa, not just of a kingdom within it. She also received gifts from the emperor of various cloths, jewels, and mirrors. Her own gifts to him included slaves, cloths, and cinnabar.

According to the Chinese historians she died in 248 at the age of 65, accompanied by 100 sacrificed slaves. Chaos followed her death, till a 13-year-old girl named Iyo, a relative of Himiko, eventually came to the throne after the abortive accession of a male ruler whom the people refused to obey.

Yamatai was the centre of power in Japan, with many if not most other kingdoms giving allegiance to it. It has also long been the centre of controversy as to its location, for surprisingly this is not clear. The description of the journey in the *Wei Chih* is open to very different interpretations. Most experts equate Yamatai with Yamato in the Nara Basin area, which was to be the site of the first Japanese state a few hundred years later, but others see it as located in north Kyūshū.[35]

The descriptions of Wa/Japan found in the *Wei Chih* and other Chinese documents represent a significant distinction between the Yayoi period and earlier periods—a shift from prehistory to recorded history.

The period itself was an intense and even revolutionary one of great change over a relatively short span of time. It witnessed a leap from hunting and gathering to cultivation, and from stone tools to metal tools. Settlements became fixed, and society became clearly stratified. These changes created the economic and technological base for a social and political unification into a state.[36]

1.5 THE EARLY STATE EMERGES: THE KOFUN/YAMATO PERIOD (CA 300–710)

When Queen Himiko was buried with her 100 slaves it was obvious that a large tomb was needed—100 paces in diameter, according to the *Wei Chih*. This was to set the fashion for some centuries. As society became more stratified, those at the top wanted to show their status beyond the span of their mere mortal life. As with the pyramids in ancient Egypt, huge tombs were erected. In Japan's case they were usually raised mounds (*kofun*) surrounded by hollow clay figurines known as *haniwa* ('clay rings').

The *haniwa* are rather mysterious, but seem to have been a combination of tomb markers and status objects. There were also objects inside the tomb, probably for the afterlife. Many of these, too, were status objects, but it was not all a case of mere ostentation. The tombs also contained large numbers of weapons, leaving no doubt as to the ability of the ruling elite to maintain their position by force if necessary.[37]

The burial mounds are convenient physical symbols of this period. The most important feature of the period, however, is the emergence of the Yamato state, named after its power-base at Yamato in the Nara Basin.

The pre-eminence of Yamato forms the substance of the *Kojiki* and *Nihon Shoki* accounts. We saw earlier that these do not reveal much about the actual process, other than a triumph over a rival power-base at Izumo by what appears to have been negotiation. Dates are also unreliable. Most experts now believe the first verifiable emperor was Suijin. The *Nihon Shoki* lists him as the tenth emperor and gives his death as equivalent to AD 30, whereas the *Kojiki* gives it as AD 258. In fact, 318 seems most likely.[38]

Some believe that Suijin may have been the leader of a group of fourth-century invaders from Korea known as the 'horse-riders', and that it was these horse-riders who established the Yamato state.[39] This is not impossible, but it seems more likely that Suijin was of the Yamato clan, and that his clan increased their power and authority by a gradual process of degree. In this they relied heavily on negotiation and persuasion—and no doubt threat and coercion—rather than simple military confrontation. Their preferred method seems to have been to incorporate local chiefdoms already established in Yayoi times, and give the chieftains themselves places within the Yamato hierarchy. Ranks and titles were used by the Yamato court to give potentially troublesome members of formerly independent local regimes a personal stake in the emerging imperial system.[40]

The tactic of where possible incorporating a powerful threat rather than directly confronting it, and of drawing on a potential opponent's strengths rather than trying simply to destroy them, is still widely seen today as a basic Japanese preference.[41] Its identification at such an early stage of Japanese history is testimony to the depth of such a tradition.

The ranks and titles given to those local kings and chiefs incorporated into the Yamato camp were important in a status-conscious age. The Yamato administrative system was strongly hierarchical.[42] This, too, is a continuing characteristic of Japanese preferences.

Exact dates remain unclear. It is probable that during the fourth and fifth centuries Yamato authority was not absolute but rather 'first among equals' among a coalition of clans. By the early sixth century, however, the Yamato imperial family seems to have emerged as the single prevailing line. It was at this point that rulers of the Izumo region started to send tribute to the Yamato ruler.[43]

A sense of statehood is also suggested in a poem attributed to the late fifth-century emperor Yūryaku (r. 456–79):[44]

> Your basket, with your pretty basket,
> Your trowel, with your pretty trowel,
> Maiden, picking herbs on this hillside,
> I would ask you: Where is your home?
> Will you not tell me your name?
> Over the spacious Land of Yamato
> It is I who reign so wide and far,
> It is I who rule so wide and far.
> I myself, as your lord, will tell you
> Of my home, and my name.

The Yamato state soon entrenched its position by the adoption and promotion of Buddhism. This was especially favoured by the Soga, a particularly powerful clan within the Yamato structure. The Soga were of Korean descent, like many of the aristocratic families of the day, and probably felt more of an affinity with Buddhism than did native Japanese. It was from Korea—specifically priest-scholars from the Korean kingdom of Paekche—that Buddhism was introduced in the mid-sixth century. Its adoption was greatly aided by the practice of writing, which had also been introduced by scholars from Paekche a century earlier.[45]

The Soga saw Buddhism as a means of developing a state religion that would further their political control, which by means such as inter-marriage they were starting to assert over the imperial family. They were undoubtedly a persuasive element in the acceptance of the religion by the imperial family from Emperor Yōmei (r. 585–7) on.

For its part, the imperial line also saw Buddhism as politically very useful. It provided a unifying ideology for the new nation. Its identification with the imperial family also meant that the spread of Buddhism helped spread acceptance of imperial authority. Moreover, and very importantly, it conferred a degree of Chinese-style dignity and civilisation on the newly emerging state.[46]

Japan did very much want to be taken seriously. This was not just as a deterrent against possible further invasion. It was a genuine wish to achieve the best, to become a strong nation. To this end it was soon to adopt a range of Chinese practices, till eventually it could feel it had out-done China and had nothing left to learn. Here again we see an early example of the incorporation of the strengths of others, combined with a willingness to learn and emulate.

During much of Japan's Kofun period China was not at its strong-est. In fact, it was in considerable turmoil, with a multiplicity of chang-ing power-bases and dynasties between the end of the Late Han period in 220 and the start of the T'ang in 618. For some of this time the country was divided into the three kingdoms of Wei, Wu, and Shu Han.

The Korean peninsula, which was generally the closest point of 'for-eign' contact for Japan, was also characterised by the coexistence of three major kingdoms between 300 and 668. These were Paekche and Silla in the south, and Koguryo (from which the modern name Korea derives) in the north. Wedged between Silla and Paekche there was also a small area called Kaya (Mimana in Japanese), which was a confedera-tion of some half-dozen chiefdoms or minor kingdoms.

The *Nihon Shoki* treats Kaya as a Japanese colony, but this is unlike-ly.[47] So, too, is the claimed invasion of Silla by the legendary 'Empress'

Jingū, a fourth-century shaman-ruler. Many aspects of Japan's relations with these Korean kingdoms are unclear, but its relations with both Kaya and Paekche were generally strong and beneficial. Japan benefited not only from the introduction of writing and Buddhism but also from access to valuable sources of iron ore.

Its relations with Silla were not so good, and as Silla rose to dominance on the Korean peninsula from the mid-sixth century Japan's involvement there waned. It came to a definitive end a century later in 663 when the Japanese fleet was destroyed by Silla's fleet in a naval battle off Korea. Silla then went on to establish control over the Korea peninsula, bringing the period of the Three Kingdoms to an end a few years later. Fortunately for the new Yamato rulers, Silla does not seem to have been interested in following up its victory by attempting to invade Japan—though the Japanese did take the precaution of building a fortified defensive base in north Kyūshū, known as the Dazaifu, which was to become an important centre over the next few centuries.

Japan's emulation of China was particularly seen in the activities of Yōmei's second son, Prince Shōtoku (Shōtoku Taishi, 574–622), who was half Soga by blood. Probably the best-known figure of those times, from 594 till his death in 622 Shōtoku was regent under Empress Suiko (r. 593–628). He greatly contributed not only to the promotion of Buddhism by the building of numerous temples but to the promotion of all things Chinese. Among other things he was responsible for re-establishing missions to a now reunified China, and for introducing the Chinese-style 'cap rank' system in which, as the name suggests, the rank of officials was indicated by their hat.

Shōtoku is also credited with drawing up the so-called Seventeen Article Constitution of 604, which was intended to strengthen central government. It had a strong Chinese flavour, particularly in its Confucianism.[48] Though deemed a constitution it was, however, largely a set of guidelines for officials, with a particular emphasis on harmony (*wa*) and loyalty to the divine and therefore legitimate authority of the imperial line. Something of its nature can be seen from the opening words of Article One, which quote Confucius and state that 'Harmony is to be valued', and from the opening words of Article Eight, which are of a less grand and more specific character: 'Let the ministers and functionaries attend the court early in the morning, and retire late.'[49]

The Soga clan was the major influence in the early Yamato court, often controlling the imperial line itself. However, in 645 it was overthrown in a coup led by Fujiwara no Kamatari (614–99). The Fuji-wara were to dominate court life in Japan for some centuries to come. But they did not change the Soga clan's promotion of things Chinese. Along with the future Emperor Tenji (r. 661–71), Kamatari put in place a number of ambitious reforms based on the Chinese model of central government. These reforms are known collectively as the Taika (Great Change) Reform(s) of 645.

One major reform was the nationalisation of land. Paddies were henceforth to be allocated by the government. Every six years all free adult males received approximately 0.3 acres, and females 0.2 acres. Other reforms included taxation in the form of produce and not simply labour, a restructuring of ranks, and, in contrast to the previous practice of shifting capitals, the establishment of a permanent capital (at Nani-wa, present-day Osaka, though in practice this did not remain the capital for more than a few years). Moreover, orders were given for the surveying and registering of land and population. Taxation prac-tices and claimed ranks of various local officials were investigated with a view to eliminating corruption. Unauthorised weapons were confiscated.

Chinese-style law codes were drawn up in connection with these reforms. They emphasised the authority of the emperor and thus the centralisation of power, and they also addressed the rationalisation of bureaucracy. These various laws are known generically as *ritsuryō*, *ritsu* being essentially penal sanctions and *ryō* being instructions for offi-cials.[50] Though not always carried out as intended, *ritsuryō* law during the eighth century permitted a small group of around 400 officials to control a country of about 5 million people.[51]

The population had grown markedly through the Yamato period from the estimated 2–3 million at the end of the Yayoi period. Though small relative to China's population of more than 60 million, the 5 million or so people in Japan at the end of the seventh century rep-resented a huge figure compared to European populations of the time.[52]

Population growth seems to have progressed in waves. The birth rate was high but so too was the mortality rate, especially among infants. A major factor in this were the waves of epidemic disease such as smallpox transmitted through extensive contact with the continent, against which the insular Japanese had developed little or no immunity.[53]

Some idea of the helplessness of people in the face of the ravages of these diseases is seen in the poetry of Yamanoue Okura (ca 660–733). An official eventually elevated to the rank of minor aristocrat but of humble origin, Okura was one of the few poets before modern times to write of everyday life, including subjects shunned by other poets such as illness and poverty. Moreover, he was a true family man, one of the few 'manager-officials' ever recorded in Japan's history to leave a function early and openly in order to spend time with his family.[54] He is thus a valuable source of information on 'real life' around this point in history. He writes as follows on the death of his young son Furuhi.[55]

> The seven treasures
> Prized by man in this world—
> What are they to me?
>
> Furuhi, the dear white pearl
> That was born to us,
> With dawn would not leave our bed,
> But, standing or lying,
> Played and romped with us.
> With the evening star,
> Linking hands with us,
> He would say
> 'Come to bed, father and mother,
> Let me sleep between you,
> Like sweet daphne, triple-stalked.'
> Such were his pretty words.
> For good or ill
> We should see him grow to manhood—
> Or so we trusted,
> As in a great ship.
> Then, beyond all thought,
> Blowing hard, a sudden crosswind
> Of illness
> Overwhelmed him.
> Lacking skill and knowing no cure,
> With white hemp I tied my sleeves,
> Took my mirror in my hand
> And, lifting up my eyes,
> To the gods in heaven I prayed;
> My brow laid on the ground,
> I did reverence to the gods of the earth.
> 'Be he ill or be he well,

It is in your power, O gods.'
Thus I clamoured in my prayers.

Yet no good came of it,
For he wasted away,
Each dawn spoke less,
Till his life was ended.

I stood, I jumped, I stamped,
I shrieked, I lay on the ground,
I beat my breast and wailed.
Yet the child I held so tight
Has flown beyond my clasp.
Is this the way of the world?

Though life for the ordinary person was far from easy, the Yamato state was in place, and the nation Japan had been formed. State-level societies are generally characterised by effective unification, by social stratification and differentiation of population categories, and by the legitimisation of power through a militia, criminal code, and legal constitution, with the ruler governing with the aid of written law.[56] All of these requirements were in place by the end of the Kofun period. The modern name Nippon or Nihon (Source of the Sun) was also coming into use by the end of the period.[57]

This does not mean of course that everyone recognised the nation as such, for some of those geographically far removed from the Yamato power-base continued to consider themselves independent for some centuries to come.[58] However, at least the structure was in place.

The imperial family was also well entrenched, for towards the end of the period Emperor Temmu commissioned the chronicles that would legitimise the imperial line by giving it a divine heritage. In fact, it became so well entrenched that it still survives today, the world's longest imperial lineage.

It may seem strange that an imperial family that officially espoused Buddhism should legitimise itself through the gods of Shintō, but this is simply another example of Japanese pragmatism. To this day the Japanese continue to particularise religion, following one religion in one context and another religion in another context. This 'pragmatic religiosity', like the avoidance of moral distinction between good and evil that in other cultures is usually based on religious values, clearly has deep roots.

REVIEW OF PART ONE

In Part One we have seen the development of civilisation in Japan from a primitive land of Palaeolithic hunter-gatherers to a sophisticated court-centred state. The 1,000 years from around 300 BC to around AD 700 have been seen to be particularly important, spanning key developments such as those outlined in Table 1.1 below.

Table 1.1   Key developments in the period ca 300 BC–ca AD 700

Development	Approximate Time
Shift from hunting and gathering to relatively stable rice-based agriculture	300 BC–AD 0
Arrival of immigrants from the continent	300 BC
Introduction of metal	300 BC
Emergence of kingdoms	AD 0?
Establishment of social stratification	AD 0 on
Continued contact with continental cultures	AD 50 on
Emergence of the Yamato state	AD 300–AD 500
Introduction of writing	AD 450
Introduction of Buddhism	AD 550
Adoption of Chinese political-legal-administrative systems	AD 600–700
Production of a mythology to legitimise Yamato rule by attributing divine authority to it	AD 700

Many matters are still unclear, such as the nature and scale of Yayoi immigration. However, knowledge of ancient Japan is increasing. Many earlier assumptions are now known to be incorrect.

There is now recognition of the diversity and change within Japan's ancient past. But there are also elements of continuity. The establishment of the Yamato imperial line, the world's longest imperial lineage, provides a constant element through all succeeding historical periods until the present day. Certain policies and preferences, such as a desire to learn from others in order to strengthen oneself, and an avoidance of judgement as to good or evil, also have great bearing on present-day Japanese behaviour. These policies and behavioural patterns are based on values and practices summarised in Table 1.2.

Table 1.2   Key values and practices in the ancient period

- avoidance of moral judgements as to good or evil
- pragmatic behaviour particularised to the situation rather than based on universal principles
- incorporation of potential threat
- adoption of the strong points of others
- desire to make Japan a strong and respected nation
- willingness to learn
- preference for ranking and hierarchy
- practical approach to religion

We have seen, in short, the birth of a nation, a nation with distinct characteristics.

Part Two

Of Courtiers and Warriors: Early and Medieval History (710–1600)

2.1 LEARNING FROM THE CHINESE—WITHIN LIMITS: THE NARA PERIOD (710–794)

The Yamato state needed a capital. Without this its centralised system of control would have no real core. In the final stages of the Yamato period there had been a few attempts to establish a permanent capital, but these had all failed for one reason or another.[1]

Then, in 710, the capital was moved to Heijō, better known now as Nara. Nara was modelled on the T'ang Chinese capital, Ch'ang-an. It was a similar rectangular grid pattern, but at 20 sq km was only about a quarter of Ch'ang-an's area.

In less than a hundred years the capital was to move again. Nara proved not to be the hoped-for permanent site. Nevertheless, it represents the high point of the Japanese effort to learn from China. Physically, China's influence was seen not only in the design of the city but also in grand buildings such as the Tōdaiji Temple—the largest wooden building in the world—and the huge bronze statue of Buddha it contained. In broader terms, the age of the Nara capital may have been brief, but it shows most clearly the workings of the *ritsuryō* and other Chinese-inspired political and legal reforms.

And it was during the age of Nara that Chinese writing led to the appearance of the first real books produced in Japan, the *Kojiki* and *Nihon Shoki* chronicles of 712 and 720. These were followed shortly afterwards by the first poetry anthologies, the *Kaifūsō* (Fond Recollections of Poetry) of 751 and the *Manyōshū* (Collection of Ten Thousand Leaves) of 759. Some documents were even printed—another Chinese influence.[2]

However, the respect for things Chinese did not lead to indiscriminate imitation. More often than not there were distinctive Japanese modifications to Chinese 'imports'.

For example, the 'cap rank' system introduced earlier by Prince Shōtoku was in theory based, as in China, on merit not birth. However, in practice, and particularly during the Nara period, both rank and position in the Japanese bureaucracy quickly became determined by inherited family status rather than by individual merit.[3] That is, the examination-based meritocracy of China's bureaucratic world was not too palatable to the Japanese. This is ironic in view of the prominence of examinations in present-day Japan, but understandable from the perspective of an established elite wishing to safeguard control and stability.[4]

The *Kojiki* and particularly the *Manyōshū* already show the embryonic development of a distinctly Japanese writing system, albeit based on Chinese characters. The law codes, too, show significant modification, such as in the leniency of punishments in morally tolerant Japan relative to those in China.[5] The land allotment system also differed, particularly in that women were allotted land in Japan but not at all in T'ang China.

Another very important modification of Chinese practices was that of the 'mandate of heaven'. In China an emperor ruled with the mandate of heaven only while he acted virtuously. He could be removed if he was felt to have strayed from the path of virtue. This was 'overlooked' in Japan, where the Yamato rulers preferred to be legitimised by divine descent rather than the judgement of the people.

The use of the male pronoun above is deliberate, for the Chinese preferred their emperors to be male. This was one thing that was not modified in Japan. Although there were half-a-dozen reigning empresses in very early Japan, from 770 to the present only two females were to ascend the Japanese throne, both briefly and both in name only.[6]

Life was not, of course, confined to the courts. For all the great advances of the day, there was much suffering and hunger among the common people. A document of 730, for example, lists no fewer than 412 out of 414 households in Awa (in present-day Chiba Prefecture) as existing at what was considered the bare 'subsistence level. Similar figures, of 996 out of 1,019, are recorded for households in what is now Fukui Prefecture.[7]

Only around 1.8 million acres of land was cleared for paddy, so there was simply not enough land for the allotment system to work properly for very long. And agricultural technology was inefficient, which meant that land clearance and utilisation left much to be desired. Even much of the cleared land soon became barren.[8]

Peasants suffered too from a heavy tax burden, in no small part thanks to the unusual Buddhist zeal of Emperor Shōmu (r. 724–49).

Shōmu commissioned not only the Tōdaiji but also a temple in every province, at huge expense. His zeal was partly due to the massive suffering of his people during one of Japan's worst epidemics, the Great Smallpox Epidemic of 735–7. This virtually exterminated local populations in some areas and reduced Japan's overall population by around a third.[9] Shōmu felt himself in some way responsible for this and a number of famines and other disasters during his reign, and turned—with what seems to have been genuine piety—to Buddhism.[10]

At times there was famine relief, and during particularly serious disasters such as the Great Smallpox Epidemic there was even tax exemption for peasants. In an attempt to increase incentives for land reclamation, a law change in 743 allowed peasants who cleared land to hold it in their families in perpetuity. This revision was part of a trend that saw land increasingly returning to private ownership.[11]

However, in general the tax burden worsened for peasants, who comprised 95 per cent of the population at the time. They were not helped by having to compensate for tax exemptions given increasingly to landowning religious institutions and noble families. Troubled by poor crops and heavy tax demands, many peasants simply walked off their allotted land, seeking instead the security and lesser demands of working land in the private tax-free estates of the temples and nobles. In actual fact, however, life on the tax-free estates was not necessarily better for them. Private landowners could exact their own dues from those working their land, and some were harsher than the government.

Yamanoue Okura, the socially-concerned *Manyōshū* poet who wrote much of his poetry in the early years of the Nara period, again offers a glimpse of life for the common people. One of his poems, 'A Dialogue on Poverty', takes the form of a dialogue between a poor man and an even poorer one. The poorer man's account is given below.[12]

> Wide as they call heaven and earth,
> For me they have shrunk quite small.
> Bright though they call the sun and moon,
> They never shine for me.
> Is it the same with all men,
> Or for me alone?
> By rare chance I was born a man
> And no meaner than my fellows,
> But, wearing unwadded sleeveless clothes
> In tatters, like weeds waving in the sea,
> Hanging from my shoulders,

And under the sunken roof,
Within the leaning walls,
Here I lie on straw
Spread on bare earth,
With my parents at my pillow,
My wife and children at my feet,
All huddled in grief and tears.
No fire sends up smoke
At the cooking-place,
And in the cauldron
A spider spins its web.
With not a grain to cook,
We moan like the night thrush.
Then, 'to cut', as the saying is,
'The ends of what is already too short',
The village headman comes,
With rod in hand, to our sleeping place,
Growling for his dues.
Must it be so hopeless—
The way of this world?

Okura's poems give further valuable insights into general life in those times, such as the prevalence of illness, or a cheerless Buddhist view of the impermanence of human life and material things. One surprising observation is a widespread lack of respect for the elderly. As an aged Confucianist, Okura was particularly sensitive to this deviation from Confucian principles—a deviation which again shows there was a Japanese limit to the adoption of Chinese ways. In his 'Elegy on the Impermanence of Human Life' he laments the passing of youth, the onset of old age, and the life of old people:[13]

...with staffs at their waists,
They totter along the road,
Laughed at here, and hated there.
This is the way of the world...

The greatest victim of the age, however, may have been the central government. Its overall tax revenue was dwindling. The increasing independence of the private estates also eroded respect for central authority. No doubt aggravated by ongoing intrigues among court factions, by the end of the period there was already a certain sense of decay in the authority of central government.[14] This was ironic, for the period was the heyday of the *ritsuryō* system, which was meant to spread central imperial authority throughout the land.

2.2 THE RISE AND FALL OF THE COURT: THE HEIAN PERIOD (794–1185)

Emperor Kammu (r. 781–806) was particularly unhappy in Nara, and in 784 he decided it was time to move the capital again. No one quite knows why. He may have felt oppressed by the increasing number of powerful Buddhist temples in the city. Or, since there had been so many disasters in recent times, he may simply have felt it was ill-fated. In any event, he left in a hurry.

After a few years' indecision a new capital was finally built in 794 a short distance to the north, in Heian—present-day Kyōto. Like Nara, it was built on Chinese grid-pattern lines. Unlike Nara, it was to remain the official capital for more than a thousand years.

At Heian the court was in many ways to reach its zenith. In its refinement, its artistic pursuits, and its etiquette, it rivalled courts of any time and place in the world. However, the more refined it became, the more it lost touch with reality, and that was to cost it dearly.

The Heian court gave the world some of its finest early literature. For example, around 1004 the court lady Murasaki Shikibu wrote the world's first novel, *Genji Monogatari* (Tale of [Prince] Genji). Many of its thousand pages reveal a life of exquisite refinement:[15]

> It was late in the Third Month. Murasaki's spring garden was coming ever more to life with blossoms and singing birds. Elsewhere spring had departed, said the other ladies, and why did it remain here? Genji thought it a pity that the young women should have only distant glimpses of the moss on the island, a deeper green each day. He had carpenters at work on Chinese pleasure boats, and on the day they were launched he summoned palace musicians for water music. Princes and high courtiers came crowding to hear.

The princes and courtiers had little else to do. By this stage the court had lost its real functions of government, and occupied itself instead with dilettantish pastimes.[16] Nobles of the day debated the merits of flowers or seashells, or floated wine cups to each other along miniature waterways, or composed delicate verses. Their values centred not on matters of state but on the correct protocol, the proper costume, the perfect phrase.

Meanwhile, in the real world, provincial warriors—the early samurai—were growing ever more powerful. Their power grew in proportion to the loss of power by the central government.

A main cause behind this change in the power structure was the continuing increase in private land ownership. Public land allotment ceased by the tenth century, and by the end of the period about half of all land was to be privately owned.[17] Much of this private land was exempt from tax, meaning a serious decrease in taxation revenue for the government.

Private land could be acquired in a number of ways, including purchase, but most importantly by the opening up of virgin land. In practice this ended up making powerful families even more powerful, for usually they alone possessed the wherewithal to acquire tools and hire the necessary labour. Even those smallholders who did manage to acquire land by reclamation often commended it to more powerful persons who could ensure its protection.[18]

There is a need to be careful about the term 'powerful', for in Japan there has long been a distinction between nominal power (authority) and real power. A major noble family based in the capital may well have had sufficient wealth and 'power' to mobilise resources in order to reclaim land, but this did not mean it had the actual power to maintain real control of that land. That actual power was more likely to be held by a minor local noble, such as those appointed as estate-managers.

The owners of large provincial estates were invariably away at court for much or all of the time. Absentee ownership, with actual control in the hands of estate-managers or custodians, became standard practice, particularly as the period progressed.[19] This separation of ownership and possession was another cause behind the rise of the local warrior at the expense of the central noble.

Even court-appointed governors of provinces also tended in time to send deputies to the provinces in their charge. In this way the court grew increasingly removed from provincial matters, and central control over people and land became ever weaker in real terms.

It was not simply a case of the court losing power relative to the provinces. Within the court itself, the emperor lost much of his personal power. There were two main reasons for this.

The first was the use of regents. This was taken to extremes by the highly influential Fujiwara family, who dominated the court for much of the period. The family had long provided imperial consorts and empresses. Then in 858 Yoshifusa (804–72), the head of the family, arranged the enthronement of his seven-year-old grandson and promptly declared himself regent. The practice of Fujiwara regency continued after him, becoming the norm till the late eleventh century despite occasional resistance from the imperial family. Typically, emperors were born of Fujiwara mothers. One famous member of the Fujiwara family, Michi-naga (966–1028), achieved the distinction of having no fewer than four daughters who married emperors.

The second reason was early abdication. As with the tactic of the Fuji-wara regents a junior would be enthroned, but this time he was control-led by an abdicated emperor rather than a regent. This practice (*insei*, or 'cloister government') was seen occasionally in earlier times, but became very common from the late eleventh century. It was used by retired emperors such as Shirakawa (1053–1129, r. 1073–87) to combat the domination of the court by the Fujiwara family.[20]

These practices of regencies and cloister government, along with numerous other power-plays and court intrigues, inevitably damaged the cohesion and effectiveness of central government, and contributed further to the decline in real central control of the nation.

The decline of the court and central government went hand-in-hand with a decline in things Chinese. Even well into the second half of the period it was still a sign of class for a male aristocrat to be versant with Chinese language and literature, but this was now in the sense of a 'clas-sical education'. When Japanese now thought of China, they thought of the China of old, not of contemporary China. At the time, China too was in a period of dynastic decline, with the T'ang period coming to an end in 906. Official embassies to China had already ceased in the ninth cen-tury, and no further missions were to take place for some centuries. It was felt that Japan had little left to learn from China at this stage.[21]

As Chinese influence receded, a distinctly Japanese identity emerged all the more clearly. Chinese script was modified into the Japanese *kana* script, largely thanks to aristocratic women who were discouraged from using Chinese.[22] Distinctive forms of painting appeared. So too did dis-tinctive forms of poetry, particularly based on groupings of syllables into patterns of seven and five, and characterised by understatement and suggestion rather than the ornateness and richness of Chinese poetry.

Distinctive aesthetic values also emerged, such as *okashi* and particu-larly *(mono no) aware*, aesthetics which are still very much alive in mod-ern Japan. *Okashi* refers to something unusual and generally amusing, often in a relatively trivial sense, such as a breach of etiquette. *Mono no aware*, which is usually expressed through the symbolism of nature, rep-resents a view that life is beautiful but ephemeral. It translates literally as 'the sadness of things'. This aesthetic is also found elsewhere—as in the Latin term *lacrimae rerum* (the tears of things)—but is particularly prevalent in Japan. The term *aware* occurs more than a thousand times in the *Genji Monogatari*, but its flavour is perhaps best illustrated by an earlier poem by the ninth-century poetess Ono no Komachi:[23]

> The blossoms have faded,
> While I grow old idly,
> Watching the rain.

The attitudes to life underlying both *okashi* and *mono no aware* seem to reflect Buddhist influence, particularly *mappō* ('last law'). This predicts the final decline of humankind, the final proof that human existence is, in itself, without substance. This final phase was expected to begin in Japan in the latter half of the Heian period, and presentiment of it was not confined to the court alone. A sense of the imminent coming of *mappō* pervaded much of society.[24]

Many of the major nobles at court certainly seem to have lived lives without substance, but the same could not necessarily be said of those minor nobles sent as managers to the provinces, or other powerful local leaders. Displaying a more realistic approach to life, they concerned themselves with acquiring real power. In fact, these minor aristocrats were often heads of offshoot branches of the Fujiwara or imperial families, and included the 'shed' imperial-line families Minamoto (also known as Genji) and Taira (also known as Heike).[25] Excluded from rights of accession, they often bore grudges towards the central nobles.

They were allowed to maintain armed guards, who were themselves often of aristocratic descent. These armed forces, known as *bushi* (warriors) or *samurai* (retainers), grew increasingly powerful through alliances. Eventually they were powerful enough to intervene in central court affairs.

Their involvement in court affairs was eventually to lead to the collapse of the central government. In 1156, rival claimants to the headship of the Fujiwara family—still influential though past its heyday—were struggling for control of the court. They enlisted the help of rival provincial military groups, the Taira and the Minamoto. The Taira were led by Taira no Kiyomori (1118–81), whose base was in the Inland Sea region to the west. The Minamoto were led by Minamoto no Tameyoshi (1096–1156), whose base was in the Kantō region to the east.

In the military clash that followed, the Taira group was victorious, partly because of inner divisions within the Minamoto camp. Tameyoshi was executed. Kiyomori now started to establish himself in the capital, perhaps not quite as supreme ruler but certainly in a very powerful position.

However, the Taira camp too was divided. Its ranks in fact included a Minamoto, Tameyoshi's eldest son Yoshitomo (1123–60). Yoshitomo was seen by many as the main contributor to the victory over his father, but he felt insufficiently rewarded. As a result, in 1159 he attacked the Taira forces in the capital, but was defeated and killed by Kiyomori.

What followed shortly afterwards—whatever the precise details— was to change the history of Japan.

By many accounts Kiyomori seems to have had a great passion for women, particularly Yoshitomo's concubine, Tokiwa.[26] He is said to have threatened to kill her three children by Yoshitomo unless she gave herself to him. She duly surrendered to his 'advances'. Kiyomori's own stepmother, Ike no Zenni, also seems to have pleaded for the lives of Yoshitomo's children (six in all).

Whether or not this particular interpretation of events is true, it is a fact that Kiyomori spared all six children.[27] It was a deed of humanity uncharacteristic of his usual ruthlessness. It was also exceptional by the standards of the day, for it was common practice—even sanctioned in law—to eliminate the family of vanquished rivals.[28]

Most importantly, it was eventually to lead to the downfall of the Taira. Two of the spared sons, Minamoto no Yoritomo (1147–99, the son of a priest's daughter) and Minamoto no Yoshitsune (1159–89, one of Tokiwa's three sons), were to vanquish the Taira, ushering in a new era in Japanese history.

After his victory over Yoshitomo, Kiyomori settled in the capital and over the next twenty years or so immersed himself in court life, dominating it. In 1180, at the peak of Taira power, Kiyomori enthroned his own 2-year-old grandson, Antoku (1178–85, r. 1180–3).

An aggrieved rival claimant, Prince Mochihito (1151–80), called for Minamoto support for his cause. Yoritomo, who had been in exile in the Izu Peninsula, readily responded. Perhaps aided by a general feeling that Kiyomori had 'lost touch' with the provinces, Yoritomo soon attracted large numbers of provincial warriors to his side, including his half-brother Yoshitsune.

Mochihito was killed that same year, and Kiyomori died the following year of fever, but Yoritomo continued the campaign against the Taira. There was some delay in the fighting due to widespread famine and pestilence, but in 1183 Minamoto forces seized the capital. The Taira, now led by Kiyomori's son Tomomori (1151–85), fled westwards, taking the young Antoku with them. The Minamoto pursued them, and Yoshitsune inflicted the final defeat in 1185 in a naval battle at Dannoura, off the western tip of Honshū. Tomomori threw himself into the sea rather than surrender. A similar fate awaited Antoku. He was held in the arms of his grandmother, Kiyomori's widow, as she too jumped into the sea.

An almost contemporary account of the death of Antoku reveals a strong element of Buddhistic fatalism, especially when his grandmother explains to him why she must end his life:[29]

> Your Majesty does not know that he was reborn to the Imperial throne in this world as a result of the merit of the Ten Virtues practiced in former lives. Now, however, some evil karma claims you.... Japan is small as a grain of millet, but now it is a vale of misery. There is a pure land of happiness beneath the waves, another capital where no sorrow is. It is there that I am taking my Sovereign.

It was not necessarily a passive or negative fatalism. As the struggles for power show, some people of the day were not only active, they were positively assertive. But the outcome of things was attributed to fate. Though Buddhism does hold people ultimately accountable for their actions, and for the creation of their own fate, the insertion of karma and fortune into the cause and effect of events helped diffuse the issue of immediate moral responsibility.[30] It was easier to avoid issues of conscience when the outcome of events could be blamed on an earlier life. This fitted in nicely with deep-rooted Japanese preferences for the avoidance of moral judgement.

The famine and pestilence that brought a temporary halt to the fighting were just part of a series of natural disasters during the last few years of the Heian period, adding to the man-made disasters of warfare. There was also, for example, a severe typhoon in 1180, a major earthquake in 1184, and a number of serious fires and floods around the same time. These events were described graphically in a work written some thirty years later by a retired priest, Kamo no Chōmei (c. 1155–1216). His *Hōjōki* (The Ten Foot Square Hut) of 1212 describes the famine and pestilence of 1181–2:[31]

> ...beggars filled the streets and their clamour was deafening.... Respectable citizens who ordinarily wore hats and shoes now went barefooted begging from house to house.... And by the walls and in

the highways you could see everywhere the bodies of those who had died of starvation. And as there was none to take them away, a terrible stench filled the streets.

With the combination of natural disasters and the Genpei (Minamoto-Taira) War it must certainly have seemed to many that the world was being turned upside-down, and perhaps that the final phase of humankind predicted in *mappō* was indeed imminent.

The general gloom and melancholy of these troubled times is reflected in the world-weary poetry of Saigyō (1118–90). An aristocrat and one-time imperial guard, who had met both Taira no Kiyomori and Minamoto no Yoritomo, Saigyō renounced the world to lead the life of a reclusive monk. One of his best-known poems speaks far more than its few lines:[32]

> In a tree standing
> Beside a desolate field,
> The voice of a dove
> Calling its companions—
> Lonely, terrible evening.

He is more direct in another:[33]

> Times when unbroken
> Gloom is over all our world,
> Over which still
> Sits the ever-brilliant moon:
> Sight of it casts me down more.

These times of unbroken gloom were now dominated by Minamoto no Yoritomo. The changes he put in place were to mark a new era in Japan's history.

2.3   THE WARRIOR STATE: THE KAMAKURA PERIOD (1185–1333)

In 1185 Minamoto no Yoritomo was the most powerful figure in the land. However, he did not seek the throne for himself or his descendants, nor seek to destroy it. Instead, he sought from the court legitimisation of his power through the title *seii tai-shōgun* ('barbarian-subduing great general'), generally abbreviated to *shōgun*.[34] This was granted to him in 1192.

The particular nature of the relationship between legitimacy (formal authority) and actual power in Japan is an ongoing feature of the nation's history and society.[35] Typically, a high authority does not wield a similarly high degree of actual power, but instead confers legitimacy— often in the form of some title, and often under pressure—on those who do hold actual power and claim to use it in the name of that higher authority. The fact that the higher authority is the guarantor of the power-holder's legitimacy gives the higher authority too a certain guarantee of protection. The recipient of legitimacy may in turn confer legitimacy on those below them, and so on. It is in one sense a diffusion of respons-ibility, and in another a hierarchical ordering of authority. Yoritomo provides an especially clear example of the process.

Mainly because of this need for legitimacy—but also partly because it has long been a practice in Japan to maintain some degree of continuity with the past amidst change—his government was a mixture of old and new. It became known as the *bakufu* (tent headquarters), a term used of the headquarters of commanders in the field, and in theory was merely the military arm of the imperial central government. The old central institutions were left largely intact, though seriously weakened. Old titles were retained, though often given a new meaning. Kyōto still remained the official capital, and the court stayed on there.

However, in practice the real power of government was now with the *bakufu* (shōgunate). It was based not in Kyōto but in Kamakura in the Kantō region. This was Yoritomo's traditional support-base, and he was moreover suspicious of the intrigues and undesirable influences in Kyōto. He preferred to keep himself a safe distance from the court.[36]

What was also new was that the core of the government was now a single lord–vassal group, spread rather thinly throughout the nation.[37] Yoritomo rewarded his loyal vassals with estates and offices such as *jitō* (steward) and *shugo* (protector or constable). They administered the provinces under their charge on the basis of local custom and military house laws, rather than the centrally imposed legal codes of the previous *ritsuryō* system. They also collected dues for the *bakufu*, and were en-titled to retain a portion of the produce of the land for themselves. Through this system Yoritomo exercised a relatively direct control over much of Japan, and also further eroded the revenue of the noble court families and central government.

It was a feudal system, and in that regard Japan shared common ground with the medieval western world.[38] However, feudalism in Japan was distinctive in that it operated through the traditional central civil administration. The lord–vassal relationship was also far more personal than in the west, where the contractual type of relationship was more common. In Japan it was of a paternalistic and almost familial nature, and some of the terms for 'lord' and 'vassal' used 'parent' (*oya*) and 'child' (*ko*) respectively. At the same time, and rather paradoxically, family bonds do not seem to have counted for much in the warrior's world, and so it is perhaps more accurate to see this personalisation simply as an expression of dislike for the abstract. The strength of the family was to be greatly exaggerated by later propaganda.

Personal loyalty was a major factor in Yoritomo's control over his own men. He may not have had a particularly endearing personality, but he nevertheless seems to have had a strong personal charisma that drew men to him. However, reliance on personal loyalty as a means of control is not very successful. It is inconsistent, hard to institutionalise, and fades with time.

Partly because he realised this, and partly because he was highly suspicious by nature, Yoritomo was ever alert to any remote suggestion that his power might be challenged. This led him to suspect the worst even of close friends and family, and to take decisive steps against them.

His treatment of his younger half-brother Yoshitsune is a good example. Fuelled by jealousy over Yoshitsune's popularity and widely acknowledged military prowess,[39] and suspecting him of plotting, Yoritomo gave orders for Yoshitsune's assassination. Finally, after four years as a fugitive, in 1189 Yoshitsune was surrounded by Yoritomo's forces and killed himself, along with his wife and infant children. He was to become immortalised in Japanese literature and legend as the archetypical tragic hero.

For good measure those who hunted Yoshitsune down were themselves attacked and killed by Yoritomo shortly afterwards. More of Yoritomo's own relatives and associates were also 'terminally eliminated' as potential threats.

Stating the obvious, Yoritomo's elimination of relatives may not have been in the best interests of the family. When he was killed in 1199 by a fall from his horse—not in battle, but in rather suspicious circumstances[40]—there was no really suitable Minamoto successor. He left two sons, Yoriie (1182–1204) and Sanetomo (1192–1219), and each nominally became shōgun. However, neither of them was strong enough or mature enough to achieve real control in the chaos of murder and intrigue that followed Yoritomo's death.

It was no time or place for the faint-hearted or those swayed by sentimental concerns such as family ties. Both Yoriie and Sanetomo were controlled and eventually murdered by their own family. Behind many of the intrigues was their mother, Yoritomo's widow Hōjō Masako (1157–1225). In effect, she controlled the government, and became popularly known as the 'nun-shōgun' (*ama shōgun*, a reference to her having taking nun's vows on Yoritomo's death).

One of the devices used by Masako was the institution of a shōgunal regent. This reduced the position of shōgun to a nominal one, with manipulable court nobles generally being appointed as shōgun and real control being exercised by the Hōjō.

The Hōjō shōgunal regents became particularly dominant after 1221, when they survived a challenge to their power from the retired emperor Go-Toba (1180–1239, r. 1183–98). Go-Toba had memories of the Genpei War when he had been installed as an infant emperor after Antoku's death, and had long opposed the Minamoto and Hōjō. Following his unsuccessful challenge the shōgunate based a shōgunal deputy in the capital to help keep a check on the court. Go-Toba himself was banished to remote Oki Island, off present-day Shimane Prefecture, and was eventually to die there. He is yet another well-known tragic figure of Japanese history.

Though clearly much was happening at home, two of the most important events during the period of Hōjō supremacy were of external origin. These were the attempted Mongol invasions of 1274 and 1281. These foreign threats probably helped the Hōjō to retain power nationally, for, together with periods of national alert before and after, they created a state of national emergency that overrode any internal dissent for some thirty years.

When Genghis Khan's grandson Kublai (1215–94) came to power as Emperor of Great Mongolia in 1260, the Mongol Empire already covered Korea, northern China, and indeed much of Eurasia. Kublai's next main target was southern China, the base of the Sung (Song) forces. However, he also turned his attention to Japan. In 1268 he sent a letter to the 'King of Japan' threatening invasion if the Japanese did not recognise Mongol overlordship and agree to submit tribute to him.[41] The Japanese authorities—court and shōgunate alike—ignored this and subsequent letters, but nevertheless the shōgunate put the coast of northwestern Kyūshū, where any attack was expected to occur, on military alert.

The first attack came in November 1274. As expected, it came in northwest Kyūshū. On this occasion Kublai sent about 900 vessels from

Korea carrying some 40,000 men. They landed at Hakata, and the invaders immediately forced the Japanese defenders inland. However, instead of pressing on, that night the Mongol forces returned to their ships. Shortly afterwards these suffered extensive damage, along with considerable loss of life of those on board, when a violent storm blew up. The invaders withdrew to Korea, their numbers reduced by a third.

The Japanese were alarmed at their own inferiority in terms of weaponry and cavalry tactics,[42] and strengthened their preparations for an expected second attack.

The Mongol invasion force of June 1281, which again landed at Hakata, was much larger. It comprised no fewer than 4,400 warships and 140,000 men. By this stage Kublai had secured victory over the Sung in 1279, becoming founder of a new dynasty of rulers of China. He had also suffered the insult of having his envoys to Japan beheaded in 1275 and again in 1279. This time he was serious.

But, large as the Mongol forces were, they were met with staunch resistance and were unable to secure a real foothold. Reinforcements arrived a few weeks later from southern China, but, just as the invaders were planning a massive combined assault, another storm blew up in the form of a typhoon and destroyed most of their fleet. Once again they were forced to withdraw, this time with more than half their men lost.

The two Mongol defeats were partly due to the spirited Japanese resistance and partly to their reliance on recently subjugated Chinese and Korean troops, who had little commitment to the Mongol cause. However, the two storms also had an undeniable and very major influence on the outcome. The storm winds became known as *shinpū* or *kamikaze*—literally 'divine wind', reflecting a Japanese belief that Japan was the Land of the Gods and had been protected by them. The same term was later to be used in World War Two of the suicide pilots who gave their life in the same cause of protecting the nation.

Kublai did not give up his intention to invade Japan, and planned a number of subsequent attacks. On each occasion he was diverted by instability elsewhere in his empire. The Japanese knew of his intent and maintained an alert at least till his death in 1294, after which Mongol interest in Japan appears to have waned.

Japan's victories and survival resulted from a mixture of spirited fighting on their part, poor organisation and morale on the enemy's part, and sheer good fortune. No doubt the same applies to most military victories regardless of time and place, but in Japan's case they were particularly favoured by fortune and circumstance.

The external threats may have helped prevent internal fighting, but they also contributed to mounting discontent towards the Hōjō shōgunate. The financial cost of the defence and long-term state of military alert was very great, and severely depleted the shōgunate's finances. It was unable to pay promised rewards to warrior families, or even basic compensation for their contribution to the nation's defence. This was particularly galling to those families who felt that they themselves, rather than the Hōjō, had won the victory. Further discontent was caused by the Hōjō decision to install shōgunal deputies in Kyūshū and to concentrate even more posts into their own hands.

Despite the financial problems of the shōgunate and many warrior families, the nation's economic situation as a whole improved during the period, partly as a result of the relative peace and stability that prevailed under the *jitō-shugo* system.[43] The *shōen* (estates) became more productive, though they were still far from fully efficient. Increased productivity helped the prosperity of maritime traders who distributed rice and other goods around the nation. Guilds also became stronger.

The life of the common people during the Kamakura age was marked by the emergence of new Japanese forms of Buddhism. The most distinctive characteristic of these was their appeal to people at large, as opposed to Heian period Buddhism which had generally been esoteric and confined to the ruling class. The Jōdo (Pure Land) Sect, founded by the priest Hōnen (1133–1212), believed salvation could be attained by chanting the name of Amida Buddha. The Jōdo Shin (True Pure Land) Sect, founded by Hōnen's disciple Shinran (1173–1263), simplified this further to just one sincere invocation of Amida's name. The type of Buddhism promoted by Nichiren (1222–82) was similarly simple, but focused on the Lotus Sutra rather than Amida.

Not all forms of Buddhism established in the Kamakura period were popular in their appeal, however. Zen Buddhism, with its stress on austerity and self-discipline, appealed more to warriors than to commoners of the day. Elements of Zen had been present in Japan for some centuries, but it took particular root following two trips to China by the priest Eisai (1141–1215), and presently developed into a number of sects.

Dissatisfaction towards the Hōjō shōgunal regents came to a head under the unusually assertive emperor Go-Daigo (1288–1339). Acceding to the throne in 1318, he was determined to re-establish direct imperial rule.[44] He was inspired in this by the former emperor Go-Toba, who had shown a similar resolve—albeit unsuccessfully—100 years earlier.

Go-Daigo tried twice to challenge the shōgunate, in 1324 and 1331, but failed on both occasions. Like Go-Toba before him, he was banished to the Oki Islands. However, unlike Go-Toba, Go-Daigo soon managed to escape, and succeeded in mustering considerable support in the western part of Honshū.

In 1333 the Kamakura shōgunate sent one of its ablest generals, Ashikaga Takauji (1305–58), to deal with the situation. Takauji, the young head of a branch of the Minamoto family, was an opportunist. Realising that he and Go-Daigo had considerable military might between them, he turned traitor to the shōgunate and, declaring his support for Go-Daigo, attacked the shōgunal offices in Kyōto. Within weeks another powerful young general of Minamoto descent, Nitta Yoshisada (1301–38), also rebelled against the shōgunate and destroyed its base at Kamakura.

A new era was nigh.

2.4 A NATION AT WAR WITH ITSELF: THE MUROMACHI PERIOD (1333–1568)

In 1333 Go-Daigo returned to Kyōto, supported by Ashikaga Takauji and Nitta Yoshisada. He hoped to re-establish direct imperial rule. However, this attempt was to prove shortlived, for he soon lost Takauji's support. Takauji wanted to be granted the title of shōgun. Go-Daigo refused this, for he wanted to avoid any weakening of direct imperial rule through shōguns, regents, or retired emperors.[45] Thwarted, Takauji turned his back on Go-Daigo's central government, pointedly preferring to remain in the east after he had returned to Kamakura to put down a brief revival of Hōjō support.

Go-Daigo considered Takauji to be defying him and presently sent Nitta Yoshisada—Takauji's sometime ally, sometime rival—to bring him into line. However, it was Takauji who prevailed, defeating Yoshisada and forcing him to flee. Yoshisada was eventually killed in 1338 by one of Takauji's allies. Takauji then captured Kyōto, forcing Go-Daigo to flee to Yoshino in the densely wooded mountains some 100 km south of Kyōto. In Kyōto itself Takauji promptly installed as emperor a member of a rival imperial family branch, Kōmyō (1322–80, r. 1336–48), who in 1338 finally conferred on him his much-coveted title of shōgun.

It is undeniable that Takauji was an opportunist, prepared to shift his alliances to suit the circumstances most favourable to himself. But he was not at all exceptional in this—other than in his degree of success.

The popular belief nowadays is that samurai were men of absolute loyalty. Many undoubtedly were, and sacrificed their lives for their lords. However, it was very common among samurai of the Middle Ages to switch sides. Troop figures given in the mid-fourteenth century military tale *Taiheiki* reveal that in one engagement against Takauji (at Hakone), Nitta Yoshisada's 70,000 men were reduced to a mere 100 despite having numerical superiority over Takauji's 60,000. Even allowing for distorted figures, this can only be explained by massive defections.[46]

This clearly shows the limits of personal loyalty—and once again the prevalence of pragmatism over principle. It forms a stark contrast between reality and the popular image of the samurai. And it forms a poignant contrast between the typical medieval samurai and the typical World War Two Japanese soldier, who seems to have been far readier to fight to the death than the samurai whose tradition he somewhat inaccurately believed himself to be upholding. Like the strength of the family, the 'fanatical' loyalty of many twentieth-century soldiers reflects the fact that Japan's later leaders were to re-learn the value of indoctrination—something not so obvious in the medieval world, where fear and self-interest seem to have been greater behavioural determinants.

The *Taiheiki* not only tells us something about samurai values, it also gives an insight into the life of the medieval peasant amidst the warfare.[47] It shows them being taken away as labourers by armies on the march, or having their goods taken from them for military use. It shows them being killed over nothing by ill-disciplined warriors. And it shows them scavenging for spoils, or robbing the defeated as they fled. For they too, in their own way, were opportunists.

Against such a background, then, Go-Daigo fled Kyōto for Yoshino. Here he set up a court in exile, with the result that there were now two 'emperors' at the same time. This duality was to continue till 1392, when the rival courts, known as the Northern (Kyōto) and Southern (Yoshino) Courts, were 'reconciled'. More exactly, claimants from the southern line were promised alternate succession with the northern claimants by the then third Ashikaga shōgun, Takauji's grandson Yoshimitsu (1358–1408, r. 1369–95). Yoshimitsu was not to honour his promise, and the southern line was soon to become extinct.

Unlike the Minamoto and Hōjō before him Takauji preferred to establish the shōgunate in Kyōto, and it was eventually located in the Muromachi area of the city. Administratively, he used many of the existing structures and offices, such as the *jitō* and *shugo*.

However, his relationship with the *shugo* was problematic, for he had neither land to offer as reward nor the personal charisma of Yoritomo.

That is, he could neither buy nor command their loyalty. Some of the *shugo* were arguably as powerful as he himself was. Takauji and most of his successors also proved to be poor leaders, and exercised little real control. Disputes, even within the shōgunate itself, were numerous. In one such dispute Takauji arranged the murder of his own brother Tadayoshi (1306–52), continuing the tradition of 'family first' when it came to eliminating enemies.

With a few exceptions, actual shōgunal power declined steadily with the passing of time. Powerful *shugo* families such as the Hosokawa, who often occupied the position of shōgunal deputy, exerted great influence on the shōgunate. One *shugo* family, the Yamana, controlled no fewer than eleven of the sixty-six provinces of their day.

The main exception to weak shōguns was probably Yoshimitsu. He not only 'reunited' the dual courts, but also attempted to curb *shugo* power by the ancient Yamato state method of giving many of them court posts, obliging them to reside in Kyōto where he could keep a watchful eye on them. In order to strengthen his own personal power he created the position of 'retired shōgun', which he himself occupied in 1395 after abdicating in favour of his 9-year-old son. He then had the world-famous Kinkakuji or Golden Pavilion built in Kyōto, in the lavish style of the palaces of retired emperors of old.

In another interesting move Yoshimitsu expressed fealty to the Chinese Emperor. In a letter to the Ming court in 1403 he termed himself 'Your subject, the King of Japan'.[48] This self-designation may well have compromised Japanese sovereignty, but it also established a basis for the shōgunate to deal with foreign powers independently of the imperial court.[49]

However, after Yoshimitsu's death in 1408 shōgunal power declined particularly noticeably. Shōgunal orders were often ignored, and in some cases were even effectively overruled by the court, which was itself weak. For example, in 1443 the shōgunate forbade performances by a troupe of actors during the New Year holiday, but the court gave its permission, and the performances went ahead.[50]

Provincial families continued to become more powerful, becoming the forerunners of the *daimyō* (feudal lords) of a later age. The estates that were theoretically under the absentee ownership of noble court families were in effect dismembered as power accrued to local lords. Revenue from them was no longer paid to their absent owners. The peasants still paid their taxes, however. In fact the burden worsened leading to numerous uprisings. This was despite—or perhaps because of—increased agricultural productivity due to improvements in tools, fertilisers, and strains of rice.

Unchecked by any shōgunal power, the provincial families increasingly fought against each other as fragile alliances were made and broken. The inconclusive Onin Civil War of 1467–77 laid waste much of Kyōto, and laid bare the inability of the shōgunate to quell civil unrest. For the next 100 years—known as the Sengoku ('Warring States') era—there was to be an almost constant series of civil disturbances.

In this warrior-dominated age Zen Buddhism continued to appeal to the warrior. Zen ideals such as simplicity, restraint, discipline, and meditation formed a contrast to the actual disorder and confusion of the country. It was an age of aesthetic ideals such as *wabi* (subdued taste), *kare* (literally 'withered' or 'dry', but with connotations of 'severe', 'unadorned', and 'natural'), *sabi* (elegant simplicity), and *yūgen* (elegant and tranquil otherworldliness), ideals that still characterise much of Japanese culture today. Many of these ideals, especially restraint and *yūgen*, are also well-known characteristics of the *nō* drama that developed during this period. *Nō* plays were often based on tragic military encounters and often had a theme of retribution in afterlife.

The other-worldliness of *nō* was paralleled by an escape from the real world by a number of hermit poets and writers. They displayed an even more profound world-weariness than Saigyō in an earlier age. For example, the Buddhist monk Zekkai (1336–1405) wrote:[51]

> I have locked the gate on a thousand peaks
> To live here with clouds and birds.
> All day I watch the hills
> As clear winds fill the bamboo door.
> A supper of pine flowers,
> Monk's robes of chestnut dye—
> What dream does the world hold
> To lure me from these dark slopes?

One anonymous poem found in a funeral register, written around 1500 during the Sengoku era, is an allegory of the civil strife that characterised the nation:

> A bird with
> One body but
> Two beaks,
> Pecking itself
> To death.

It was during the particular unrest of the Sengoku era that westerners first appeared in Japan. In September 1543 a Chinese junk, blown off its intended course to Ningpo (Ningbo) in China, landed on the island of Tanegashima off southern Kyūshū. On board were the Chinese crew and three Portuguese traders.[52] They brought with them firearms, more sophisticated than the weapons of the Mongols some centuries earlier, and these were soon to be adopted and manufactured by a number of Japanese warlords. They also brought the first word of Christianity, which was to be more systematically introduced in 1549 by the Jesuit Francis Xavier (1506–52, later a saint).

These first Europeans found a land torn apart by civil war, a land of warlords who recognised no effective central government and simply grabbed as many neighbouring fiefs as they could, either by force of arms or treachery.[53] It was a land badly in need of reunification.

2.5   REUNIFYING THE NATION: THE AZUCHI–MOMOYAMA PERIOD (1568–1600)

A divided land is an easily conquered land, but fortunately for Japan the European powers of the day seem to have had no interest in attempting to conquer it. True, Columbus had set out to pave the way for exploitation of the fabled riches of Marco Polo's Cathay (China) and Cipangu (Japan), but had been sidetracked along the way by the discovery of the New World. This new land had riches of its own. Moreover, it promised to be more easily conquered and exploited than Japan, tiny and peopled with ferocious warriors.

And before long, the country was anyway to be reunified. This was largely due to the cumulative accomplishments of three successive military leaders: Oda Nobunaga (1534–82), Toyotomi Hideyoshi (1536–98), and Tokugawa Ieyasu (1542–1616). Each had their own method, reflecting their personality. There is a well-known saying in Japan that if a song-bird would not sing, Nobunaga would kill it, Hideyoshi would persuade it to sing, and Ieyasu would simply wait for it to sing.[54]

Nobunaga was a *daimyō* from Owari Province (part of present-day Aichi Prefecture). An astute tactician, he rose from relatively minor status to considerable power through a number of victories over rival *daimyō*. One of his most important victories was that over the forces of Imagawa Yoshimoto (1519–60) at the Battle of Okehazama (near Nagoya) in 1560, when his vastly outnumbered troops succeeded in surrounding the Imagawa forces.

In 1568 Nobunaga successfully seized Kyōto in support of Ashikaga Yoshiaki (1537–97), one of the claimants to the position of shōgun—a position still held, albeit nominally, by members of various branches of the Ashikaga family. Yoshiaki was duly installed as shōgun. However, it was obvious from the outset that it was Nobunaga who was the real power. He even publicly issued directives and admonishments to Yoshiaki. Then, just five years later in 1573, Nobunaga drove him out of the capital for allying with the Takeda family, traditional enemies of the Oda.

Yoshiaki continued to hold the title of shōgun till 1588, but in real terms his expulsion brought the by now almost meaningless Ashikaga shōgunate to an end.

Nobunaga was an extraordinary man. He was the ultimate warlord, without peer when it came to brutality and self-interest. He had members of his own family murdered (such as his younger brother Nobuyuki in 1557), but that was nothing special. What was special was his habit of having up to 20,000 of his already defeated enemies burned alive, including any civilians who happened to be caught up in the massacre.[55] He had a particular penchant for massacring Buddhist priests, for he saw them as troublesome and potential threats, thanks to a history of popular Buddhist-inspired uprisings over the previous hundred years or so.[56] The Buddhists were a potential threat, but not strong enough to merit any attempt on his part towards reconciliation. He preferred to try to destroy them.

European visitors of the day were astonished not only by Nobunaga's cruelty and ruthlessness, but by his massive ego. He even erected a temple where he could be worshipped, and declared his birthday a national holiday.[57] It may have been that a belief in his own absolute supremacy was the reason he did not seek legitimisation through the title of shōgun or similar, for it would place him in a theoretically inferior position to whoever conferred it.[58] Certainly, his spurning of legitimacy was unusual in Japanese history.

However, there was construction amidst the destruction. He gave captured land to his vassals and started a policy of territorial redistribution that was to be developed further by his successors. In June 1575, he deployed 3,000 musketeers to help defeat Takeda Katsuyori (1546–82) in the Battle of Nagashino. This was the first significant use of firearms in Japanese warfare, and showed Nobunaga's astuteness in realising the potential of this weapon that the Europeans had brought with them.[59] It was to set a trend. As early as 1571, in a manner reminsiscent of the Taika Reforms of a thousand years earlier, he also started a survey of the agricultural lands under his control. In 1576, again reminiscent of the Taika Reforms, he started to confiscate weapons held by peasants, and that same year he standardised weights and measures. Also in 1576 he started construction of a great castle headquarters at Azuchi, on the shore of Lake Biwa to the east of Kyōto.

His ultimate aim was inscribed on his personal seal—*Tenka Fubu*, meaning 'A Unified Realm under Military Rule'. He achieved about half of this aim before his life was cut short in an appropriately violent way, in 1582, on a campaign against the Mōri family in western Japan. Ironically for a man who burned temples, he was trapped inside a burning temple, Honnōji, after one of his officers, Akechi Mitsuhide (1526–82), turned against him. It is possible he simply burned to death, but more likely that he chose to kill himself first.[60]

Nobunaga's plan to unify the land was carried out further by his retainer Toyotomi Hideyoshi.

Hideyoshi was another remarkable figure. He rose from the humble position of footsoldier to be the most powerful person in the land. An extremely shrewd and capable man, his abilities were recognised by Nobunaga, in whose forces he served from 1558. Nobunaga also seems to have had a personal liking for him, and nicknamed him 'Monkey' (*Saru*) because of his rather simian features. He was successively promoted, recognised as a brilliant strategist, and became one of Nobunaga's leading generals.

Upon Nobunaga's death Hideyoshi pursued and defeated his lord's attacker Akechi Mitsuhide. He then made peace with the Mōri family.

Nobunaga had three sons. One of these, Nobutada (1557–82), died with him at Honnōji. Another, Nobutaka (1558–83), was disposed of the following year jointly by Hideyoshi and Nobunaga's third son Nobukatsu (1558–1630). Nobukatsu wanted to become head of the Oda family, but he was thwarted. Hideyoshi had Nobunaga's infant grandson Hidenobu (1580–1605, the son of Nobutada) recognised as heir instead, while in practice he wielded power himself. Like Nobunaga, Hideyoshi never actually became shōgun, but unlike Nobunaga he did take a number of legitimising high titles, such as regent.

Hideyoshi's power continued to expand through a mixture of alliances, as with the Mōri, and successful battles. One of his most successful campaigns was in 1587 against the ambitious and powerful Shimazu family of Satsuma Province in southern Kyūshū, who were trying to extend their power northwards. Following his victory he strategically redistributed fiefs in Kyūshū to ensure that his own loyal followers were able to keep potential enemies in check.

This policy of fief redistribution, used by Nobunaga before him, was later to become a hallmark of Tokugawa policy too. It had a twofold benefit. It not only strategically placed loyal vassals between less loyal ones; in the case of relocation of less loyal vassals it also separated them from the bulk of the people who formed their traditional power-base.

Hideyoshi's practice of keeping the families of *daimyō* as hostages at his headquarters in Momoyama (near Kyōto) also helped to some extent to quell any opposition—though family ties were clearly not always an important consideration for some warlords.

Another of Hideyoshi's policies to reduce threat—again started by Nobunaga—was his confiscation of peasant weapons nationwide, in the so-called 'Sword Hunt' (*Katanagari*) of 1588.[61] It was a move intended to reduce the threat of peasant uprising and the use of peasant militia by rival warlords. He was no doubt mindful of his own rise to military power from peasant origins.

The Sword Hunt also had the effect of separating peasant and warrior in terms of social class. This separation was further enforced by 'class-freezing' regulations that Hideyoshi issued in 1591.[62] Among other things these prevented peasants from leaving their fields to take up any other profession, and obliged samurai to live in the castle-towns that became a feature of this age. He also further revived and extended the practice of collective responsibility by threatening punishments on entire villages and towns for the wrongdoings of individuals. These stern measures of class separation and collective responsibility were clearly aimed at preventing instability and threat.

Hideyoshi continued the land surveys commenced by Nobunaga, likewise the standardisation of measures, and he carried out a population census in 1590. The following year of 1591 the provinces in the far north finally came under his control.

Thanks to Hideyoshi's various victories and policies, and thanks to the legacy of Nobunaga's achievements, by the early 1590s the reunification of the country was more or less complete. It still needed, of course, to be consolidated, and preferably under Hideyoshi himself. There had to be constant vigilance against any threat to this aim.

One suspicion Hideyoshi had was about Christian activity. Nobunaga had been tolerant of them because they were useful in his campaign against Buddhists. At first Hideyoshi too was tolerant. However, immediately following his Kyūshū campaign, when he came into close contact with Christians, he denounced Christianity in the Edict of Expulsion of 1587. He did not actually enforce this edict for some years, and it was seen as more of a warning. However, his anti-Christian attitude hardened further with the arrival of Franciscans in 1593, which ended the Jesuit monopoly and led to considerable sectarian squabbling and politicking. Then in 1597, possibly suspecting missionaries to be the advance guard of an invasion, Hideyoshi crucified twenty-six Christians, including nine Europeans.[63] The Incident of the 26 Martyrs was the first time any Europeans had been put to death in Japan for professing Christianity.

In his later years, especially after around 1590, Hideyoshi's personality seems to have changed. His suspicions about any possible threat developed into virtual paranoia. He was convinced his young nephew Hidetsugu (1568–95) was plotting against him, and he forced him to commit suicide. To be on the safe side he also executed Hidetsugu's wife and three young children, as well as his retainers. To send a message to would-be conspirators Hidetsugu's head was put on public display.

In some ways Hideyoshi became more like his former lord Nobunaga. He started to show almost Nobunaga-like cruelty, and a Nobunaga-like sense of personal grandeur. Nothing was allowed to spoil his world, and messengers who brought him bad news risked being sawn in half.[64] His great master of the tea ceremony, Sen no Rikyū (1522–91), who had also served Nobunaga and was hardly young and threatening, somehow fell foul of Hideyoshi, and was another obliged to kill himself.

Hideyoshi's world was not big enough for him, and he envisaged the conquest of China to establish a pan-Asian empire. As the first phase of this grand scheme his forces invaded Korea in 1592, but were driven back by combined Korean and Chinese forces. His campaign had not been helped by his own failure to set foot in the field. He tried again in 1597, but this campaign too was abandoned, for Hideyoshi died from illness in September 1598.

Three years prior to his death, with a view to ensuring continuity of Toyotomi hegemony Hideyoshi had established a council of five of Japan's greatest *daimyō*, the Five Great Elders. One of these was Tokugawa Ieyasu, one of the great survivors of Japanese history.

Ieyasu's career is outlined in Part Three. It can be noted here that in 1584 he had unsuccessfully challenged Hideyoshi, and the following year had acknowledged Hideyoshi as his overlord. Though they were allies in a number of campaigns, Hideyoshi was never quite sure of Ieyasu's loyalties. In 1590 he strategically relocated him from his traditional central territory near Shizuoka to more distant territory in the Kantō region. Hideyoshi probably made an error of judgement in this move, not the least because Ieyasu's new territory, at 2.5 million *koku*,[65] was bigger than that of any other *daimyō* and even bigger than Hideyoshi's own personal holdings. By 1598 Ieyasu had strengthened his position to the point where he was considered by many *daimyō* to be their overlord. In fact, he had no fewer than thirty-eight *daimyō* among his vassals.

From his deathbed Hideyoshi implored the Five Great Elders to look after his infant heir Hideyori (1593–1615), and they promised to do so. However, upon his death the promise was not kept by Ieyasu and a dispute arose over who was to be Hideyoshi's successor. Ieyasu prevailed. In the Battle of Sekigahara (near Nagoya) in October 1600 he triumphed over those who fought in the cause of Hideyori.

Was this to be the final civil war? Was the national unity so hard won by Nobunaga and Hideyoshi now to be lost, or would Ieyasu be able to maintain control and stability? Time was to tell.

REVIEW OF PART TWO

Part Two has, over a period of almost 1,000 years, followed the fortunes of the court on the one hand and warriors on the other. The centralised, Chinese-style *ritsuryō* state was at its strongest during the first half of the Nara period, but signs of decay were evident from an early stage. During the succeeding Heian period, despite court culture and artistic accomplishment reaching a peak, central power continued to decline, as did the importance of things Chinese as they were gradually 'Japanised'. Factors in this decline of central power included constant intrigues (mostly involving the Fujiwara family), loss of revenue caused by dwindling tax returns from increasingly privately owned land, and loss of personal power by the emperor as a result of regencies and 'cloister government' by retired emperors.

By contrast, the power of provincial warriors steadily increased. After clashes between the two most powerful warrior families in the land, the Taira and the Minamoto, in the late twelfth century Minamoto (no) Yoritomo emerged as the effective supreme power in the land—though he still felt a need for formal legitimisation from the court. He established the shōgunate, or military government, and ushered in the feudal

age. However, the shōgunate too, like the court before it, was soon to be
weakened by intrigues and regencies. After surviving threatened invasions and attempts at the restoration of imperial power the shōgunate
eventually lapsed, like the imperial institution, into a condition of virtually nominal meaning only. Powerful warlords vied with each other to
establish dominance, and the country was in an almost constant state of
civil warfare.

Somewhat ironically, it was during this age of the warrior that some of
Japan's most noted cultural elements and practices, such as *nō* drama,
austere aesthetics, and Zen Buddhism, became established. Agricultural productivity increased, certainly relative to the inefficiency of the
Heian period, though the life of the peasant seems to have made little
advance.

Eventually, partly benefiting from firearms introduced by Europeans in the middle of the sixteenth century, one particularly determined warlord, Oda Nobunaga, was able to establish dominance.
He started a process of national unification which was to be carried on
by his immediate successors Toyotomi Hideyoshi and Tokugawa
Ieyasu.

Key developments, greatly simplified, are summarised in Table 2.1.

Table 2.1   Key developments in early/medieval Japan

Development	Century
Chinese-style *ritsuryō* state at its peak	8th
Central state gradually loses its revenue, lands, and power, as provincial warriors increase theirs	9th on
Court 'high culture' at its peak	10th–11th
Provincial warriors take over the government, Minamoto no Yoritomo becomes shōgun	late 12th
Shōgunate loses support, civil disorder follows	mid-13th on
Constant civil war	mid-15th–late 16th
Country eventually reunified under the warlords Oda Nobunaga and Toyotomi Hideyoshi	late 16th
Tokugawa Ieyasu becomes main power in the land	end 16th

Values and practices that continue to have relevance today are summarised in Table 2.2.

Table 2.2   Key values and practices in early/medieval Japan

- distinction between formal authority and actual power
  (the latter often separated but legitimised)
- preference for the indirect
- dominance of pragmatism over principle
- diffusion of responsibility (both in terms of conscience being displaced by
  fatalism, and of the punishment of the collective for the acts of an
  individual member)
- 'Japanisation' of imported ideas and practices
- intermingling of old and new
- personalisation of relationships, though more as an expression of dislike of
  the abstract contract than as genuine respect for the family
  (at least among warriors)
- ideals of austerity and discipline among warriors
  (though not always in practice)
- self-interest rather than loyalty

The behaviour of the typical medieval samurai, the degree of self-interest, and the weakness of family bonding all run counter to modern perceptions. These modern perceptions were to result in large part from later idealisation and propaganda.

Part Three

The Closed Country: The Tokugawa Period (1600–1868)

3.1 STABILITY EQUALS SURVIVAL: ESTABLISHING THE TOKUGAWA SHŌGUNATE

Ieyasu was determined to capitalise on his victory at Sekigahara, and more generally on the accomplishments of Nobunaga and Hideyoshi. His main aim was to ensure the Tokugawa stayed in control of the nation. In this, he would be aided by his survival skills.

In some ways like the nation as a whole, Ieyasu owed much to a mixture of determination, pragmatism, astuteness, and good fortune. A remarkable survivor living in dangerous times, his life is the stuff of adventure stories and films.

He was born Matsudaira Takechiyo in 1542 in Mikawa Province (part of present-day Aichi Prefecture). His mother was just 15 years old and his father, the minor chieftain Matsudaira Hirotada (1526–49), just 16. The Matsudaira family were having trouble with their neighbours, the Oda to the west and the Imagawa to the east. They entered into an uneasy alliance with the Imagawa, and in 1547, to underpin this, Hirotada agreed to send them his young son Takechiyo as hostage. However, while on his way to the Imagawa base at Sunpu (Shizuoka), Takechiyo was captured by Oda forces and taken to the Oda base at Nagoya. Upon his father's death in 1549 a truce was declared between the Oda and Matsudaira families, and Takechiyo resumed his role as hostage to the Imagawa.

Takechiyo stayed with the Imagawa till 1560, seemingly quite settled. While with them he married and became a father in his teens, like his own father before him. He even fought with the Imagawa in their battles. Then in 1560 Imagawa Yoshimoto, the head of the family, was defeated and killed by Oda Nobunaga in the Battle of Okehazama. Takechiyo—now known as Motoyasu—was freed from his vassalage, and in fact became an ally of Nobunaga.

With the western borders of his home (Matsudaira) territory now secure through this alliance, Motoyasu turned his attention to the Imagawa territory to the east, and gradually achieved control of this by 1568. By this stage he had changed names again, to Tokugawa Ieyasu. In 1570 he moved his base to the former Imagawa stronghold in Shizuoka, and over the next decade, using his alliance with Nobunaga, was able to extend his territory. At times Nobunaga had doubts about his loyalty, but Ieyasu overcame these. In 1579 he had his own wife and first son— whom Nobunaga suspected of colluding with his old enemy the Takeda family—killed as evidence of his loyalty.

When Nobunaga died in 1582 Ieyasu made use of the ensuing turmoil to occupy Takeda territory in the provinces of Kai and Shinano (present-day Yamanashi and Nagano Prefectures). He was now a major force for Nobunaga's successor Hideyoshi to reckon with.

In 1584 Ieyasu tried to challenge Hideyoshi's authority, but failed, and the following year acknowledged Hideyoshi as his overlord. They then formed an uneasy alliance, which in 1590 helped overcome the Hōjō in the Kantō region (unrelated to the earlier Hōjō). Hideyoshi rewarded Ieyasu with territory taken from the Hōjō, but, still concerned about his loyalty, obliged him to take up this territory at the expense of his existing territory. Ieyasu had little choice but to agree. However, instead of moving into the Hōjō's former base at Odawara, he chose instead the little fishing village of Edo, which was more centrally located within the territory. This obscure little village was later to become one of the world's largest cities and major economic capitals, Tōkyō.

Over the next few years Ieyasu consolidated his huge holdings, which in effect comprised all the Kantō Plain. Among other things he built Edo Castle, which was later to form the foundations for the Imperial Palace. He was acknowledged by many *daimyō* as their overlord, and felt strong enough to break his promise to the dying Hideyoshi to safeguard Hideyoshi's infant heir Hideyori. Having triumphed at Sekigahara in 1600 he was effectively the greatest power in the land.

To legitimise his position, in 1603 Ieyasu received the title of shōgun—unused since 1588—from Emperor Go-Yōzei (r. 1586–1611). He was now 61 years old. In the manner of earlier emperors and shōguns, just two years later he resigned in favour of his son Hidetada (1579–1632). Though Hidetada was no infant, Ieyasu himself continued to wield actual power. By this early abdication Ieyasu helped ensure the continuity of his line—a continuity further helped by Hidetada's own similar abdication in 1623.

Hideyori was still a potential threat. It took Ieyasu some years, but in 1615 he finally managed to destroy Hideyori's base at Osaka Castle. Still only 22, Hideyori committed suicide when defeat was imminent. His captured 7-year-old son Kunimatsu was executed by beheading.

The same year of 1615, Ieyasu also issued sets of laws to control both the court and the military houses. Though the court had legitimised Ieyasu's own position and he treated it with some respect, he made it clear that its authority was merely formal and ceremonial. It was made subject to the control of the shōgunate, which reserved the right to approve all court appointments. Military houses were controlled by the enforcement of the status quo, down to fine detail.[1] They were required to ensure that:

- no person should take up residence in a new domain;
- all criminals should be expelled;
- all marriages involving *daimyō* should have shōgunal approval;
- no new castles were to be built at all, and even repairs to existing ones should have shōgunal approval;
- innovations being planned or factional conspiracies being formed in neighbouring domains should be reported immediately;
- *daimyō* processions should include given numbers of retainers matching the *daimyō*'s rank;
- *daimyō* should follow specific dress codes;
- unranked persons should not ride in palanquins.

Ieyasu clearly believed that enforced stability and orthodoxy were important to continued control. Change was undesirable because it was hard to predict. Mobility was a threat. The more people acted in a set-tled and prescribed manner, the less of a threat they posed. Failure to act as expected was even punishable by death. Ieyasu is said to have defined 'rude behaviour'—for which a samurai could lop off the miscre-ant's head—as 'acting in an other-than-expected manner'.[2]

Ieyasu died of illness the following year, 1616, and was deified as the manifestation of the Buddha of Healing. How much he had healed the nation was a matter of some debate, but he had certainly helped keep it unified.

His policy of orthodoxy and stability was pursued by his son Hidetada and most of his successors, all of whom were Tokugawa. In many cases it was possible simply to build on policies already put in place by Hideyoshi.

The regulations for military families were soon followed by regu-lations for other classes. These prescribed not only such matters as type and place of work and residence, and type of clothing, but such minute details as what type of present a person of a particular class could give to their offspring of a particular sex and age, what type of food they could eat, and even where they could build their toilet.[3]

Hideyoshi's freezing of the classes was an important means of enforcing orthodoxy and stability. It was now extended to a formal Chinese-inspired hierarchical system known as *shi-nō-kō-shō*, meaning 'warrior-peasant-artisan-merchant', in descending order of status.[4] Peasants ranked higher than artisans and merchants because in Confucian terms they were seen as essential producers. Within each class, particularly the samurai class, there were numerous sub-rankings.

Court nobles, priests, and nuns were outside the classes, while below the classes were two 'outcast' sub-classes, *eta* ('great filth', nowadays *burakumin*, or 'hamlet people'), and *hinin* ('non-persons'). They were engaged either in despised 'impure' activities[5] such as butchering, leather-work, and burial, or in 'suspicious' activities such as peddling and acting. *Burakumin* continue to this day to be segregated from mainstream society.

Class was in theory determined by birth, and movement between the classes was difficult—though in practice not impossible as is popularly believed.[6] A main division was between the samurai and the non-samurai. Samurai accounted for only about 6 per cent of the population, and included most bureaucrats since in effect that is what they became. Non-samurai were basically divided into those who lived in the country and those who lived in the towns.

The Tokugawa also valued Hideyoshi's policy of domain redistribution. The shōgun himself owned about one-quarter of cultivated land, along with major cities, ports, and mines. The remaining land was strategically divided between the 275 or so *daimyō* on the basis of whether they were *shinpan* (relatives), *fudai* (traditional retainers), or *tozama* ('outer *daimyō*' of questionable loyalty). Though numbers fluctuated, typically there were around 25 *shinpan*, 150 *fudai*, and 100 *tozama*.

Nor could a *daimyō* relax after being given a domain (*han*). Although in theory they were allowed considerable autonomy in matters such as taxation rights and internal administration, including law enforcement, in practice they were expected to follow the examples and guidelines established by the shōgunate. In effect, local government became their responsibility, and they had to carry out their responsibilities to the shōgunate's liking. The shōgunate constantly monitored their behaviour. At the least suggestion of insubordination they were punished. In just the first fifty years of Tokugawa rule no fewer than 213 *daimyō*—the great majority—lost all or part of their domain for offences either real or alleged. In the same period 172 new *daimyō* were given domains as rewards for loyal service, there were 206 instances of domains being increased as a similar reward, and on 281 occasions *daimyō* were relocated.[7]

Hideyoshi's practice of keeping the families of potentially trouble-some *daimyō* hostage was extended by the Tokugawa into a system known as *sankin kōtai* (alternate attendance). With just a few excep-tions, this obliged each *daimyō* alternately to spend a year in Edo and a year in his domain, while his family remained permanently in Edo. The great expense involved in maintaining a residence in Edo as well as in their domain, and in proceeding to and from Edo on a regular basis with the requisite number of retainers, also helped prevent the *daimyō* from accumulating too much financial power. In fact, it consumed around half their income or more.[8] They were also obliged to travel not only on specific dates but also along specific routes, which were always guarded by shōgunate troops.

Other measures taken by the Tokugawa shōgunate to restrict mobility and limit potential instability amongst the general population included:

- checks on land travel, with officially approved travel documents having to be obtained and shown at the barriers between do-mains;
- a curfew system that prevented people moving around at night without proper authority, especially outside their own town wards;
- the destruction of most bridges, thereby channelling movement and making it more manageable;
- the effective banning of wheeled transport;
- the use of secret police to report on any suspicious movements or happenings.

Punishment for offenders was usually severe, particularly for those in the major towns in territory controlled directly by the Tokugawa. Execu-tion was common for petty theft or even for negligence in letting your own house catch fire—fires being a particular danger to communities of mostly wooden houses. Whole families, and even neighbours, were sometimes executed along with the miscreant, for Hideyoshi's principle of collective responsibility was applied with vigour. In particular, heads of families and neighbourhood associations were held responsible for the misdeeds of their members.

Punishments in Europe at the time were also severe by modern standards, but the severity of those in Japan was enough to shock many European visitors of the day. The Frenchman François Caron, who spent many years in Japan in the first half of the seventeenth century, wrote that:[9]

Their punishments are rosting, burning, crucifying both waies, drawing with four Bulls and boyling in Oyl and Water.

An Italian visitor, Francesco Carletti, remarked:[10]

...many suffered crucifixion on the slightest pretext, such as the theft of a radish.... Sometimes also they crucify women, with babies at the breast, and leave them both to die in agony together. Their punishments are indeed extremely cruel, barbarous, and inhuman....

They both omit beheading, which was not uncommon, but was by no means the final use of the blade on executed commoners. In a practice known as *tameshigiri* ('trial cut'), samurai tested the efficiency of their swords on the corpses of executed criminals until, as Carletti observed, 'the wretched body is chopped into mincemeat, being left there as food for the dogs and the birds'.[11] A good blade could cut through three corpses in one blow, with seven the record—and testing was not confined to corpses.[12]

Condemned samurai and nobles sometimes suffered a similar fate, but in most cases were allowed the 'privilege' of committing suicide by ritual disembowelment, known as *seppuku* or *harakiri* ('stomach cutting'). This was a practice that had arisen in the Heian period and was meant to show the purity of the victim's soul, which was felt to reside in the stomach. It was by this stage often ritualised or even tokenised, with the victim's head being cut off by an honoured friend immediately after the incision.

The severity of the punishments makes an interesting contrast to the relative leniency of the *ritsuryō* system almost 1,000 years earlier, and suggests one difference between court rule and martial rule. At the same time, however, punishment continued to be based on disobedience and disruptiveness, rather than moral judgement.

The principle of collective punishment made people very cautious about welcoming any strangers into their midst. Strangers were suspicious enough anyway in an age of controlled movement, but when a community could be punished or even executed for the misdeeds of a stranger then it made sense not to accept them at all.[13] This has considerable bearing on the continuing general Japanese reluctance to become involved with strangers.[14]

Collective and severe punishments also applied in theory and sometimes in practice in the countryside of the *daimyō* domains, but life there was often easier. This was because many *daimyō* were generally happy not to interfere in the affairs of any village in their domain provided its collective taxes were paid, and provided there was no blatant law-breaking or defiance. Discipline in the villages was, except for serious cases, generally left to the headman or village council, and punishments were usually in the form of a fine or imposition of a duty, with ostracism being one of the worst punishments.[15]

Villagers therefore made sure they presented a reassuringly peaceful and inoffensive front to *daimyō* officials, whatever the actual state of turmoil in their village might be. This idea of deferential 'lip service' was to be another important legacy for modern Japan. It is another element in the relationship between formal authority and actual power,[16] and also in the commonly noted continuing Japanese distinction between outward appearance (*omote* or *tatemae*) and inner reality (*ura* or *honne*). If one gave the appearance of 'toeing the line' and respecting authority, and if one did not cause any real disturbance, then the chances were that one would be left in peace—and even with a degree of 'freedom within limits'. The same could be said of Japan today.

Westerners always presented a problem. They were not familiar with Japanese ways, behaved unpredictably and often defiantly, spoke strange languages that were hard to monitor, and had strange ideas about some divine power that transcended emperors and shōguns alike. Their trade was useful, true, and they had some useful technology, but they were simply too much of a threat for the shōgunate's peace of mind. In particular, the challenge that their uncompromising God presented to the authority of the shōgun was a major problem—not so much in theological terms, but political ones.

Had westerners kept their Christian beliefs to themselves, and not tried to assert the authority of their God—and their God alone—through preaching and moral judgements, they may well have received better treatment. Japan was (and still is) a land of religious tolerance. Nobunaga's campaigns against Buddhist institutions were based on political rather than religious grounds, and the same was true of the actions by Hideyoshi and then the Tokugawa against the Christians.

Though the Japanese did not concern themselves overly with the theological distinction, Catholicism was seen as more of a threat than the newly emerged Protestantism.[17] This may have been because Catholics comprised the great majority of the Christians in Japan—and virtually all the converted Japanese—or because they were more outward and assertive in the expression of their faith than the Protestants. Most likely, however, it was largely because the shōgunate was aware of the vigorous empire-building being pursued by Catholic nations in the New World. Columbus himself had come from a Catholic nation. Moreover, the Catholic Church even had its own state, the Vatican, with popes who often became involved in politics. This all clearly suggested that the Catholic Church was not merely spiritual.

In any event, Christianity came to symbolise the western presence and threat to shōgunal power and authority. It became a focal point for shōgunal action against that threat. This action applied not only to westerners themselves, but also to those Japanese who had been converted to Christianity. Like the punishments of the day, it was harsh, particularly against Japanese Christians.

Persecution intensified through the early 1600s. Many suspected Christians were asked to demonstrate their rejection of Christianity by stepping on a copper tablet that bore an image of a crucifix or similar Christian symbol. Some remained steadfast in their faith even though the tortures used to persuade them to renounce it were horrific, including, for example, eye-gouging and the torturing of young children in front of their parents.[18] The executions were similarly horrific, involving methods such as crucifixion, beheading by saw, or throwing into boiling thermal pools.

The culmination of persecution was the Shimabara Massacre of 1638, near Nagasaki, in which as many as 35,000 people—men, women, and children, and most of them Christians—were killed by shōgunate forces. This was not purely a persecution of Christians, but was at the same time the quelling of an uprising partly caused by discontent over taxation and an unpopular *daimyō*.[19] Nevertheless, the causes became conveniently blurred, and it brought an effective end to the open presence of Christianity in Japan (though 'hidden Christianity' was to persist among some, especially in the Nagasaki region). From 1640 all Japanese were obliged to register at Buddhist temples to prove their non-Christianity, a practice which also helped keep a check on the population at large.

Christian missionaries had been expelled in 1614, but western traders had been allowed to continue to visit and even reside in the country. Gradually, however, the shōgunate came to feel that the disadvantages of foreign trade outweighed the advantages. It was not only a constant worry in terms of national security, but a perceived indirect threat to the Tokugawa through the enriching of certain *daimyō* participating in foreign trade. Even at such an early stage, the shōgunate also had an economically motivated wish to preserve domestic merchants from excessive competition.[20]

By 1639 all westerners had been expelled or had left voluntarily, with the exception of the Dutch, who were allowed only on the small island of Deshima in Nagasaki Harbour.[21] Along with the Chinese and Koreans, they were the only foreigners formally allowed to trade with Japan as it effectively withdrew from the world for the next two centuries. This was the period later described as the *sakoku jidai*, or 'closed country period'.

It was not just a case of foreigners being banned entry into Japan, for the shōgunate seemed to reject almost any form of 'foreignness'. From 1635, with very few exceptions, Japanese were not allowed to travel overseas, and those Japanese who were overseas at the time—who numbered in the tens of thousands, mostly in southeast Asia—were banned from returning on pain of death.[22] The building of large vessels capable of ocean travel had also been banned by that stage. Ships authorised for coastal trading had to display an official shōgunate seal.[23]

The arrival of westerners had helped generate a national consciousness in Japan,[24] aided by the process of reunification that followed shortly afterwards. It was during the 1600s that the Ryūkyū Islands to the south and Hokkaidō to the north began to be incorporated into the nation, giving it a geo-political identity very close to present-day Japan. Japanese world-maps of the time, in another example of adaptation from the Chinese, show Japan—not China—as the centre of the world.[25] Clearly, for the time being at least, Tokugawa Japan was not interested in too much involvement with the lesser nations of its world. A closed country was also a much safer country for its Tokugawa rulers.

3.2 SAMURAI AND ETHICS

As the country entered an enduring phase of stability and peace, without even any real foreign threat, warriors became superfluous. There were a number of peasant uprisings to put down, their lords' honour to uphold, and a bit of policing, but little work for real warriors. Instead, they became bureaucrats and administrators. Their battles became mere paper wars.

These men who occupied the top class in the social order were acutely embarrassed by their almost parasitic life. They seized the least chance for real action to prove their valour, and they went to almost absurd lengths to justify their existence. As a rather ironic result, it was during this age of the redundant samurai that some of the clearest expressions of the samurai ideal, *bushidō* ('way of the warrior'), were to emerge.

Every Japanese knows the story of the Forty-Seven Rōnin. A *rōnin* (wanderer) was a samurai made masterless either by dismissal or by the execution or demotion of his lord. There were quite a few of them in Tokugawa Japan who roamed the countryside causing trouble for villagers and disquiet for the authorities. The forty-seven in question, however, are seen as the embodiment of samurai virtue.

In 1701 their lord, Asano Naganori (1665–1701) of Akō in Harima (Hyōgo Prefecture), had been insulted by Kira Yoshinaka (1641–1703), the shōgun's chief of protocol. Asano had drawn his sword in the shōgun's castle—a capital offence. He was made to commit *seppuku*, and his domain was confiscated from his family. Forty-seven of his now masterless samurai retainers vowed to avenge his death by killing Kira. They hid their intent for two years, pretending to lead a life of dissipation, then attacked and killed Kira in an unguarded moment, placing his severed head on their lord's grave.

Though their behaviour was considered exemplary *bushidō* they were nonetheless ordered to kill themselves for having taken the law into their own hands. Amidst scholarly discussion and public controversy they killed themselves in a mass *seppuku*. Their graves at Sengakuji Temple in Tōkyō are now a major tourist attraction.

Descriptions of *bushidō* from this period that are still popular today include *Hagakure* (In the Shadow of Leaves) of 1716 and *Gorin no Sho* (The Five Rings) of around 1643. However, one of the most interesting was written by Yamaga Sokō (1622–85), who was himself a *rōnin*. He had also been a teacher of one of the Forty-Seven *Rōnin*.

Yamaga was perhaps the first to see *bushidō* as a comprehensive philosophy.[26] In his various writings he stressed aspects of it such as loyalty and self-discipline, as well as the importance of learning and cultivation of the arts and the rounded development of the whole man. Knowing one's role in life, and knowing how to properly conduct relations with others, are particularly stressed. But he also struck a defensive note in his justification of the samurai's apparent lack of functional usefulness to the society of the day. Yamaga argued that the samurai's freedom from occupation proper allowed him to concentrate on perfecting his moral virtue and thus to serve as a model for the rest of society, disciplining the imperfect if necessary:[27]

> The samurai dispenses with the business of the farmer, artisan, and merchant, and confines himself to practising this Way; should there be someone in the three classes of the common people who transgresses against these moral principles, the samurai summarily punishes him and thus upholds proper moral principles in the land.

There is here a reference to morality, but it is a different morality from the western concept. It is still not a question of good and evil, but of doing the expected thing in the context of social relations and orderliness. Step out of line, and one is summarily punished.

Yamaga's account also has a heavy Confucian tone. Confucianists were very much concerned with knowing one's place, honouring relationships, respecting order, and doing one's duty. Because of these values, Confucianism was revived and promoted by the Tokugawa shōgunate. In some aspects, however, it was modified to suit Japan. For example, Chinese Confucianism allowed for showing loyalty to conscience, but in Japan this became narrowed to loyalty to one's superior. A Confucian adviser to the shōgun was appointed, and a Confucian college was founded in Edo with shōgunal support. The period produced many noted Confucian scholars, such as Hayashi Razan (1583–1657), Yamazaki Ansai (1618–82), Arai Hakuseki (1657–1725), and Ogyū Sorai (1666–1728).

One major influence of Confucianism was on gender perceptions and by extension sexual relations. Texts such as *Onna Daigaku* (Great Learning for Women) of 1716 preached the 'five infirmities' of women—indocility, discontent, slander, jealousy, and silliness—and placed them in a greatly inferior position to men. *Onna Daigaku* observed that:[28]

> Without any doubt, these five infirmities are found in seven or eight out of every ten women, and it is from these that arises the inferiority of women to men.

This lowly view of women was one reason why so many—if not most— samurai preferred homosexual relationships.[29] Moreover, according to the sometimes-followed Chinese philosophy of *yin* and *yang*, too much association with the female *yin* could seriously weaken the male *yang*.

Confucianists and the shōgunate did not really approve of homosexuality, but turned a blind eye to it. The shōgunate was particularly prepared to be tolerant because in Japan's case physical male homosexuality invariably reflected social rank, with the active partner always the senior.[30]

Confucianism was not always good for the shōgunate. One of its ironies was that it encouraged ideas of merit and learning. This was allowed for in concepts of hierarchy and rank in China, which permitted some mobility on the basis of learning and meritorious achievement, and in later centuries this was also to some extent to be allowed for in Japan. However, encouragement of merit and learning did not necessarily work in the best interests of the Tokugawa shōgunate and its policy of unquestioning orthodoxy and stability. Over time rather more critical and questioning attitudes emerged in some quarters than the shōgunate wanted—though this should not be overstated, for obedience was still the norm.

The children of samurai and nobles were educated at home or at special domain schools, and wealthy merchants also set up private schools. Increasingly the children of other classes had the opportunity to study at small schools known as *terakoya* (literally 'temple-child building'). These were originally set up under the auspices of village temples but soon spread to the towns. Tuition was usually very cheap or free, since the teacher was often a priest who taught as an act of benevolence or a samurai who taught for a sense of self-worth. As a result of this widespread education the literacy rate in the later part of the period is estimated to have been 45 per cent for males and 15 per cent for females, giving an overall rate of 30 per cent. This was arguably the highest in the world at the time. It set an enduring trend, for Japan still has the highest literacy rate in the world at 99 per cent.

Another point of Confucianist irony was that its encouragement of obedience to the ruler inevitably raised the question of who exactly the ruler was. It did not escape the notice of an increasingly educated population that in China the ruler was the emperor. This effectively meant the shōgun could be seen as a usurper.

Doubts about the shōgunate intensified from the 1700s with the revival of Shintō, and early texts associated with it such as the *Kojiki*. Shintō and the *Kojiki* were seen as something purely Japanese, and became part of *kokugaku* ('national learning'). In some ways this was a continuation of the emergence of national consciousness, prodded by the occasional reminder of the outside world in the form of castaways, or foreign ships seeking reprovisioning rights or similar. It was also an expression of a feeling that Japan was a little too Chinese. *Kokugaku* scholars included figures such as Motoori Norinaga (1730–1801) and Hirata Atsutane (1776–1843). Motoori produced an annotated version of the *Kojiki* and was openly critical of things Chinese. Hirata argued the superiority of Shintō and Japan and was to be part-inspiration for later Japanese nationalism and imperialism.

The idealisation of the way of the samurai, the revival of Confucianism, the spread of education, and the emergence of nationalism were all to play a part in the formation of modern Japan. So too, of course, did the conformism and orthodoxy that formed their setting.

3.3   COMMONERS, CULTURE, AND THE ECONOMY

Edo soon became a bustling centre. The location there of the shōgunate, and the alternate attendance of the *daimyō* and their retainers, made this inevitable. By the end of the eighteenth century it had a population of around a million, making it the biggest city in the world at the time. It was such a part of life of the age that the whole period is often popularly called the Edo period.

But it was not the only busy centre. Osaka and Kyōto both had around half a million residents. Towns sprang up along the routes taken by the *daimyō* and their processions to provide for their many needs. Exchange centres developed where *daimyō* representatives could convert their domain's rice crop into cash. And despite the restrictions on travel, and the harshness of punishments for town dwellers, many peasants flocked to the towns to seek their fortune amidst all this new economic activity.

These various townspeople (*chōnin*) helped form a new and vibrant culture. Their dynamism helped offset the staid orthodoxy preferred by the shōgunate.

Wealthy merchants in particular played a part in this new bourgeois culture. Not for them the refined and restrained *nō* drama of the aristocrats. They preferred the colour and ostentation of *kabuki*, with its exaggerated movements, simple melodramatic plots, and stage effects such as trapdoors and revolving stages. Or else they flocked to the 'puppet drama' of *bunraku*. Not for them the refined sensibility of aristocratic poetry. They preferred shorter and often humorous verses such as *haiku* and *senryū*.[31] They liked witty books (*sharebon*), popular romances (*yomihon*), merchant success stories (*chōninmono*), and sexually titillating books (*kōshokubon* or *ukiyo-zōshi*).[32] They liked colourful woodblock prints, often sexually explicit. These were known as *shunga* ('pictures of spring') or more generally as *ukiyo-e*, 'pictures of the floating world'. The 'floating world' was originally a term used by priests to refer to the transience of life, but in the age of Edo it came to mean the world of human relations, especially sexual relations.

The sexuality of the age was often downplayed to western visitors of later times, but it was a major part of bourgeois culture in particular.[33] Early *kabuki* actresses were barely distinguishable from prostitutes, and performances often degenerated into orgies. The shōgunate, alarmed at the unruliness of it all, banned females from the stage.[34] However, the male actors who replaced them had exactly the same effect. The shōgunate ordered them to tone down their act, and kept an eye on performances, but for once was really unable to do much about it.

It was also the age of the *geisha* ('artistic person'), who were often male. In most cases—male and female alike—the *geisha* were little more than artistically talented prostitutes, for although they played the *shamisen* and could recite verses they also sold their bodies. The shōgunate managed to exercise at least some degree of control by confining *geisha* and prostitutes to specified 'pleasure quarters' in each city, such as Yoshiwara in Edo.[35]

While the townspeople generally prospered, this was not always the case with the peasantry, who comprised the majority of the population. There were a number of crop failures and famines due to climatic instability. The tax burden in many domains was high and the cause of a number of uprisings. Poor administration in some domains contributed to their woes. There were also many who could not cope with the economic vagaries of increasing crop specialisation and commercialisation in agriculture, as in cash crops such as silk, cotton, tobacco, sugar, and tea.[36] In practice unsuccessful farmers often entrusted their lands to others and became tenants, despite laws to the contrary. The gap between rich and poor grew as a result.

However, overall, the degree of distress of the peasantry has been exaggerated. The levelling out of population growth from around the middle of the period, at some 30 million, has often been attributed to infanticide among poor farming families. This certainly did happen, but it was not always done out of desperate poverty. It was often done simply to improve living standards, just as many modern-day families limit the number of their children. In other words, it was often a form of 'postnatal contraception'.[37]

In a similar way, family size was sometimes adjusted upwards by adoption in order to improve economic efficiency, for each family was a unit of production.[38] Just as villages were whole units responsible to the domain lord for crop production and taxes, within villages it was extended families (*ie*) who were the units, and not individuals. Blood ties were not particularly important to these extended families.

Overall, despite cases of failure and hardship, living conditions throughout the period improved for the peasantry as a whole, as for society at large.[39] In fact, the various laws to regulate consumption passed throughout the period are in themselves an indication that wealth was increasing. A decree issued by the shōgunate in 1788 stated:[40]

> For long it has been the custom among peasants to wear simple cloth-ing and tie their hair with straw. However, of late, they have become accustomed to luxuries and forgetful of their status. They wear cloth-ing befitting those of higher status and use oil and *motoyui* [cord] to tie their hair. They now use umbrellas and *kappa* [raincoats] in the rain instead of straw hats and *mino* [straw covers]. As expenses rise because of all this, villages decline and people leave the villages.... The peasants should at no time forget their station in life. For peasants to engage in trade or for villages to have hairdressers is to be disrespectful. Henceforth, all luxuries should be avoided by the peasants. They are to live simply and devote themselves to farming.

Improved living standards indicated a healthy economy. The reasons for this state of health reflected a mixture of astuteness and circum-stance:

- the rate of increase in production was greater than the rate of increase in population—to some extent the result of an awareness of the link between economic efficiency and size of family (the product-ive/consumptive unit), but also the result of improved agricultural technology;[41]
- the high rate of literacy and numeracy helped the spread of new technology and the efficiency of commercial activity in general;
- the alternate attendance system gave rise to the need for *daimyō* to obtain liquid assets to meet their huge and varied expenses, leading to sophisticated brokering and exchange mechanisms, and to an advanced monetary economy;[42]

- as a result of increased economic activity there was increased diversity and specialisation (in terms of both region and worker), which boosted efficiency, commercialisation, and monetarisation still further;
- national stability in terms of peace and political structures provided a helpful environment;
- owing to the class system merchants were not taken particularly seriously by the shōgunate, were given a considerable degree of autonomy, and were relatively lightly taxed.[43]

The rise of the merchant was particularly important for Japan's future. It was in this period that certain huge merchant houses such as Mitsui and Sumitomo developed.[44] The whole idea of profit-making, which was once scorned by the ruling class as undignified, became gradually more acceptable. Ishida Baigan (1685–1744) even developed a philosophy that extolled profit-making and the role of the merchant.[45]

The rise of the merchant, however, was also one more factor that ultimately helped undermine Tokugawa policy. Clearly, a class system that placed merchants at the bottom was losing touch with reality. In that reality, it was not uncommon for *daimyō* to be greatly in the debt—and in some cases control—of merchants. Some merchants were allowed samurai privileges, and some samurai engaged in commerce. The frozen class system, a pillar of Tokugawa policy, was inevitably starting to thaw.

3.4 THE RETURN OF THE FOREIGN DEVILS AND THE FALL OF THE SHŌGUNATE

A degree of contact with the west was maintained through the Dutch presence in Nagasaki. There was still an interest in 'western learning' (*Yōgaku* or *Rangaku*), especially the sciences, and even considerable admiration.[46] Physician-scholars such as Engelbert Kaempfer (1651–1716) and later Philipp Franz von Siebold (1796–1866)—both actually German, but both employed as physicians to the Dutch colony in Nagasaki—left a particularly strong impression.

From time to time unauthorised westerners did land in the closed country, sometimes intentionally, sometimes not. With very few exceptions they were either expelled or executed. From around the end of the eighteenth century, as western powers grew more active in the Pacific and eastern Asia, a number of nations made official attempts to reopen relations—at least to the extent of obtaining reprovisioning rights for their vessels. These too were doomed to failure. Russia tried and failed in 1792 and again in 1804. Britain tried in 1797, 1808, and 1818. America, whose whaling ships were active in waters near Japan, tried in 1791, 1797, and 1837, and particularly seriously in 1846 and 1849.[47]

By the middle of the nineteenth century the shōgunate had realised that westerners were probably not going to leave Japan alone. However, having seen what was happening in China, with its western-induced Opium Wars, it was even more determined to keep them at bay. Aided by staunch nationalists, it even tried to prevent debate about the issue of relations with westerners. Takano Chōei (1804–50) was imprisoned and later forced to commit suicide for his 'audacity' in urging the opening of the country to foreign contact. Even the compromise view of Sakuma Shōzan (1811–64), who advocated a blending of Japanese and western strengths and coined the slogan 'Tōyō no dōtoku, Seiyō no gakugei' ('Eastern ethics, Western science'), was enough to bring about his assassination.

The more extreme nationalists popularised the slogan 'sonnō jōi' ('Revere the emperor, expel the barbarians'). The anti-foreign sentiment may have found favour with the shōgunate, but the other half of the slogan was not so welcome, for it suggested an ominous lack of respect for the shōgunate itself.

From around the 1830s in particular, there was a growing feeling that the shōgunate was losing control, and with it came a loss of respect. It had failed to respond constructively to a severe famine during 1833–7.[48] In 1837 there was even a call for insurrection led by Oshio Heihachirō (1793–1837), a Confucian official in Osaka who had long been upset by the inefficiency and corruption of officialdom. Oshio's uprising was small-scale in itself, but it caused further loss of respect for the shōgunate due to the incompetence shown in the attempt to suppress it.[49] Oshio himself, though obliged to commit suicide, became a symbol of the fight of the common people against corrupt and inefficient officialdom and the greedy merchants tolerated by the regime. The shōgunate did pass a number of reforms, but these were ineffective.

By extension the samurai, who were in most cases one and the same as the officials, also lost respect. This added to their earlier frustrations about being deprived of their role as warriors. And even their military competence was now being called into question.[50]

Matters were brought to a head by the visit in July 1853 of US Commodore Matthew Perry (1794–1858), who sailed—or more exactly steamed—into Edo Bay with four ships. Perry had official orders to request three things: more humane treatment for castaways, the opening of ports for provisions and fuel, and the opening of ports for trade.

He was a determined man, prepared to use force if necessary, and he made sure the Japanese were aware of his determination and the potential of his armed force.[51] Having presented the Japanese with a letter from the American president to the emperor of Japan, he left, promising to return the following year for an answer.

There was much confusion and argument after Perry's departure. The shōgunate even took the unprecedented and humiliating step of requesting advice from the *daimyō*. However, it was effectively powerless to resist. When he returned in February 1854, with a larger fleet of nine ships, the shōgunate agreed to a treaty. In the Treaty of Kanagawa of March 1854 the shōgunate accepted American requests, including the right to station a consular official in Japan. The first consul, Townsend Harris (1804–78), duly took up his post in the port of Shimoda in 1856. The doors of the closed country had been forced open.

Similar treaties with other powers followed rapidly, such as with Britain in October 1854 and Russia in February 1855, and France and Holland soon after. Further concessions to any one power brought similar concessions to the others, for all were granted 'most favoured nation' status. Japan lost control over its own tariffs. These 'unequal treaties' won by 'gun-boat diplomacy' were humiliating to the Japanese. One particularly galling concession was the right of extraterritoriality, by which foreign nationals who broke the law were tried by their consul rather than the legal authorities of the host nation. This was a clear relegation of Japan to 'uncivilised' status, and it hurt Japanese pride and sensibilities greatly, for it was the western devils—not the Japanese—who were supposed to be the barbarians.

Western traders and adventurers also arrived in number.[52] They were not always the best behaved or the most politically correct of diplomats, but some nationalists—particularly among the samurai—needed little or no provocation to attack them.[53]

The inability of the shōgun to deal effectively with the foreign 'threat', despite his supposed role as military protector of Japan, sounded the death knell for the shōgunate. Opposition to it mounted, its opponents representing a mixture of political opportunism and genuine concern for the welfare of the nation.

Not surprisingly, major opposition came from *tozama* domains, especially Satsuma in southern Kyūshū and Chōshū at the western tip of Honshū. Satsuma and Chōshū were large and powerful domains, sharing a bond of antipathy towards the shōgunate though traditionally they were not well-disposed towards each other.

Chōshū nationalists were especially fervent. One of their men, Yoshida Shōin (1830–59), had unsuccessfully attempted to stow away on one of Perry's ships in order to learn about the west and thereby strengthen Japan. Soon afterwards he was executed for plotting to assassinate a shōgunal representative, becoming a martyr for the cause of *sonnō jōi*.

In July 1863 and again in September 1864, angered at the shōgunate's inaction, Chōshū even began firing at foreign vessels in the Strait of Shimonoseki (adjacent to its domain). It suffered armed reprisals from British and American forces, losing many of its ships and having many of its military land bases destroyed. The shōgunate decided it too needed to punish Chōshū, and sent punitive forces in 1865 and 1866. However, the regrouped Chōshū forces—now using peasant militia as well as samurai—successfully resisted these shōgunal forces.

Chōshū's epoch-making stand against the Tokugawa shōgunate—the first time a domain had successfully defied it—was aided by Satsuma's decision not to join the shōgunal forces. Both domains were rivals for the favours of an imperial court that now sensed an opportunity to reassert itself after many centuries of tokenism. They had fought each other over the matter as recently as 1863, and Satsuma had prevailed. However, soon afterwards the two domains had formed an alliance. This alliance too was to be epoch-making.

In January 1867 there was a new shōgun, Yoshinobu (1837–1913, also known as Keiki). He seemed unusually capable, undertaking a number of constructive administrative reforms. He also seemed keen on a constructive *rapprochement* of shōgunate and court. The opponents of the shōgunate now had to act quickly. A delay might prove their undoing, and allow a reformed shōgunate to continue.

Helped by Iwakura Tomomi (1825–83), a court noble with Chōshū connections, an alliance of *tozama* domains led by Satsuma and Chōshū managed to obtain an imperial rescript calling for the abolition of the shōgunate. With this authority, on 3 January 1868 they occupied the palace and declared an 'imperial restoration'. Though opposition from shōgunal supporters was to continue for some time afterwards, Yoshinobu himself, after a brief period of indecisiveness and uncoordinated resistance, presently accepted this declaration. He retired to Shizuoka to live out the remaining forty-five years of his life peacefully.

The emperor who now found himself 'restored to power' was a 15-year-old boy by the name of Mutsuhito (1852–1912), posthumously to be known as Meiji ('enlightened rule'). He had acceded to the throne just a year earlier, in January 1867, following the death of his father

Kōmei (1831–67, r. 1846–67). Kōmei's death is surrounded by controversy, and he may well have been poisoned.[54] He had been less than fully supportive of the imperial restoration movement, preferring a union of court and shōgunate. His death was certainly convenient, for it enabled the all-important imperial rescript of authorisation to be obtained. It also removed the possibility of having a reluctant and difficult adult emperor and left instead a potentially manipulable boy as the head of state.

In any event, the rule of the shōguns, which had lasted for almost 700 years, was at an end. The foreign devils were back, and did not look like leaving. The closed country had finally opened its doors.

REVIEW OF PART THREE

The warlord Tokugawa Ieyasu and his immediate successors were able to consolidate the unification process started during the latter half of the sixteenth century. Building on the success and in many cases the actual policies of Oda Nobunaga and Toyotomi Hideyoshi, they were able to revitalise the shōgunate. It was occupied by the Tokugawa family for two and a half centuries. The main thrust of Tokugawa policy was to keep Japan as far as possible in a stable state of controlled orthodoxy. This included removing the western threat, symbolised by the political threat to shōgunal authority presented by Christianity, and effectively closing Japan off from the rest of the world. Other mechanisms of control included the enforced alternate attendance of *daimyō* at the shōgunate's base in Edo, strategic redistribution of domains, hierarchical separation of the classes, restrictions on travel and transport, curfews, monitoring, collective responsibility, and minute prescriptions even for everyday living. Breach of regulation usually meant harsh punishment.

However, over time significant internal changes took place despite the ideal of maintaining the status quo. In particular there were changes to the actual social order brought about by socio-economic developments. These saw the emergence of a powerful merchant class, and the general weakening of the now redundant samurai, who became bureaucrats in practice but also ironically became idealised. A new, vibrant, bourgeois culture emerged, centred on these merchants. Furthermore, the promotion of Confucianism, intended to support orthodoxy and order, also ironically improved educational levels and critical thinking.

Through its emphasis on the emperor as supreme ruler it also raised questions as to the legitimacy of the shōgunate. Partly as a reaction against what was seen as too much Chinese influence, a nationalist spirit also emerged, one that looked to the past and centred on Shintō and the emperor. These developments were by no means helpful to the shōgunate, which was also plagued by corruption and incompetence.

The shōgunate may have fallen anyway through these domestic factors, but as it happened its end was hastened by the return of western powers in the mid-nineteenth century. They demanded trade and other rights, and forced treaties that were humiliating to Japan. The shōgunate's inability to defend the nation against this foreign threat, despite the shōgun's supposed role as military protector, opened the way for an effective coup by those 'outer domains' long opposed to it, especially Satsuma and Chōshū. Their action was a mixture of opportunism and genuine nationalism. The last shōgun was forced to resign early in 1868. A teenage emperor was 'restored' to power by samurai from these domains, heralding a new period in Japan's history.

Key developments during the period are summarised in Table 3.1.

Table 3.1   Key developments in the Tokugawa period

Development	Approximate time
Shōgunate re-established	start 1600s
Foreigners removed, Christianity suppressed	early–mid-1600s
Shōgunal policies of control in place	by mid-1600s
Role of samurai changes to bureaucrat	from mid-1600s
New bourgeois culture develops	from mid-1600s
Shintō-based nationalism develops	from early 1700s
Population levels off, economy prospers	from early 1700s
Education spreads	from mid-1700s
Foreigners start to 'pester' again	from late 1700s
Rising public dissatisfaction towards shōgunate	from early 1800s
Foreigners return in force, country reopens, Japan humiliated	from 1850s
Outer domain samurai challenge shōgunate	from early 1860s
Shōgunate toppled by coup, emperor restored	late 1860s

We have also seen values and practices of continuing relevance to Japan. Some were the result of necessity, some seemingly the result of preference. They are summarised in Table 3.2.

Table 3.2   Key values and practices in the Tokugawa period

- widespread orthodoxy and conformism
- widespread obedience—at least in form—to authority, and an idea of 'freedom within limits'
- continued distinction between formal authority and actual power, and by extension between outer form and inner substance
- continued preference for equating 'wrong' with disruption and disobedience rather than evil
- 'morally relaxed' attitude towards sexuality
- collective responsibility and accountability, enforced by vigilance and harsh punishment
- cautiousness towards strangers, and strong in-group/out-group consciousness
- economic astuteness, even among many peasant families
- sense of materialism among many non-samurai
- continuing view that life is relatively cheap
- high regard for education
- revival of Japanised Confucianism
- idealisation of the way of the samurai
- a strengthening sense of nationalism, with an especially strong distinction between Japan and the rest of the world
- sense of humiliation by western powers

Some of these points, such as conformism and obedience, education and Confucianism, nationalism and unease towards strangers, have particularly obvious relevance to modern Japan. The idealisation of the samurai was also important, not only in itself but as a symbol of the masking of historical reality.

Certain other points help explain earlier paradoxes. For example, the harsh enforcement of collective accountability helped suppress the expression of obvious self-interest. This suggests the earlier medieval paradox of blatant self-interest despite legal norms of collective responsibility was due to the failure of authorities in those days to enforce the law with sufficient vigour.

Part Four

Building a Modern Nation: the Meiji Period (1868–1912)

4.1 CONSOLIDATING THE RESTORATION

The 'restored' Emperor Mutsuhito, at 15 years of age, was hardly likely to proceed without guidance in his 'enlightened rule'. Not surprisingly, his advisers were the samurai leaders who had supported his cause. These were mostly from Satsuma and Chōshū, with a few from other domains such as Tosa (in Shikoku) and Hizen (in Kyūshū). There were also a few court nobles such as Iwakura Tomomi among the group of advisers, mostly to add legitimacy to what was in effect the new government.

From Satsuma came Okubo Toshimichi (1830–78), Saigō Takamori (1827–77), and Matsukata Masayoshi (1835–1924). From Chōshū came Kido Kōin (1833–77), Inoue Kaoru (1835–1915), Itō Hirobumi (1841–1909), and Yamagata Aritomo (1838–1922). They were all young, most in their early thirties. Most of them were also originally of fairly low rank within the samurai class.

Itō Hirobumi, who was to become the dominant figure in Meiji, was a classic 'pauper to prince' story. Born into a poor farmer's family, in his early teens he was adopted (along with his father) into the family of a low-ranking samurai. For his subsequent exploits, which included the burning down of the British Legation, he was made a samurai in his own right in 1863. During Meiji he was to become prime minister on four occasions, and eventually obtained the title of 'prince'.

These young men had dual motives. On the one hand they had a genuine nationalistic desire to do the best for their country in the face of foreign threat. On the other, they had a desire to achieve personal success for themselves, a success they felt had been denied them under the old shōgunal regime.[1] They were far from shackled by dedication to the old regime, but neither were they shackled by ideological commitment to a full imperial restoration in actual practice as well as name. It was simply a question of doing whatever was best for themselves and the nation. For the moment at least, carrying the authoritative banner of an imperial restoration seemed a good way to proceed. Fortunately for themselves and the nation, they had a maturity and wisdom beyond their years. Fortunately for the imperial family, Mutsuhito did as he was told.

Their first aim was to consolidate the new regime. People had been greatly alarmed by the turbulent events of the coup. Mass hysteria was a common response to the traumatic change occurring in their long-settled world.[2] The public needed reassurance that stability—rather than the emperor—had been restored.

It was vital that lingering armed resistance was quickly put down. Edo was a centre of resistance by some 2,000 troops, but it was fully secured by July. The shōgunal loyalist Enomoto Takeaki (1836–1908) had fled Edo with a fleet of warships and taken them to Hokkaidō, declaring it a republic, but he was defeated in June the following year. Resistance was still to spring up in various forms for some years, but with the defeat of Enomoto order was effectively restored for the short term at least.

It was also vital that the emperor himself gave reassurance, especially about how Japan was going to deal with the foreign threat. In April 1868, just three months after being restored, he and his advisers issued the Charter Oath (of Five Articles).[3] This promised:

- public discussion of 'all matters';
- the participation of all classes in the administration of the country;
- freedom for all persons to pursue their preferred occupation;
- the abandoning of 'evil customs of the past' (unspecified);
- the seeking of knowledge throughout the world in order to strengthen the country (or more literally, 'to strengthen the foundations of imperial rule').

It was clear from this fifth article that the new government was planning not to confront the foreign threat but to learn from it and incorporate its strengths. The earlier xenophobic catchphrase *'sonnō jōi'* ('Revere the emperor, expel the barbarians') was soon to be replaced by more pragmatic and constructive slogans such as *'wakon yōsai'* ('Japanese spirit, western learning'). This approach to modernisation was—ironically but almost certainly consciously—similar to that of governments of the ancient Yamato and Nara periods. The past was a useful lesson for the modern.

Japan was fortunate it had the luxury of being allowed to learn at its own pace and in its own way, for just like China in those ancient times, or for that matter the Europeans in the sixteenth century, the western

powers of the nineteenth century were not really interested in colonising Japan. They had easier pickings elsewhere—not the New World this
time, for America itself was now one of those western powers, but the
ancient world of China.

In its short preamble the Charter Oath also promised a constitution.
This was actually promulgated in some haste just three months later, but
was a surprisingly low-profile affair. The so-called 'Constitution of 1868'
was to be overshadowed by a later and much better known Meiji Constitution, but it did provide in theory for a national assembly, public ballot,
and a Grand Council of State.[4] The Grand Council was the only item
to be put into effect at the time, and its various ministries and offices
further conferred legitimacy upon the young leaders of the government.

Again mirroring the practice of Japan's Yamato-Nara government,
the Meiji government wanted a single capital to be the hub of centralised power, as opposed to the 'dual capitals' of Edo and Kyōto. Edo was
chosen, and given a new name Tōkyō ('eastern capital'). The emperor
moved there from Kyōto in 1869. The new Grand Council was also
based there.

And in yet another Nara-style policy, the nation's land was nationalised. The former shōgunate's territory, which accounted for about a
quarter of the land, was the first to be nationalised. Then in March 1869
the Satsuma-Chōshū government leaders persuaded the *daimyō* of their
home domains to return their territories to the emperor, for reorganisation into prefectures. Other *daimyō* soon followed suit. In some cases
the relinquishing of their territory was not done with complete goodwill,
though they did not wish to incur the displeasure of the government and
had little real choice in the matter. In August 1871, the government
went a step further, legally abolishing the domains and replacing them
with prefectures.[5]

The *daimyō* were persuaded to accept these changes partly by generous financial arrangements and/or governorships of the new prefectures. Not only did the *daimyō* receive generous incomes, the
government took over their domain debts, and also took over responsibility for paying the stipends of their samurai retainers—which it
reduced by about a third. This generous treatment of the *daimyō* and to
a lesser extent the samurai was important politically, for it helped
reduce the risk of armed resistance against the regime.

However, such generosity did not help government finances, which
had been unhealthy from long before the Restoration. A number of
financial reforms were carried out in the first few years of the regime. A

modern mint was set up, along with a modern banking system, and a standardised decimal currency was established based on the yen. These reforms were overseen by key figures such as Okuma Shigenobu (1838–1922, from Hizen), who was minister of finance, and Itō Hirobumi, who had been sent to the United States to study currency systems and served as Okuma's assistant.

A particularly important financial reform was the introduction of a fixed land tax in July 1873, based on a percentage of the assessed value of a given plot of land. This replaced the former feudal system of variable tax linked to the harvest. Ownership of a given plot of land was now deemed to lie with the person (usually head of family) who had traditionally paid the tax on the harvest from it. This reform helped provide greater incentive to increase productivity. However, it had the less desirable effect of increasing the rate of tenancy up to as high as 40 per cent, since poorer farmers in bad years were forced to mortgage their land in order to pay the tax.[6]

Another major reform implemented by the new government to pave the way for modernisation was the abolition of the restrictive class system. This was very definitely not a reflection of Nara period influence. In keeping with the promises of the 1868 Charter Oath the restrictions on class occupations were removed in 1869. The classes were restructured from *shi-nō-kō-shō* into *kazoku* (nobles, including *daimyō*), *shizoku* (samurai descendants), and *heimin* (commoners), with the imperial family constituting an additional separate 'class', *kōzoku*. In 1870 commoners were officially allowed surnames. In 1871 the *eta* and *hinin* outcasts were in theory disestablished as specific sub-classes and given full equality with commoners, though in practice discrimination remained strong. Also in the cause of equality, universal education was proclaimed as an aim in 1872, though it was to be some years before it became a reality.

Probably the biggest blow to the old class system was the phased elimination of the samurai class. In practice, the upheaval of the Restoration meant most samurai were left with no real occupation, even of a bureaucratic nature. They were increasingly expected to fend for themselves by finding some new form of employment. Some did continue to work as administrators, this time for the government, and some did succeed as businessmen, or became policemen or farmers, but many relied on gradually decreasing stipends. However, in 1873 the government introduced conscription, meaning men of all walks of life were now officially potential military men. It also offered former samurai the option of a final lump sum payment of government bonds in lieu of stipends. This became compulsory in 1876. That same year of 1876 former samurai who had not already chosen to do so were finally banned from wearing swords.

These various reforms were substantial, and although they signalled a reassuring confidence and authority on the part of the new government, they were not always well received. Many peasants were strongly opposed to conscription—known as the 'blood tax'—and the new land tax. On more than a few occasions they expressed their feelings in violent demonstrations.

The most serious expression of dissatisfaction, however, came from former samurai, not peasants. Its culmination was the Satsuma or Sein-an (Southwest) Rebellion of 1877. Ironically, at the centre of the rebellion was one of the new government's most prominent figures, Saigō Takamori.

Saigō had suffered a political setback in October 1873. While many senior government figures such as Okubo, Kido, Itō, and Iwakura were overseas on the Iwakura Mission of 1871–3,[7] Saigō had proposed an invasion of Korea. For form's sake this was meant to be a punitive invasion, since Korea was felt by some to have insulted Japan by not directly opening relations with its new government. However, despite his involvement in the new regime Saigō was a staunch old-fashioned samurai, and it is also possible to interpret his proposal as a means of providing a sense of purpose and worth for the former samurai.[8] As it happened, following the Iwakura Mission's return in September 1873 the plan was overturned by the Grand Council.[9]

History suggests that his proposal was simply being deferred rather than rejected outright, but Saigō took it badly, and even suffered a breakdown. He returned to Kagoshima, the main city of the former Satsuma domain, along with a number of supporters. Soon he became a focal point for disenchanted former samurai and anti-government feeling in general.

Over the next few years tensions mounted in Kagoshima. The government suspected an uprising in the making, and in January 1877 sent a naval unit to the city to remove munitions. It was attacked, and from then on fighting escalated. In late February Saigō's force of some 40,000 men engaged pro-government forces at Kumamoto to the north. The ensuing battle lasted six weeks, but in the end victory went to the government's new conscript army. Saigō and some 400 troops—one-hundredth of his original force—slowly fought their way back to Kagoshima, where he committed suicide on 24 September after a valiant last charge.

Disaffection and acts of violence among former samurai did continue for a few years more. One such act was the assassination of Okubo in May the following year, by former Satsuma samurai who considered him a traitor. However, the Satsuma Rebellion was really the final action in which 'old-school samurai' participated on any significant scale. It was almost as if Saigō and those who died with him knew full well from the outset that the day of the samurai was over, and they preferred to end with it.[10]

4.2 THE WESTERNISATION OF SOCIETY

With the exception of the now dead Saigō, the new government saw westernisation as a key element in modernisation. Westernisation would make Japan stronger, better able to compete with the western powers, and perhaps even match them or surpass them. One of the many slogans of the age was to be '*oitsuke, oikose*'—'catch up, overtake'. A westernised Japan would be taken more seriously by the west, and Japan very much wanted to be taken seriously. It did not like the humiliation of the 'unequal treaties' signed during the death throes of the shōgunate, and was very keen to have them revised. It wanted Japan to be treated as an equal—or ideally as a better.

Western institutions and practices were to be introduced not only in areas such as politics, the military, industry and the economy, but into society in general. The westernisation of society was sometimes more indiscriminate than the government would have liked, but it was an important backdrop to political and economic reforms.

Western-inspired changes in everyday life were numerous and often bewildering. From 1 January 1873 the western solar (Gregorian) calendar was adopted in place of the old lunar one, meaning that dates now 'advanced' by between three and six weeks.[11] Telegraphs started operating in 1869, and a postal service in 1871. Modern-style newspapers proliferated from the early 1870s, and—a testimony to the high degree of literacy in the nation—over a hundred of them were in circulation by 1875.[12] Western dress became fashionable among progressives, and in 1872 became compulsory for government officials (including on ceremonial occasions) and civil servants such as postmen.[13] Western-style haircuts also became increasingly fashionable, and a popular symbol of modernity.[14] Beef-eating too was popular among progressives—the supposedly 'traditional' Japanese dish of *sukiyaki* developing from this—and specialist restaurants sprang up to cater to them and to the increasing number of foreigners.

Though it was only used by a select few, one of the best-known material symbols of westernisation was the Rokumeikan ('Deer Cry Pavilion'). This government-built hall near the Imperial Palace was designed by the leading British architect Joseph Conder and completed in 1883. It was the venue for balls and other social occasions involving western dignitaries, and was used in particular by Foreign Minister Inoue Kaoru. The cabinet of the day was nicknamed 'the dancing cabinet', and the term 'dance fever' (*butōnetsu*) was coined by the Japanese public many decades before its English-language equivalent.

The greatest of all physical symbols of modernisation was perhaps the railway.[15] Japan's first railway was opened in May 1872, between the foreign settlement of Yokohama and Shinagawa, and the track was extended to Tōkyō's Shinbashi in September that year. Within fifteen years 1,000 miles of track had been laid, and by the end of the century 5,000.

The effect of the railway on the movement of both people and goods—and on the economy as a result—was enormous. In the Tokugawa period a journey between Edo and Kyōto, which was almost always undertaken on foot, took on average two weeks. Even the luxury of hiring 'professional walkers' in the form of sedan bearers could save only a day or so. However, after the railroad link was completed in the late 1880s it took less than one day. Moreover, the rail fare was less than a third of the cost of the trip by sedan chair.[16]

Other transport developments in Meiji Japan included the invention of the rickshaw (from *jinrikisha*, 'human-power vehicle') in 1869, and the opening of steamship and stagecoach services—almost always owned and operated in the early years by foreigners—in 1868.[17]

The government attached great importance to transport development, for it recognised its infrastructural value to the economy and general strength of the nation. Between 1870 and 1874 one-third of the state's investments were in railway construction alone.[18] The social commentator Tsuda Mamichi (1829–1903) wrote in June 1874 that he saw the development of transport as the single most important priority in achieving national prosperity, one even that 'should certainly rank ahead of the military system and building schools.'[19]

In social and demographic terms, the spread of both intra-city and inter-city transportation brought new patterns of urbanisation. Population clusters arose around the stations, especially at intersections of routes. 'Urban sprawl' became noticeable as distance became less of an obstacle. People's worlds expanded as they could now travel quite freely. They were no longer confined to their own community.

Very importantly, the spread of transport also meant that people could now live apart from their place of work. That is, the age of commuting—for which Japan is now notorious—had begun. Within a few decades rush-hour commuting was already to become a problem. The *Niroku* newspaper complained in its 23 March 1910 issue that 'Usually the people at the end of the line and the next few stops are able somehow to get aboard, but no-one waiting at stops further along the way has a chance unless he fights like a madman.'[20] And, like Japan today, some males took advantage of the forced mixing of the sexes in crowded train carriages.[21]

At a less obvious level, thought patterns were also changing. Through translations and an increasing ability to read English and other languages, a whole wave of western writings by novelists, philosophers, and scientists flooded into the country, from Goethe to Darwin to Mill to Rousseau. This created a maelstrom of often contradictory and irreconcilable ideas and influences that were not necessarily recognised as such.

Japanese literature of the day showed particular confusion, blurring romanticism and naturalism, utilitarianism and escapism. But it also showed the authority of things western. Just as—in time-honoured fashion—the young leaders of the Restoration needed the authority of the emperor to legitimise their acts, so too did many writers seek the authority of western figures to add weight to their thoughts or justify their own circumstances. Even fictional works of the day are littered with references to this and that western writer or thinker. This was not only among authors who positively promoted western models of one sort or another. Remarkably, western models were also used to portray the frustrations and failures of those Japanese unable to cope with the bustling dynamism of the westernisation process itself. The Russian literary concept of the 'superfluous man' appealed particularly to those Japanese who felt bewildered and left behind by all the changes.[22]

The superfluous man in Japan was a loser in a tough world of winners and losers, a world where people were suddenly left largely on their own to succeed or fail on their own strengths. The rigidly prescribed orthodoxy of the Tokugawa era had at least meant that people had a fixed place, and were told how to think and act. That security had now gone. Freedom proved a two-edged sword.

Not surprisingly, the related ideas of 'survival of the fittest' and 'self help' were very popular. Samuel Smiles' work *Self Help* (1859), on the theme of 'Heaven helps those who help themselves', was one of the first English works to be translated into Japanese, in 1871. It was a best-seller.

The self-help philosophy fitted perfectly with the sentiments of Fuku-zawa Yukichi (1835–1901), one of Meiji Japan's most influential edu-cators and advocates of westernisation.[23] In his work *Gakumon no Susume* (An Encouragement of Learning) of 1872, he wrote:[24]

> There are no innate status distinctions between the noble and base, the rich and the poor. It is only the person who has studied diligently, so that he has a mastery over things and events, who becomes noble and rich, while his opposite becomes base and poor.

Darwin's theories on evolution and natural selection were very popular in Meiji Japan, and so was social Darwinism. This is seen in the appeal of the British philosopher Herbert Spencer (1820–1903), who coined the term 'survival of the fittest'.[25]

Spencer was held in such esteem that he was privately consulted by the highest levels of the mid-Meiji government for advice as to the best policies for the nation. His reply, in a letter of 26 August 1892, was at his request kept secret till after his death, for he feared it would upset his countrymen.[26] Among other things he advised that 'the Japanese policy should be that of keeping Americans and Europeans as much as pos-sible at arm's length.' There should be prohibitions on foreign ownership of property and restrictions on foreign business rights, and the Japanese race should be kept pure by not interbreeding with foreigners. In short, he recommended many of the things for which the Japanese govern-ment is to this day criticised by Britons and other foreigners.

As it happened, many of the steps he recommended had already been taken anyway by the Japanese government. For example, in 1873 a law had been passed prohibiting the purchase of land by foreigners.[27] Spen-cer's advice therefore came more as an endorsement.

The Japanese government called upon numerous western experts and specialists in addition to Spencer. Many of them were invited to Japan. They included experts in mining, navigation, coin-minting, trans-port, banking, law, political science, agriculture, education, and even the armed forces.[28] Their role was usually confined to technical matters and they had relatively little scope for making major decisions. By 1875 there were around 520 foreign employees in government employment. Foreign employment then gradually shifted to the private sector, with around 760 being in private employment by 1897.[29] According to some estimates as much as 5 per cent of total government expenditure during Meiji went on salaries and other expenses related to the employment of foreigners.[30] They also accounted for one-third of the budget of Japan's first modern university, Tōkyō University, which was established in 1877 and was a particularly prominent employer of foreign experts.[31]

In addition to westerners being invited to Japan to teach, Japanese people visited the west to learn. There were a number of official or semi-official missions to America and/or Europe, the largest and best-known being the Iwakura Mission of 1871–3. This had some fifty official members, including key political figures such as Itō, Okubo, Kido, and Iwakura himself, and had at least as many persons again (mostly students) accompanying the mission unofficially. That such a major mission could be sent out of Japan—taking so many leaders out of effective operation—so soon after the Restoration is testimony to the confidence of the new government. As with other missions, many of those who went published their thoughts and impressions when they returned to Japan, disseminating the knowledge they had gained. The accounts of their trips were widely read by a literate nation, a nation keen to learn from the west but still a little confused by it all.

4.3 HARNESSING THE ENERGIES OF THE PEOPLE

The self-help philosophy emerging in the 1870s was a potential problem for the new regime. If individuals became too strong and independent, they could prove difficult to control. Their endeavours could become disorganised and wasted. The authority of the government might even be affected. This would weaken the country and make it vulnerable to the foreign powers, should they start thinking after all about colonising Japan.

On the other hand, it was not easy to make a strong nation out of weak and uncommitted people, and the government very much wanted to lead a strong nation. People had to be encouraged to become strong and able to achieve aims, but, Tokugawa-style, it had to be within limits. Their newly liberated energies had to be harnessed.[32]

Nationalism was an ideal cause. It tapped nicely into the revived sense of national identity and crisis triggered by the return of the foreign threat, and built on earlier *kokugaku*. It was easy to spread among the public, by methods such as catchphrases. Become strong and build a strong nation. Make your own success the success of the nation. Become strong and show the westerners that Japan is no nation to be toyed with.

The cry was not only *oitsuke, oikose* ('catch up, overtake') but also *fukoku kyōhei*—'rich nation, strong army'.[33] Successism (*risshishugi*) was the order of the day.

Nationalism needed symbols as well as catchphrases. That too worked out nicely for the men whose power was legitimised by the emperor, for the emperor himself could become the main symbol. Support for the emperor meant support for them, his champions.

In an age when so many different ideologies were competing with each other, it was not necessarily an easy task to bring all public thinking into line. However good the causes might seem, a few determined detractors might create problems. A key tool was indoctrination, but ironically this was hampered by one of Japan's few real strengths of the day—the nation's high rate of literacy and education. It would be a pity to sacrifice that. In fact, it was essential to the building of a strong modern nation.

The answer was obvious. Education itself had to be controlled. What people read had to be controlled, or better still, written to order. Controlled education would in time mean people's entire world-view—the way they perceived life—could be controlled.[34]

Universal education had been proclaimed as an aim in 1872. By as early as 1879 almost two-thirds of all boys and one-quarter of all girls were receiving education to at least elementary school level. Initially many school texts were translations of western texts, and students were therefore exposed to such ideas as egalitarianism and individual rights.

However, no less a person than the emperor drew attention to the undesirability of this. During a tour of central Honshū in 1878 he came to the conclusion that the adoption of things western had gone too far, and at the expense of values such as filial piety. From this point, guided by the imperial tutor and Confucianist Motoda Eifu (1818–91), education was to give increasing importance to appropriate moral instruction, and especially to Confucianist and nationalist/Shintō values. The state was to exert increasing influence over the selection of texts, till by the end of Meiji it had total control.[35]

Western heroes in school texts were replaced by figures of Confucian virtue, such as the industrious Ninomiya Sontoku (1757–1856, also known as Kinjirō). The flag of Japan started to appear at the head of each chapter of each text. The singing of morally uplifting songs was introduced into school assemblies.

In some regards Japan was simply producing its own version of the sort of nationalistic expression that dominated classrooms in Great

Britain or other imperial nations. However, it went a step further in indoctrination, severely restricting the world-view of its students. A major move was the issuing in October 1890 of the *Imperial Rescript on Education*, which was in practice drafted largely by Motoda Eifu and Yamagata Aritomo.[36] It was intended as a message for society at large, not just those in schools:

Know ye, Our subjects,
    Our Imperial Ancestors have founded Our Empire on a basis broad and everlasting, and have deeply and firmly implanted virtue; Our subjects ever united in loyalty and filial piety have from generation to generation illustrated the beauty thereof. This is the glory of the fundamental character of Our Empire, and herein also lies the source of Our education. Ye, Our subjects, be filial to your parents, affectionate to your brothers and sisters; as husbands and wives be harmonious, as friends true; bear yourselves in modesty and moderation; extend your benevolence to all; pursue learning and cultivate arts, and thereby develop intellectual faculties and perfect moral powers; furthermore, advance public good and promote common interests; always respect the Constitution and observe the laws; should emergency arise, offer yourselves courageously to the State; and thus guard and maintain the prosperity of Our Imperial Throne coeval with heaven and earth. So shall ye not only be Our good and faithful subjects, but render illustrious the best traditions of your forefathers.
    The Way here set forth is indeed the teaching bequeathed by Our Imperial Ancestors, to be observed alike by Their Descendants and the subjects, infallible for all ages and true in all places. It is Our wish to lay it to heart in all reverence, in common with you, Our subjects, that we may all attain to the same virtue.

The *Rescript* had to be memorised by all students and was read aloud on major occasions. Not all the public accepted it readily, especially teachers, and the path to national unity that it represented was not entirely smooth.[37] Nevertheless, the ideology it contained gradually became more firmly entrenched.

The youth of the day were thus urged to be diligent, respectful, to work for the public good, and to serve the state and the emperor. The *Rescript*'s Shintō values merged emperor and state, and made this union one and the same as the origin of life itself. Its Confucianist values made the emperor a benign father figure, and also helped promote a respect for the family not always seen in Japan's earlier history. Harmony begins at home.

The Constitution provided for religious freedom, and the *Rescript* seemed to breach this by its stress on Shintō. (Confucianism was not a problem since, lacking a deity, it was an ideology rather than a religion.) However, criticism was circumvented by declaring Shintō to be an expression of patriotism, not a religion as a such. This was 'State Shintō'.

The *Rescript* did not use alarmist terminology about the foreign threat. But it did give people a nationalistic sense of purpose, for even those who failed to make a dazzling success in business or any specific field could still feel they had achieved something by faithfully serving the emperor and his family-nation. Did the *Rescript* not say that this was what Japanese had done since the beginning of the world? Was this not their way of life? To serve the emperor was to be a true Japanese. It was a privilege not extended to those of other nations, who by implication were lesser beings.

In many ways it was a reinforcement of the legitimacy of the emperor reminiscent of the *Kojiki* and *Nihon Shoki* of more than 1,000 years before. The *Rescript* and similar documents formed in a sense Japan's 'modern myths'.[38] The antique terminology in which it was couched was no coincidence, and yet again we see a parallel with the Yamato-Nara age.

The Meiji government had relearned from the nation's ancient leaders the value of indoctrination.

4.4   MOVES TOWARDS DEMOCRACY—OF SORTS

However much it was harnessed for the national good, the self-help movement was still a potential problem for the new government. It encouraged ideas of human rights and democracy. These were unheard of in Japanese history. Such ideas could hamper the government in its business of co-ordinating the nation.

On the other hand, the western powers clearly seemed to value such ideas. Politically, it would be helpful to Japan to at least play along. The western nations would be more inclined to take seriously a nation that espoused their own political principles. This would help hasten revision of the unequal treaties, a goal which had become a symbol of Japan's success in modernisation and acceptance by the world powers.

It was clear that democracy, like its bed-fellow self-help, should be promoted, but in a controlled fashion and within limits.

Christianity was a related potentially troublesome issue. The Meiji government knew that westerners often thought Christianity and democracy went hand-in-hand, and that they even tended to evaluate the degree of civilisation of a nation in terms of its attitude to Christianity. It had looked at one stage as though this might be going to prove a major problem. Some 60,000 'hidden Christians' had emerged in the years immediately before the Restoration, and some samurai had even been converted. In some alarm the new government had reaffirmed the ban on Christianity in 1868, but the foreign powers had protested and it was lifted in 1873. Social commentators such as Tsuda Mamichi had even suggested it might be helpful to Japan to adopt Christianity officially, since it was the religion of the western powers.[39]

However, fortunately for the new regime, the threat did not materialise. Christianity simply did not catch on, and was never to appeal to more than 1 per cent or so of the population. Even when it did appeal to potentially influential Japanese, it was often 'Japanised' by being made more flexible and stressing selected values such as duty and hard work.[40] Before long Japan was able to proclaim to the west that it was perfectly happy to welcome Christianity, safe in the knowledge that it wasn't really going to prove a problem.

More of a problem were the non-Christians who were involved in the 'freedom and human rights movement' (*jiyū minken undō*) that was developing in the 1870s and early 1880s.[41] By 1880 there were some 150 local popular rights societies. The following year the Liberal Party (*Jiyūtō*) was founded—Japan's first major political party. And just a year later a second major party was formed, the Constitutional Reform Party (*Rikken Kaishintō*), calling for a British-style constitution and parliament.[42]

Nor did those in the movement forget the promise by the government in 1868 to work towards establishing a national assembly. By the end of the 1870s the League for Establishing a National Assembly claimed to represent around 130,000 members nationwide. There was a widespread interest in politics at the time, reflected not only in the popularity of novels with a political theme but also in numerous 'home-grown' suggestions for a new and proper constitution.[43]

The democratic movement was not a simple one. It undoubtedly contained a genuine element of desire for a more democratic form of government. Some of this was driven by grand ideals and visions. It also contained an element of frustration towards the government leaders, who kept power to themselves—in the emperor's name—and were blatantly an oligarchy (rule by a few). Some of this, by contrast, was driven by self-interest and pragmatism. Both the founders of the two major parties, Itagaki Taisuke (1837–1919) and Okuma Shigenobu respectively, had been part of the government, but neither was from Satsuma or Chōshū and both had personal ambitions and frustrations among their motives.[44]

The oligarchs were not deaf or totally unsympathetic to the various messages. They knew, whether they liked it or not, that democracy had to make an appearance. Such an appearance would have political value not only in impressing the western powers but also in dampening anti-government sentiment. But it all had to be done at a controlled pace and only within certain limits—ideally as an appearance that did not necessarily match the substance, in a time-honoured Japanese fashion. It had to be democracy on the oligarchs' terms, an 'authoritarian democracy'.

Management of a self-contradiction was no easy task, and it did not always go smoothly. Eventually, however, aided by a long-standing Japanese ability to bring together conflicting elements as well as a Tokugawa period tradition of 'freedom within limits', a balance of sorts was achieved. Often that balance took the form of almost simultaneous acts of repression and liberalism.

In 1875 the government introduced harsh laws to curb freedom of speech. Yet the same year the emperor again promised that a national assembly would be formed, and the government agreed to establish a senate for the discussion of legislative matters, to establish the forerunner of the Supreme Court, and to hold a conference of prefectural governors. The governors' conference led within a few years to the introduction of the principle of election to office in prefectural assemblies. The right to vote in these elections was restricted, as was the power of the prefectural assemblies. Nevertheless these bodies, first convened in March 1879, were the first 'popularly' elected political bodies to operate successfully outside the western world.[45]

In 1880 another harsh, undemocratic law was passed. It restricted public meetings, and prevented the unauthorised involvement in politics of people in certain occupations, such as policemen, teachers, students, and soldiers. And yet, almost immediately afterwards the government allowed the formation of two major political parties. And in 1881 Itō again promised there would be a national assembly and a new constitution. This time he gave a specific indication when this would happen—within ten years.

But in a classic display of authoritarian democracy the constitution was not to be left to the public, despite their many constructive suggestions. Itō obtained imperial authority to draw the thing up by himself.

If there was going to have to be a constitution, Itō wanted it to be on German/Prussian lines, not the British lines preferred by Okuma. A Prussian-style constitution would retain considerable power for the emperor (or those advising him) and limit party involvement in cabinets. German influence already prevailed in the military, under the control of Yamagata Aritomo, and was also to prevail in the legal code.[46] The general mood of the government leaders was pro-German, and not as pro-British as commonly believed.

To this end Itō went to Europe the following year to study various constitutions, confirmed his preference for the Prussian model, and on his return to Japan worked on the draft constitution with a number of appropriate German advisers.[47] Work on the draft constitution went relatively slowly, at a pace Itō preferred. It gave him time to put in place safeguards to counterbalance the imminent risky experiment in democracy.[48] In 1884 he created a peerage to fill the seats in the anticipated House of Peers, most peers being former *daimyō*. He himself was eventually to attain the highest rank, prince. In 1885 the senate was replaced by a cabinet comprising ministry heads, who were largely the oligarchs themselves. Itō himself took the position of prime minister, the first person in Japan's history to occupy this western-style position. Then, when the draft was finished in April 1888, Itō promptly established a supra-cabinet Privy Council to discuss and approve it on the emperor's behalf. He resigned as prime minister so that he himself could head this new body and thereby make sure his own handiwork was approved.[49]

The finished document, the first ever full and formal constitution adopted outside the western world, was promulgated on 11 February 1889.[50] This date was the anniversary of the claimed date—according to the ancient *Nihon Shoki*—of the founding of the Japanese state, 11 February 660 BC. The timing was deliberate. Both the date and the constitution itself were part of the machinery creating Japan's modern myths.

Respect for the emperor was vital for this. In fact, not only did the first article of the constitution stress the immutable sovereign rights of the emperor, the very constitution itself was presented in the form of a gift from the emperor to his people. An imperial oath that accompanied the promulgation stressed that the lineage of the document went back to the Sun Goddess Amaterasu herself, and that the constitution was merely a reiteration in modern form of precepts that had always been followed by the imperial rulers of the land.

Although outwardly great reverence was displayed for the emperor, a closer reading shows his position was in fact ambivalent. He was in theory given absolute power but was in practice constrained.[51] All imperial decrees required the counter-signature of a minister of state. The government did, after all, have to govern, and it couldn't risk having an emperor get in the way.

A bicameral Diet (parliament) was provided for, consisting of an upper and lower house. The House of Peers was to comprise higher-ranking nobles, elected lower-ranking nobles, and imperial appointees (typically scholars), while the House of Representatives was to comprise elected members only. However, the right to vote was given only to adult males paying at least 15 yen per annum in taxes, which meant about 2 per cent of the adult population. Ministers were not responsible to the Diet but to the emperor. The military was also, in matters of command, answerable only to the emperor, the supreme commander of the army and navy. Various popular rights were guaranteed, such as freedom of speech, religion, association, and so forth, but on the other hand these were offset by qualifications such as 'within limits not prejudicial to peace and order'.

The constitution was in some ways a step forward for democracy, but one that still left the oligarchs, who acted in the name of the emperor, with the upper hand. It allowed the popular parties to have their say, but did not oblige the oligarchs to listen. It did not allow for effective party government.[52]

The nature of the cabinet *per se* was not fully clear in the constitution but was explained the following day by Prime Minister Kuroda Kiyotaka (1840–1900):[53]

The government must always steadfastly transcend and stand apart from political parties, and thus follow the path of righteousness.

The cabinet was, according to Kuroda, 'transcendental' (*chōzen naikaku*), since it transcended the partisan interests of party politics.

A few days later Itō said much the same:[54]

The emperor stands above the people and apart from every party. Consequently, the government cannot favor one party above the other.

The first election for the Diet was held on 1 July 1890, and the Diet convened on 25 November that year.

In October that same year, as if by way of balance to these risky democratic steps, the *Imperial Rescript on Education* was issued. Freedoms and rights had to be channelled to the right ends.

The *Rescript* certainly seemed to be needed. The election showed that the oligarchs had underestimated the party politicians, many of whom had developed considerable electioneering skill through their experiences in prefectural assemblies. Out of 300 seats in the House of Representatives, a re-formed Liberal Party took 130, while 41 went to the Progressive Reform Party. This did not bode well for the oligarchs. Many other independents and minor party representatives also indicated they were by no means going to accept uncritically any authoritarian pronouncements by the oligarchs.[55]

In the Diet itself there was open criticism of the high-handed nature of the oligarchy, and the elected members used every possible means to exert their influence. The first budget, for example, was resisted in the Diet, and had to be slashed by over 10 per cent with particular effect on the salaries of the oligarchs and the elite bureaucrats who supported them.

Over the next few years the oligarchs resorted to questionable or even downright illegal methods to force their policies through.[56] Itō on occasion used the tactic of morally obliging support by couching proposals as personal requests from the emperor. Kuroda's successors as prime minister, Yamagata and then Matsukata, both resorted to bribery and intimidation. In the notorious February 1892 election, which Matsukata tried to manipulate and which involved blatant and brutal government interference,[57] twenty-five people were killed.

Matsukata resigned a few months later and Itō became prime minister for a second term (till 1896). Itō was becoming ever more pragmatic, and was now thinking that he should—in traditional Japanese style—not simply confront the foe but learn from it, and to an extent even align with it, blurring the divisions. He almost immediately started constructive and co-operative negotiations with the Diet, and even suggested the formation of a government party with the aim of winning seats in the Diet. However, Yamagata and other hard-line oligarchs were alarmed by this apparent softness, and Itō's party plans were held in check. An uneasy and tense atmosphere prevailed in the political arena. Authoritarianism and democracy did not sleep easily in the same bed.

4.5   WAR AND POLITICS

When internal issues become troublesome it is often helpful to switch the focus to external ones. The threat of attempted colonisation by the western powers had largely but not entirely passed by the 1890s. The powers were still actively expanding on the Asian mainland, and there was still a popular saying that Korea was 'a dagger pointed at Japan's heart'—a dagger for western use, not Korean.

The Japanese government had not approved Saigō's proposal of 1873 to invade Korea, but it had maintained a strong interest there. By using the same 'gunboat diplomacy' the west had used against Japan itself, it had obtained its own 'unequal treaty' in the form of the Kangwha Treaty of 1876. This gave it trade privileges and the right of extraterritoriality. Japan had since involved itself in Korean politics, including an attempted coup in 1884. It was particularly heading for a showdown with China, which also had interests in Korea.

Following a time-honoured tradition Japan preferred to avoid confrontation with a stronger power if at all possible. However, it did not see late nineteenth-century China, weakened by fragmentation and western interference, as a stronger power. In fact, Japan seems to have been spoiling for a war with China over Korea.[58]

In spring 1894 the Korean king called for military aid from China to put down a rebellion led by a powerful religious sect. China duly sent troops. So did Japan. Though the rebellion was soon quelled both parties refused to withdraw their troops. The Japanese seemed determined to fight and in July initiated military action against China by sinking a ship carrying Chinese troops. Japan officially declared war later, on 1 August. The Sino-Japanese War had begun.

In the engagements that followed, Japan proved superior both on land and sea, but the most decisive element was its superiority in naval tactics, which were modelled on the British. The Chinese fleet was severely crippled at the mouth of the Yalu River in September, the naval base of Port Arthur in south Manchuria was seized in November, and the Chinese fleet was finally destroyed at Weihaiwei in February 1895.

In the ensuing Treaty of Shimonoseki of April 1895, China had to pay a huge indemnity, abandon its official interests in Korea, and cede territory to Japan including Taiwan and the Liaotung/Kwantung (Liaodong/Guandong) Peninsula in southern Manchuria.

This was the first major step in Japan's empire-building in Asia, and the western powers took note. Russia in particular, which had its own designs on Korea and Manchuria, acted very quickly. Less than a week after the Treaty of Shimonoseki it persuaded Germany and France to join it in advising Japan, in the Tripartite Intervention, to renounce the Liaotung Peninsula on the grounds that not to do so would cause instability in the area. Anxious to retain the goodwill of the western powers the Japanese government followed this advice, much to the displeasure of the Japanese public.

This displeasure soon turned to outright indignation when, just a few years later in 1898, the same three western powers started dividing up parts of China among themselves. There was particular bitterness towards Russia, which obtained, under a 25-year lease, the very same Liaotung Peninsula it had obliged Japan to give up.

By this stage, through its political reforms and victory over China, Japan had succeeded in earning the respect of western nations. It had also succeeded in getting the unequal treaties at least partly revised. Just weeks before the Sino-Japanese War Britain had agreed to relinquish its right to extraterritoriality, and had partially restored Japan's tariff autonomy. The other major nations followed suit by 1897, though full restoration of tariff control did not come till 1911.

However, victory in the Sino-Japanese War and success with treaty revision did not bring the hoped-for degree of stability to the political situation in Japan. In some regards it worsened as a result of the Liaotung Peninsula affair, which earned severe criticism for Japan's leaders.

The political arena degenerated into a merry-go-round.[59] Parties formed, disbanded, re-formed, changed names, re-adopted former names, or deliberately took the names of other parties and prefixed their own version with the term 'Real' or 'True'. Politicians regularly changed parties and/or allegiances (the two not always going together). Resignations and returns to office were commonplace. Between mid-1896 and mid-1901 the premiership changed seven times, three times due to Itō Hirobumi's resignations from that office.

One major development was that Itō managed to form his new political party in 1900, a government party under the name *Rikken Seiyūkai* (Association of Friends of Constitutional Government). However, he still incurred the displeasure of stauncher conservatives such as Yamagata, and his fourth resignation from the premiership in May 1901 was to be his final one. He was weary of politics, though he remained

Seiyūkai president till 1903. His party was to remain an effective force till just before World War Two.

After Itō's resignation in 1901 Yamagata was again offered the position, but he too had already been prime minister more than once and he too was weary of it. Instead, the position went to his protégé, Katsura Tarō (1847–1913). Though born into a Chōshū samurai family, and only a few years younger than Itō or Yamagata, Katsura was usually considered a 'second generation' man. The age of the oligarchs, or *genrō* ('original elder') was passing.[60]

Katsura also brought a relative stability to politics, surviving in office for four and a half years—the longest of any Meiji prime minister. One reason for this was that another external event overrode domestic issues, and that was the Russo-Japanese War of 1904–5.

Trouble had been brewing between Japan and Russia ever since the Tripartite Intervention of 1895. Russia had continued its expansionist policies in northeast Asia, symbolised by extensive rail tracks. In 1900 the anti-foreign Boxer Rebellion broke out in north China, and was quelled by the combined troops of eight nations including Japan and Russia. However, Russia refused to withdraw its troops after the rebellion, to the consternation of most of the other powers and Japan in particular.

The pragmatist Itō wanted Japan to come to a 'trade-off' arrangement with Russia: Japan would recognise Russian interests in Manchuria in return for Russia recognising Japanese interests in Korea. However, Russia opposed this. So did Yamagata and Katsura, who were convinced that war with Russia was inevitable. They preferred to secure the support of Britain. This was achieved in the Anglo-Japanese Alliance of January 1902. It was an epoch-making alliance, the first ever military pact concluded on equal terms between a western and non-western nation.

The alliance did not recognise Japan's control of Korea, though it did recognise its 'special interests' in that country. Nor did it mean that Britain would fight alongside Japan if and when it went to war with Russia. But it did give Japan the confidence that other western powers would be unlikely to act against it in such a war.

The resolution to go to war was made in January 1904. Japan's military might was now considerable, with more than half its national budget since 1897 having been allotted to military expenditure. Nonetheless there were many in Japan—including in the military—who were still uncertain as to the outcome of hostilities with a major power like Russia. Not a few hoped that success in initial engagements would bring an intervention in Japan's favour from the other powers.[61]

Japan broke off diplomatic relations with Russia on 6 February 1904, attacked Russian ships in Port Arthur on 8 February, and then declared war on 10 February. Over the next month Japanese troops landed in Korea, advancing north and crossing the Yalu River into Manchuria in May. At the same time, sea-borne forces landed on the Liaotung Peninsula and took Nanshan and Dairen. In August siege was laid on Port Arthur, though this did not fall till January 1905. In March 1905, after heavy fighting that saw around 70,000 Japanese casualties and a similar number of Russian casualties, Japanese troops took Mukden, the Manchurian capital, though it was not a decisive victory.

Both sides were now finding it hard to carry on. Russia was particularly disadvantaged by a revolution at home,[62] and had to summon its Baltic Fleet. The British denied the fleet access to the Suez Canal, meaning it had to make a very long detour. In late May, when the fleet attempted to make the final leg of its marathon journey by a dash into Vladivostok, it was intercepted and destroyed in the Straits of Tsushima by the Japanese Combined Fleet, under the command of Admiral Tōgō Heihachirō (1838–1934). This decisive victory put Japan in a position of strength when it secretly asked President Theodore Roosevelt of the United States to mediate.[63]

Roosevelt did mediate, successfully. It was an effective victory for Japan. The ensuing Portsmouth Treaty of September 1905 restored China's sovereignty in Manchuria (though in practice this was to be largely nominal), recognised Japan's interests in Korea, and gave Japan the Russian lease on the Liaotung Peninsula and much of the Russian-built South Manchurian Railway. Japan had incurred huge expenses in the war, having to borrow heavily from Britain and the United States. It was therefore anxious to obtain an indemnity from Russia. However, to the indignation of the Japanese public, this was not obtained. Instead Japan received the southern half of the island of Sakhalin (Karafuto) to the north of Hokkaidō.

The war had caused Japan much suffering in human as well as financial terms, but it had earned the nation great respect internationally. Russia was by no means the strongest of the western powers, but it was the largest, and Japan's victory over it was the first-ever victory over a western nation by a non-western nation.

Japan had now achieved its aim of matching and being taken seriously by the western powers. Far from being faced with the threat of colonisation by imperialist powers, as it had feared a few decades earlier, it was now poised to take its place amongst them. It already had Taiwan, and now it had obtained territory in Manchuria, part of Sakhalin, and in effect a free hand in Korea. Western outposts such as New Zealand were now even starting to fear colonisation by the Japanese. Japan had learned well how to play the game of becoming a world power—so far.

Japan lost no time in establishing its control over Korea. In November 1905 the Korean government was 'persuaded' to become a Japanese protectorate. The fact that Japanese soldiers were occupying the royal palace probably helped it make the decision. Itō Hirobumi himself became resident-general. Korean officials were replaced by Japanese nationals. The Korean army was disbanded, enforcing the need for Japanese 'protection'. Korean protests to the western world were ignored. So too were the 1,450 armed suppressions of Korean riots by Japanese troops between 1908 and 1910.[64] The Koreans did manage to assassinate Itō in 1909, but in August 1910 Japan went the next step and annexed the nation with no international opposition.

Back in Japan, the aftermath of the Russo-Japanese War was similar in some ways to that of the Sino-Japanese War. The victory itself was glorious, but the government was severely criticised for the humiliation of not gaining an indemnity from Russia. There were demonstrations, with up to a thousand casualties in Tōkyō alone, and martial law had to be declared.[65] Katsura was forced to resign in January 1906.

He was replaced by one of Itō's protégés, the court noble Prince Saionji Kinmochi (1849–1940), who had also become president of the *Seiyūkai* party. Like Itō in later years, Saionji was reasonably well-disposed towards party politics. Under him Japanese politics entered another phase of relative stability for the remainder of the Meiji period. At one stage the harder-line Katsura even returned to office. Relations between the still transcendental cabinet and the Diet were reasonably trouble-free, with party politicians feeling they were making slow but steady gains.

However, particularly under Katsura's return to office in the years mid-1908 to mid-1911, there were reminders that democracy in Japan still had an authoritarian flavour to it.

In 1910, in what was known as the High Treason Incident, hundreds of left-wing sympathisers were interrogated in connection with what the authorities felt to be a widespread plot to assassinate the emperor. Twenty-six were secretly tried. Evidence against the five main suspects seemed quite strong, but was questionable for the others. Nevertheless, twenty-four were sentenced to death. Twelve had their sentences commuted. The remaining twelve were executed in January 1911.

The incident followed a series of repressions of left-wing activity during the last decade of Meiji. Party politics was one thing, but socialism was another. Like Christianity, it never seems to have taken root in Japan, though it can be argued that it was never given a chance. In any event, socialists had to keep a very low profile in Japan till the end of World War Two.[66]

As a result of the High Treason Incident, a Special Higher Police Force was established in 1911. This was the notorious 'thought police'. While democracy might be advancing in terms of outward structure and institution, the same was not necessarily true of the inner substance. This duality was merely the continuation of a long tradition. So too was the lack of real democracy.

4.6 GUIDED ECONOMIC DEVELOPMENT

Japan's economic development was another aspect of the nation's modernisation that impressed westerners. Japan already had a number of key factors of production in place at the start of the period, and it made the most of these, as well as developing others. It had:

- a large workforce
- an educated workforce
- a generally obedient workforce
- an agricultural workforce of such size that a significant portion could be shifted into the industrial sector
- accumulated capital in the private sector (mostly merchants)
- established business practices of some sophistication
- despite overall limitations in its natural resources, a reasonable initial supply of basic energy sources in the form of wood, water, and to some extent coal and even iron (ironsands).

What it lacked was technology and entrepreneurs.

The deficiency in technology, which included both equipment and expertise, was fairly rapidly made up. This was largely done by importing foreign equipment, employing numerous western technical advisers, and sending Japanese overseas on study tours. Japan had missed out on the Industrial Revolution but on the other hand it benefited from being a 'late developer'. It could make use of 'state of the art' technology that other nations had only developed after a century or more of costly trial and error.

As for entrepreneurialism, this could clearly not be left to foreigners. It should be Japanese people themselves who established and kept ownership of at least the major modern industries. In general the merchant houses from the Tokugawa period were not especially willing to take up the challenge of establishing modern industries, which they saw as too risky. Mitsui and Sumitomo were in fact the only major houses to do so. Rather, in most cases entrepreneurial initiative was taken either by the government itself or by the same 'class' of lower-ranking samurai—often with peasant associations—who formed the government.

Meiji Japan's two best-known entrepreneurs, Iwasaki Yatarō (1835–85), the founder of Mitsubishi, and Shibusawa Eiichi (1840–1931), the founder of the Osaka Spinning Mill and many dozens of other companies, both came from this type of peasant-samurai background. Both of them represented self-help in action. Shibusawa in particular was favoured by the government, for he frequently proclaimed that business success should be achieved for the good of the nation as well as the individual. This was exactly what the government wanted to hear. His philanthropism, such as in founding schools and homes for the elderly, also made him popular among the public. He helped greatly to remove for good the stigma that had often been attached to money-making in Tokugawa times. The government was again grateful to him for this, for such a stigma could have proven a problem for Japan's successful economic development.

However, at least in the early years, the government was disappointed at the lack of private entrepreneurs. It ended up having to establish many enterprises by itself. The hope was that these would serve as successful models for private industry to follow, but in practice results were often poor and uninspiring. The railway was one success, and whereas in the 1870s almost all railway construction had been by the government, by 1890 some 75 per cent of it was being done by the private sector. On the other hand, the government's ventures in the textile industry were notoriously unsuccessful. Fortunately, in their stead, Shibusawa's privately built and owned Osaka Spinning Mill proved a successful model. During the 1870s the government also set up factories in industries such as munitions, brick, cement, and glass, and took over a number of mines and shipbuilding yards.

Despite the government's hopes and efforts the economy did not fare too well in the early years of Meiji, and the nation was facing a financial crisis by the end of the 1870s. Causes included not only the poor performance of some of the government's own enterprises, but heavy expenditure on foreign advisers, the payments to former *daimyō* and samurai, the expenses incurred in the Satsuma Rebellion of 1877, and a relative lack of hard currency to back up paper currency. Serious inflation set in. Rice prices, for example, doubled between 1877 and 1880.

As one counter-measure the government announced in 1880 the sale of non-strategic government-run industries. There were few takers, and eventually the government had to dispose of the industries at well below cost—in some cases below even 10 per cent of their cost value.[67] Sales were often made informally, without tender, to people with whom the government already had associations and were considered reliable. These people obviously felt an obligation towards the government, which helped the already growing bond between government and big business interests. The sale also helped concentrate much of industry into the hands of a small number of increasingly large organisations—later known unflatteringly as *zaibatsu*, or 'financial cliques'.

Other counter-measures included the establishing of a central bank (the Bank of Japan, in 1882) and a budget surplus that would build up hard currency reserves. The tight measures caused some hardship in the agricultural sector in particular, but on the other hand this helped shift labour into the more modern industrial sector. By 1886 Japan had a stable financial system, with low interest rates, and the economy entered an upswing. From this point on gross national product (GNP) was on average to grow steadily by over 3 per cent per annum till the end of the Meiji period. Exports, which the government was keen to promote, were also to grow steadily, rising from around 6–7 per cent of GNP in the late 1880s to around 20 per cent by the end of Meiji.[68]

Despite the advance of industrialisation, the Meiji economy overall was dominated by agriculture, which occupied more than half the workforce throughout the period. Nevertheless, the value of agriculture as a proportion of gross domestic product (GDP) fell steadily, from 42 per cent in 1885 to 31 per cent at the end of Meiji. By contrast, the manufacturing sector's proportion over the same period more than doubled from 7 per cent to 16 per cent.[69]

Within manufacturing, the light industry of textiles was particularly important. The government promoted domestic textile production as a means of cutting down on imports, often encouraging potential entrepreneurs by providing cheap equipment. Mill owners could also make use of very lowly paid female labour, and could locate their premises in rural centres. This meant cheap site costs and ready access to local agricultural workers wanting convenient by-employment. Textile output rose from around 25 per cent of total manufacturing output in 1880 to 40 per cent over the next 20 years.[70] In a survey of non-government factories in 1884, 61 per cent were found to be in textiles.[71]

During the last decade or so of Meiji, electrical goods quickly developed as another important manufacturing industry. Though western ownership was discouraged, Japanese companies in the field often formed joint ventures with western companies in order to acquire western technology. Today's well-known giant NEC (Nippon Electric Company) was started in 1899 as a joint venture between the American company Western Electric and its Japanese agent. Another giant, Tōshiba, started from a joint venture in the early 1900s between America's General Electric and two Japanese companies, Tōkyō Electric and Shibaura Electric (part of the Mitsui group).[72]

In the 1870s Japan was overwhelmingly an importer of manufactured goods (91 per cent of all imports, of which most were textiles) and an exporter of primary products (including raw silk, 42 per cent of total exports). By World War One, just after the end of Meiji, this was reversed. By that stage more than 50 per cent of all imports were primary products, and around 90 per cent of all exports were manufactured goods (of which around half were textiles).[73] Japan was so successful in promoting the cotton textile industry as a means of import substitution that by the end of the period it was able to export the product, even though Japanese-grown cotton itself was of poor quality and raw cotton had to be imported. The key point is that value was added in Japan. It had become a processing nation.

Heavy industry also developed strongly towards the end of the period, partly in line with Japan's military campaigns. The strategically important industry of shipbuilding was vigorously promoted during the last fifteen years or so of Meiji. From the mid-1890s the government provided heavy subsidies for purchases of Japanese-built iron and steel ships. During that 15-year period shipping and shipbuilding together received a massive 75 per cent of all government subsidies.[74] The iron and steel industry—which, like cotton textiles, relied heavily on imported raw material—was given a major boost by the government's establishment of the Yawata works in North Kyūshū in 1901. The plant was to produce over half of Japan's domestic output of iron and steel through to the 1930s.

Throughout the Meiji period the government played an important guiding role in the economy, developing and maintaining relations with the business world, and offering assistance in areas it favoured and to those companies it favoured. The exact nature of that role is the subject of considerable debate, for the Meiji period just as it is for the present day.[75] The government's guidance may not always have been particularly helpful, for they certainly made mistakes and were not always consistent. Though they had goals, the path to achieving these was often far from smooth. Nevertheless, one thing was certain—the government was reluctant to leave economic development purely to market forces. It still is.

4.7 AN ERA COMES TO AN END

Emperor Mutsuhito died of diabetes on 30 July 1912. On his death he was given the name of the momentous period he had overseen, the age of 'enlightened rule'. Japan's 'modern myths' had given the emperor a central role in the prosperity of the nation, though in practice it is questionable how much he personally was involved in the achievements of the age.[76]

Nevertheless, as a symbol of the age he was mourned on his passing. On the day of his funeral, 13 September, General Nogi Maresuke (1849–1912) even committed ritual disembowelment, in the idealised samurai tradition of *junshi* (following one's lord in death). His wife Shizuko (1858–1912) also killed herself, following her own lord. *Junshi* had been banned for some time and there was some criticism of Nogi's act as anachronistic, but in general the public were moved at this ultimate display of samurai spirit. As the novelist Tayama Katai (1872–1930) remarked in his memoirs, it was the same spirit that had been shown by those who had given their lives in battle for their country to help make Japan the great international nation it now was.[77]

Neither Emperor Meiji nor the achievements of Meiji Japan had been unreservedly admired by all. It was very rare—and a treasonable offence punishable by death—to criticise the emperor personally, but this had happened from time to time. In a famous poem of 1904, on the occasion of the Russo-Japanese War, the female poet Yosano Akiko (1878–1942) had publicly criticised him for cowardice in not going to the front himself.[78]

Most criticism, however, was not aimed at Emperor Meiji personally but rather took the form of reservations about what exactly had been achieved in his name. The most famous Meiji novelist, Natsume Sōseki (1867–1916), felt that westernisation had introduced a cold type of egoism, and produced lonely individuals divorced from roots and kin.

He also thought changes had all been made at too frenetic a pace for them to be properly digested. In a work of 1909, *Sore Kara* (And Then), when Japan was arguably at the peak of its international prestige, he wrote:[79]

> Look at Japan....She tries to force her way into the company of world class powers.... She is like a frog trying to grow as big as a cow. Of course, she will soon burst. This struggle affects you and me, and everybody else. Because of the pressure of the competition with the West, the Japanese have no time to relax....No wonder they are all neurotics....They think of nothing except themselves and their immediate needs. Look all over Japan, and you won't find one square inch that is bright with hope. It is dark everywhere.

A less popular figure may have found himself in front of the authorities for expressing such views. Someone more informed about Japan's own long history of self-interest may not even have formed quite the same views in the first place.

But it was understandable that an era of such massive change would bring about a degree of uncertainty, disorientation, anxiety, and a feeling of helplessness at being caught up in something beyond one's control. Self-parodying of Japan's westernised modernisation was not uncommon. A number of popular songs of the day also contained negative sentiment.[80] And it is clear there was almost a public readiness to express anger over government failure to gain adequate rewards for military victories, or to make sufficient progress in undoing the unequal treaties. Such readiness suggests tension and frustration, but at the same time intense national pride.

Despite the unmistakable reservations and pessimism, it was national pride and optimism that formed the prevailing view as the era came to an end. Tayama Katai positively gushed with nationalistic pride when, on the occasion of the emperor's death, he thought back over the achievements of the Meiji period:[81]

> Who could fail to be moved to tears by the illustrious life of His Majesty Emperor Meiji, 'Mutsuhito the Great', Lord of the Restoration, who despite being raised in adversity surmounted all manner of obstacles and perils to lead Japan to the state of wonderful international nationhood it enjoys today?

...I had participated in the war with Russia as a member of a photography unit. I saw an awesome display of the Emperor's august and virtuous power as it spread afar. I positively leapt for joy when I saw the Rising Sun flag flying from the enemy strongholds at Chin-chou and Nanshan, and realised how the blood in my veins too was Japanese blood. Ideologically I am a free-thinker, but my spirit is that of a Japanese nationalist....

And now...our dear, beloved, gracious Emperor Meiji, our strength and support, was dead!

Divine though they may be, even emperors die. The question now was what would become of the nation? Would it be content with its achievements and enter a phase of consolidation? Or would Sōseki's fabled frog continue to grow and finally burst?

REVIEW OF PART FOUR

Japan entered the Meiji period in a state of considerable uncertainty. It was not clear whether the imperial restoration would succeed, or even whether foreigners would try to take over the country. Fortunately the foreigners did not seem interested in invading, at least for the moment, and the boy-emperor was not troublesome. The young samurai who led the coup in his name were able to consolidate their control of the government and bring a certain stability to the country beneath all the changes.

Their aim was to build up a strong nation that could match and even perhaps eventually outdo the west. To start with it was important to make the western powers take Japan seriously, at least seriously enough for them to be deterred from any possible later thoughts of colonisation and for them to undo the humiliating treaties of the late Tokugawa period. This meant modernisation, which in turn meant a great deal of westernisation—a process which would not only help win recognition from the west but, if done judiciously, would enable Japan to adopt the strengths of the western powers in order to make itself stronger and more competitive.

It was not just a question of learning from the west, however, for in some cases these modern nation-builders appear to have been mindful of useful policies from Japan's own past.

Early reforms undertaken by the new government included the relocation of the imperial capital with a view to centralising power, and to the same end the nationalisation of feudal domains to replace them with prefectures. The restrictive feudal class system was abolished, including the samurai class from which the government leaders themselves came. This was not done without creating some dissatisfaction, which came to a head in the Satsuma Rebellion of 1877. At the same time, removal of samurai traditionalists as a result of the rebellion made it easier to modernise along western lines.

To win recognition by the western powers it was particularly important to follow a number of potentially risky paths. These included being receptive to Christianity, adopting western economic and political institutions, and demonstrating military might. Opening the nation to Christianity proved less of a risk than had been feared, because it simply did not appeal to most Japanese even when they were exposed to it. In the economy, with the help of western advisers and technology, and a good measure of 'Japanese-style' government guidance and support, Japan was able to capitalise on its existing strengths and become a significant economic power in a very short space of time. By the end of the period it was established as a processing nation with a developing heavy industrial sector.

Political westernisation proved more difficult, and had to be pursued with great caution. Reforms were made with an impressive outward show of democracy, especially the establishing of a new constitution and a parliament, but these were invariably counterbalanced by curbs and checks. The cabinet of oligarchs remained 'transcendental'—a law unto itself—and freedoms were very much within limits. Individuals excited by western ideas of self-help and survival of the fittest were encouraged to achieve not only in their own right, but at the same time in the greater cause of national prosperity. Through indoctrination centred on the emperor and state, embodied in the *Imperial Rescript on Education* and school texts, self-help became nationalistic successism, as the energies of the newly liberated and rather disoriented population were harnessed and directed to national ends.

Militarily, Japan learned fast how to fight western-style with modern weapons and a conscript army. After a fortunate opportunity to practise against its own discontented samurai in the Satsuma Rebellion, it was able to defeat a weakened China and then an inconvenienced Russia. Territories gained directly or indirectly by these victories, especially Korea, were milestones on the road to empire-building.

Japan's modernisation had not always been smooth. There had been more unplanned developments, more trial and error, and a greater role for chance than the nation's leaders would have liked. They borrowed, improvised, studied and planned as best they could, and were helped by good fortune and sheer determination to succeed. Not all the nation's people were happy or proud, but most were, and if succeeding was to be measured in terms of being recognised as a strong western-style power with a colony or two, then Japan had succeeded.

The main developments in its path to success are summarised in Table 4.1.

Table 4.1   Key developments in the Meiji period

Development	Time
Imperial rule restored in theory, oligarchs rule in practice	late 1860s on
Main early reforms enacted, such as nationalisation of land and abolition of feudal classes	late 1860s–mid-1870s
Westernisation of society and economy, helped by western advisers	early 1870s on
Self-help ideology grows strong	1870s–1880s
Ideas of 'freedom and human rights'	1870s–1880s
Government sells industries to private industrialists	early 1880s
Political parties formed	early 1880s on
Individual achievements channelled to national ends, especially through the medium of education, and especially centred on emperor	early 1880s on
Constitution proclaimed, parliament convened	1889–90
Imperial Rescript on Education issued	1890
Heavy industry develops, Japan becomes a processing nation	1890s on
Sino-Japanese War, Japan victorious	1894–5
Japan wins major revision of unequal treaties and recognition by western powers	mid-1890s on
Anglo-Japanese Alliance	1902
Russo-Japanese War, Japan effectively victorious	1904–5
Japan annexes Korea	1910
Repression of socialism in Treason Incident	1910–11

The Meiji period has also revealed many values and practices of great relevance to present-day Japan, usually at the same time showing a continuity with Japan's past. These are summarised in Table 4.2, in what is a rather long list.

Table 4.2   Key values and practices in the Meiji period

- incorporation of the strengths of a potential threat
- ability to mix old and new, native and foreign
- 'Japanisation' of many foreign elements
- pragmatism
- 'freedom within limits'
- distinction between formal authority and actual power
- distinction between outer form and inner substance
- willingness to learn
- determination to succeed
- single-mindedness of purpose
- Confucianism (Japanese-style)
- idealisation of family values
- strengthening nationalism
- revival of reverence for emperor
- dislike of Christian-type religious inflexibility
- economic astuteness
- widespread tendency to be guided by authority even in the pursuit of individual goals
- distrust of socialism
- control of world-view through propaganda and education

In a mere half-century Japan had gone from being virtually dismissed by the west as an obscure and rather backward country to being recognised as a major world power. It was arguably the most remarkable achievement of any nation in world history.

Part Five

The Excesses of Ambition: the Pacific War and its Lead-up

5.1 THE FRAGILE DEMOCRACY OF TAISHŌ (1912–26)

When Emperor Meiji's son Yoshihito (1879–1926) acceded to the throne in 1912, things were looking good for Japan. The auspicious name 'Taishō', meaning 'Great Righteousness', was chosen to mark the new era. It suggested self-assurance as a world power, and promised wisdom and justice.

For Yoshihito personally, however, things did not look so promising. There were increasing doubts about his fitness of mind and body. This was generally attributed to meningitis just after birth, but he was now in his thirties and the effects of such an illness would have long since stabilised. Almost certainly, it was some other—and presumably more embarrassing—disorder that was now troubling him. Doctors passed him fit to assume the throne, but his condition soon deteriorated markedly. Within three years he was unable to walk or talk properly. The awkward situation continued for a few years, till his son Hirohito (1901–89) took over as regent in November 1921.

Yoshihito's uncertain reign started with a political crisis. Late in 1912 the Saionji cabinet refused to agree to extra divisions for the army, which was keen on expansion. The army minister resigned and the army refused to replace him, bringing the cabinet down. Approached by Yamagata and the other oligarchs, Katsura Tarō agreed to form his third cabinet. However, he was an unpopular choice with the public and with the political parties, who saw him as a symbol of continued oligarchic authoritarianism. The main parties now included not only the (*Rikken*) *Seiyūkai* but the newly formed (*Rikken*) *Kokumintō* ('Constitutional Nationalist Party'). These two parties initiated the Movement to Protect Constitutional Government (*Kensei Yōgo Undō*), which attracted many thousands of supporters from amongst the public.

These same two parties also brought a motion of no confidence against Katsura, who responded by persuading the new emperor to order the withdrawal of the motion. The emperor's order was ignored— testimony to the exceptionally low esteem in which he was already held. Presently, in February 1913, thousands of angry demonstrators surrounded the Diet building, obliging Katsura to resign after less than two months in office. This was the first time in Japanese history that the voice of the people had helped bring down a government.

The man who followed Katsura as prime minister, Admiral Yamamoto Gonbei (1852–1933), was a political neutral and was well-disposed towards party politics. Parties gradually strengthened their representation in cabinet, but it could not be said that party politics became established. The aged Okuma Shigenobu, who succeeded Yamamoto in 1914, may have been a party man in the past but by this stage he was much under the influence of the oligarchs. He in turn was followed in 1916 by Terauchi Masatake (1852–1919), who was firmly opposed to party politics and was an unpopular prime minister.

The first real party-dominated cabinet was that of the *Seiyūkai*'s Hara Takashi (1856–1921, also Kei), who succeeded Terauchi in 1918. However, he was not necessarily the ideal representative of democracy. Though widely known as the common man's politician he was in fact of high-ranking samurai descent and very well-connected. He had only become prime minister after close vetting and approval by the oligarchs, was an early exponent of pork-barrel politics, and was not above resorting to undemocratic methods such as the use of professional 'muscle-men' to physically intimidate his opponents.[1] After his assassination in 1921 he was followed by a number of non-party cabinets.

This was the pattern of politics in the Taishō period. As with the Meiji period, there were advances for democracy and liberalism, but these were invariably counterbalanced and checked by authoritarianism and repression.

On the one hand Minobe Tatsukichi (1873–1948), an influential professor of law at Tōkyō University, was able to advocate democratic constitutionalism. He could also promote his view of the emperor as an organ of the state, as opposed to the absolute nature of the emperor's authority promoted by the government in the Meiji period. On the other hand, another professor of law at Tōkyō University, Uesugi Shinkichi (1878–1929), contended that the emperor was absolute.

At least this was debate. However, in 1925 a repressive Peace Preservation Law was passed, in effect making it a crime to advocate basic changes to the national political structure. But yet again, this was the same year that the right to vote was extended to all males of age 25 or over. It was like an interplay of light and dark.

One of Taishō Japan's darkest moments came in September 1923, in the aftermath of the nation's greatest natural disaster, the Great Tōkyō Earthquake. This killed over 100,000 people, with many more injured. More than 3 million people lost their homes, most of these in the fires that followed rather than the earthquake itself. Rumours spread very quickly that Korean residents had been responsible for some of the fires. They were also said to be exploiting the opportunity to loot and inflict further damage on the Japanese by poisoning wells and so on. Some Japanese even believed the very earthquake itself was caused by Koreans upsetting the gods by their presence on Japanese soil. In the relative state of lawlessness of the days immediately after the earthquake (martial law had in fact been declared), as many as 6,000 Koreans are estimated to have been murdered by vigilantes.[2] Anti-Korean members of the public were not the only ones to avail themselves of the lawlessness: the military police killed a number of radicals and those associated with them, including the well-known anarchist Osugi Sakae (1885–1923) and his wife and 6-year-old nephew.[3]

In the international arena too, Taishō Japan was to experience light and dark. At times there were budgetary restraints imposed by the government on military expenditure and growth. There were also moments of belief in diplomacy rather than military might. This was particularly so in the last few years of the period, when Shidehara Kijūrō (1872–1951) was Foreign Minister. However, the idea of aggressive expansionism backed by military force was far from dormant. World War One, in which Japan was nominally involved as a British ally but in practice was hardly involved at all, obviously occupied the attention of the European powers. Japan was not slow to capitalise on this. It rapidly seized German territory in the Shantung (Shandong) Peninsula in China, as well as various German-owned Pacific islands.

Its most extreme action, however, was the presentation of the Twenty-One Demands to China early in 1915. These demands not only sought Chinese recognition of Japanese footholds, such as the newly acquired territory in Shantung, and further concessions in Mongolia and Manchuria. They also called for the appointment of Japanese advisers within the Chinese government, armed forces, and police. Effectively this would have placed China under Japanese control. China was outraged and appealed to the western powers, who were unable to take any decisive action. Eventually China was obliged to sign under duress a revised version of the demands, from which the demands for Japanese appointments had been withdrawn.

The Twenty-One Demands caused considerable concern in the west as to Japan's motives, as well as in China. America in particular reacted negatively, and from that point on viewed Japan with great suspicion.[4]

Nevertheless, as a member of the victorious allies Japan had a significant place at the Versailles (Paris) Peace Conference in 1919, having an equal vote with the other victorious powers. It similarly took its place at the Washington Conference of November 1921–February 1922. This was aimed at producing a new and more stable world order by focusing on multilateral rather than bilateral agreements between nations. One of the Washington resolutions obliged Japan to agree to a naval limitation of three Japanese capital ships to five American and five British. This was considerably ahead of France and Italy's 1.75 (each), but still upset many Japanese at home, who felt they should have equal naval status with America and Britain.

A sense of unequal treatment was to be a constant irritant to Japan during the interwar years, often with some justification. In 1920 Japan was one of the founding council members of the League of Nations. In this particular aspect of internationalism it led the United States, which was never a formal member of the League. Soon afterwards Japan was greatly upset and disillusioned that it did not succeed in its proposal to have a racial equality clause put into the League's charter. This was in large part due to opposition from Australia, which had been operating its 'White Australia' policy for some decades by this stage.[5]

One major source of upset to the Japanese was a series of race-based exclusion acts passed in the United States. In particular, the 1924 Immigration Act effectively banned Japanese immigration (by relating immigrant quota eligibility to a naturalisation act of 1870). Japanese migrants had been entering the United States in large numbers since the 1880s, especially after the US annexation of Hawaii in 1897. By World War One there were well over 100,000 in California alone, which had for some time been the scene of considerable anti-Japanese sentiment as a result of the volume of immigration. Voluntary restraints were unsuccessful, leading to the 1924 Act, which was deliberately tightened so as to have particular effect on the Japanese.[6] This caused outrage among the Japanese people, and greatly weakened the arguments of those who advocated co-operation with the United States in the new world order set up under the Washington treaties.[7]

The Japanese themselves were hardly paragons of virtue when it came to racial attitudes, as their treatment of Koreans in particular showed. It was only when they themselves were the actual or potential victims of racial discrimination that they talked of racial equality. Nevertheless, Japan was getting a message that it was not going to be treated as an equal after all. It was respected for its achievements, and accepted in the world community as a major power, but it would never be accepted as a real equal because its people were simply not white. It could do things western-style for ever and a day, but it would never be a proper white nation.[8] So why bother any more? Some western things were still useful for making and keeping Japan a strong nation in a western-dominated world. But whether this uncomfortable thing called democracy was one of them was another question.

5.2 A TROUBLED START TO SHŌWA

Hirohito became emperor on his father's death on 25 December 1926. Though only in his mid-twenties he had gained significant experience as regent, and had also travelled widely abroad. Partly through admiration for the British monarchy, and partly through the influence of Minobe Tatsukichi, he was keen to function as a constitutional monarch.[9] An immediate problem here was that the constitution was very ambivalent regarding the role of the monarch.

However, constitutionalism was not the only influence on Hirohito. As a child he had been raised under a strong personal military influence, first from General Nogi and then from Admiral Tōgō. His tutors also included the nationalist Sugiura Shigetake (1855–1924). As an individual Hirohito was aloof and far removed from the public. He was a god in name, and in practice an elitist who knew next to nothing about the lives of his common subjects.

Hirohito's reign was given the name 'Shōwa', meaning 'Illustrious Peace'. In fact it was characterised virtually from the outset by crises and drama at home and abroad.

At home, the economy was not in good shape. World War One had been good to Japan, enabling it to fill market gaps in Asia left vacant by the warring western powers. During the war years industrial production had grown five-fold, exports had more than trebled, and the economy as a whole had grown by some 50 per cent.[10] With such a command over supply, Japan had also been able to experiment with new technology and diversification.[11] The *zaibatsu* in particular had profited from the war. However, after the war prices had collapsed and an enduring recession set in. The so-called 'dual economy' grew worse, as the gap between the huge *zaibatsu* and the smaller companies grew ever wider. Reconstruction after the Tōkyō Earthquake in 1923 provided a brief boost, but this was followed in 1927 by a financial crisis that saw a quarter of Japan's banks fail. Silk still formed a substantial export item, but prices slumped by more than half in the late 1920s. The rural sector was further hit by a similar fall in rice prices in 1930, and in general it was the rural sector that bore the brunt of Japan's share of the world depression of that time. Between 1926 and 1931 rural cash incomes fell from an index of 100 to 33, which was more than twice the fall in urban incomes.

The urban population was growing fast, which was itself a source of social problems. In 1895 only 12 per cent of the then 42 million Japanese had lived in towns or cities of more than 10,000 people, but by the mid-1930s this rose to 45 per cent of the then 70 million Japanese.[12] Of course, not all urban dwellers were wealthy and enjoying a high quality of life, but in general there was a significant discrepancy between rural and urban life.[13] Rural Japan was characterised by lower living standards and traditional ways, and urban Japan by at least the promise of wealth, and by modernity and westernness, symbolised by the *moga* and *mobo* (from 'modern girl' and 'modern boy'). The greater disaffection was among the rural communities. This was to work to the advantage of the military, whose forces were heavily drawn from the rural sector and who shared with the rural population a basically conservative and less internationalised outlook on life.[14]

The military, and many members of the public, were increasingly angry about economic and political developments. There was a widespread belief that big business had too much influence in politics, to the point of corruption. Even the politicians themselves accepted this. The *Seiyūkai* government of 1927–9 was labelled a 'Mitsui cabinet' by the major opposition party, the (*Rikken*) *Minseitō* (Constitutional Democratic Party, basically a derivative of the *Kokumintō*). In return, the *Minseitō* government of 1929–30 was labelled a 'Mitsubishi cabinet' by the *Seiyūkai*.[15]

Many pointed to western influence as the real source of corruption, lumping together as western evils such things as parliamentary institutions, big business, individualism, and the relatively liberal urban lifestyle.[16] There was growing dissatisfaction with what exactly Japan had achieved by its adoption of western economic and political systems, especially when these had clearly failed to stop the great depression in the west. By contrast, the rise of the Nazis in Germany and the Fascists in Italy was a sign that perhaps a less democratic approach would be more effective, and that even some western nations themselves had started to realise this.

As discontent and intolerance towards democracy mounted, there were increased calls from the military for a policy of territorial expansion as a solution to Japan's woes. Eyes turned to China. As the politicians dithered, the military took matters into their own hands.

In June 1928 extreme elements in Japan's Kwantung Army deliberately blew up a train near Mukden, killing the warlord Chang Tso-lin (Zhang Zuolin, 1873–1928). The plotters blamed Chinese bandits, hoping to use this as justification for initiating Japanese military action in the area. Moderates in the army stopped the situation from escalating, but the plotters received only token punishment. Hirohito rebuked Prime Minister Tanaka Giichi (1864–1929) for failing to take firm action, causing him to resign, but he himself took no action against the plotters either.

Tanaka was followed as prime minister by Hamaguchi Osachi (1870–1931). He too was soon facing a crisis. At the London Naval Conference of 1930, which was intended to update the Washington Conference agreement on naval limitations, he failed to achieve any significant improvement to Japan's ratio. This caused widespread outrage back in Japan. Hamaguchi was shot by a fanatical right-wing youth, eventually dying of his wounds. A few years later Japan withdrew from all agreements on naval limitations.

In September 1931 came the Manchurian Incident. It was a virtual repeat of the tactic used by the Kwantung Army in 1928. Once again a railway near Mukden was blown up by Japanese troops, and once again the Chinese were blamed, in the hope that this would provoke a crisis enabling Japan's military position to be strengthened. It was carried out by a group of middle-ranking officers, led by Lieutenant-Colonel Ishiwara Kanji (1889–1949), but this time it had the tacit approval of high figures in the military command.[17]

This time moderates did not prevail. Unlike the case in 1928, Japanese military intervention followed swiftly, in fact within hours. The government was powerless to stop it. The *Minseitō* cabinet, led by Hamaguchi's successor Wakatsuki Reijirō (1866–1949), resigned a few months later over their inability to resolve the crisis. Wakatsuki was followed by the *Seiyūkai*'s aged Inukai Tsuyoshi (1855–1932), who tried to control the military but was assassinated by ultra-right naval officers after just a few months in office. Inukai was the last party prime minister till after World War Two.

Hirohito was said to be alarmed by the army's actions in Manchuria and was urged to intervene by his brother Prince Chichibu (1902–53), but refused to do so.[18] To what extent he actually approved or disapproved of the army's actions may never be clearly established, but his lack of action and his public silence led the public at large to conclude that he supported the army's actions in Manchuria.

Japanese military intervention in Manchuria soon led to the establishment of the Republic of Manchukuo (Manshūkoku) by the Kwantung Army in March 1932. This army-created nation was formally recognised by Japan's government in September that year, and redesignated the Empire of Manchukuo in March 1934. Its emperor was China's famous 'last emperor', the puppet ruler Pu'i (Puyi, 1906–67).

The Manchurian Incident brought a reaction from the League of Nations. A commission headed by Britain's Lord Lytton went to Manchuria early in 1932 to investigate. Based on its report, in February 1933 the General Assembly of the League of Nations condemned Japan's actions. Japan promptly withdrew from the League.

The military was now virtually unchecked, with opposition cowed. The 'thought police' were active, and assassinations of those with the wrong thoughts were commonplace. The emperor himself seemed to present no obstacle to the military's plans for expansion. Indeed, the military took it upon themselves to protect him from 'evil advisers' with the wrong ideas, advisers who were too western and liberal in their outlook. Among the many casualties was Minobe Tatsukichi, whose views on constitutionalism earned him a charge of treason. Many of his writings were also withdrawn.

The general movement to restore Japan to proper health was often referred to as a call for a 'Shōwa Restoration', though this term meant different things to different people. During the early and mid-1930s in particular there were a number of assassinations and even attempted coups in the cause of this restoration.

The best-known attempted coup, the 'February 26th Incident' or '26–2–36 Incident', took place in the early hours of 26 February 1936. Some 1,400 troops led by junior officers stormed several government buildings, killing and wounding a number of leading political figures and imperial advisers. Their aim was to install a military government more sympathetic to their ultra-nationalistic ideas. However, there was by no means full support for them, and the top levels of the military were divided over their action. A decisive factor in the eventual outcome was, to the surprise of many, Hirohito. The rebels had declared themselves absolutely loyal to the emperor and had their cause severely weakened when Hirohito, outraged at the attacks on his advisers, refused to have anything to do with them and insisted they be brought to trial as traitors. He also denied them the right to commit ritual suicide. The rebel leaders hoped the trial might provide a forum for their views, but even this was denied them, for it was conducted in secret. Nineteen were eventually executed and seventy others imprisoned. However, none of the senior officers who had openly shown sympathy was convicted.

The February 26th Incident was a rare case of firm intervention by Hirohito, and of the military being curbed. In general, the first ten years of Hirohito's Shōwa had seen the military gain control of the nation at the expense of parliamentary government. Their aggressive anti-western, anti-liberal mood, shared by many members of the public, did not make an auspicious start to the era of Illustrious Peace.

5.3   THE IDEOLOGIES BEHIND EXPANSIONISM

Among those executed for complicity in the February 26th Incident was the radical nationalist Kita Ikki (1883–1937), a leading thinker in the Shōwa Restoration movement. He wanted a military coup to rid Japan of its incompetent government leaders so as to restore the emperor to a direct relationship with his people. He saw the emperor as absolute but, interestingly, not as divine—which may have been his undoing. In any event, Kita believed the emperor should suspend the constitution, and free himself from the corrupting influence of politicians and businessmen in order to guide the fair redistribution of national land and assets. Kita also saw Japan as having a special destiny as the liberator of Asian nations in the yoke of western imperialism. Once Japan was restored to health and vitality, then it could lead a united and free Asia.

Kita's beliefs were just part of a set of ideologies of the day that were used to justify Japanese expansionism. Particularly widespread were the concept of an absolute and divine emperor, and the idea of Japan occupying and controlling Asia in order to liberate it—a peculiarly Japanese idea of anti-imperialist imperialism.[19]

The concept of the absolute and divine emperor owed much to the ideology behind the *Imperial Rescript on Education* of 1890. This was greatly intensified during the 1930s. Its culmination was the *Kokutai no Hongi* (Cardinal Principles of the Nation), the bible of the 'emperor system' (*tennōsei*). This book-length document was published by the Ministry of Education in March 1937. It used very similar terminology to the *Rescript*, and was similarly intended to be used by schoolteachers and other persons in authority to instil the correct attitudes in their charges. In 1937 no fewer than 36 per cent of the population were within the age-range for compulsory education and therefore a very worthwhile target for indoctrination.

It was a document that appealed to the emotions and not the intellect. Full of inconsistencies, its deliberately stilted language put detailed analysis of it beyond the ability of most readers. At the same time, such language gave it an aura of antiquity and authority. Its main thrust was to stress the divine origin of the emperor and the importance of total self-sacrificial obedience to his will, to such an extent that loyal service to the emperor and his nation became not so much a duty but the object of life itself.[20]

The text defines the Japanese nation as follows:[21]

The unbroken line of Emperors, receiving the Oracle of the Founder of the Nation, reign eternally over the Japanese Empire. This is our eternal and immutable national entity. Thus, founded on this great principle, all the people, united as one great family nation in heart and obeying the Imperial Will, enhance the beautiful virtues of loyalty and filial piety. This is the glory of our national entity.

The emperor is a 'deity incarnate', a 'direct descendant of Amaterasu', and serving him is 'not a duty as such, nor a submission to authority', but a 'natural manifestation of the heart'. Unlike western nations, whose citizens are 'conglomerations of separate individuals' with 'no deep foundation between ruler and citizen to unite them', the emperor and his subjects 'arise from the same fountainhead'. The relationship between the emperor and his subjects is 'in its sympathies, that of father and child. This relationship is a natural relationship', not a merely contracted one such as that between ruler and citizen in the west. Indeed, Japan follows the way of nature, with 'nature and man united as one'. It is also characterised by harmony, for 'harmony is a product of the great achievements of the founding of our nation'. The ultimate harmony is that between emperor and subject, more exactly in *'the climax of harmony in the sacrifice of the life of a subject for the Emperor'* (my italics). In recent times there has been corruption by 'western individualism and rationalism', and 'we must sweep aside the corruption of the spirit and the clouding of knowledge that arises from ... being taken up with one's "self", and return to a pure and clear state of mind'. This is not only for the sake of Japan, or even Asia, but the whole world: 'This should be done not only for the sake of our nation but for the sake of the entire human race, which is struggling to find a way out of the deadlock with which individualism is faced.'[22]

Many westerners who encountered Japanese during the decade or so following *Kokutai no Hongi* were surprised that not only the masses but also many high-ranking and highly intelligent Japanese appeared to believe this propaganda—even some of those who had helped create it.[23] It is true that by the late 1930s all Japanese younger than 50 years or so had been educated in a controlled environment of emperor-centred world-view following the 1890 *Rescript*. This included many in quite senior positions. Some of them may genuinely have become confused between myth and reality. And no doubt many if not most of the 'masses' were quite genuinely indoctrinated. But at the same time, to question the emperor system was to risk one's life. Fear also played its part.

The important role of the emperor in Japan's prewar ideology has sometimes led to other aspects of the *Kokutai no Hongi* being overlooked. One of these was promotion of the idea that the Japanese were 'united with nature' and enjoyed a purer and more natural existence than western nations corrupted by individualism. The idea of a special Japanese harmony with nature was almost certainly given such an important place in the document by one of the members of the drafting committee, Watsuji Tetsurō (1889–1960), a well-known philosopher with a particular interest in environmental determinism. Though it may not have been his exact intention, it was used as one more justification for Japan's expansion on the Asian continent. Japanese were able to claim that their expansion on the Asian mainland was intended not just to throw off the shackles of western political and economic systems, but at a deeper level to restore harmony between humans and nature.

This natural harmony was known as *musubi*, a complex term. It combined meanings of 'bonding', 'harmony', and 'coupling' in the biblical sense. It had connotations of 'procreation' and 'generation' and by extension 'vitality' and 'life force', as well as the 'pristine purity' associated with new life.

One of the clearest English-language descriptions of *musubi* is found in Kawai Tatsuo's work *The Goal of Japanese Expansion*, of 1938:[24]

In the course of their evolution as a distinct race, the Japanese, under the influence of their natural environment and their varying and exhilarating climate, acquired a love of beauty and purity. They lived close to nature.... As children of the gods, our ancients lived in harmony with nature, acquiring a free and liberal social outlook which has developed into the ideal of universal brotherhood. At the same time, perceiving in the forces of nature the operation of a mysterious power, they formulated the philosophy of *Musubi*. . . . By observing the unbroken rotation of the seasons and the happy multiplication of living creatures, our ancestors perceived the existence of a power or principle which operates in nature, creating, nourishing, and multiplying all manner of things. They called this power *Musubi*. . . . The history of the Japanese nation is nothing but a record of the development of their faith in nature—the harmonization and self-identification of the race with its natural environment. . . . Preserve nature and rediscover oneself!—so teaches the philosophy of *Musubi*.

Kawai goes on to explain how the Japanese are aiming to restore the spirit of *musubi* to a degenerate China, in the interests of China itself and Asia as a whole:[25]

Following the dictate of *Musubi*, Japan, together with a resurrected China, will identify herself with the cosmic force that creates and fosters life and will help to promote its endless process in the beautification and sublimification of Asiatic life. Herein lies the foundation of Japan's China policy.

Not all Japanese went to such flowery philosophical lengths to justify Japan's China policy. Many simply referred Nazi-style to the need for *lebensraum*, 'room to live', ignoring the still under-utilised spaces of Hokkaidō. The 'room to live' view was often linked to a clearly selective argument that there were only three ways to ease the pressure of surplus population: emigration, advance into world markets, and territorial expansion. Japan was supposedly left with no alternative but the third since the west, with its anti-Japanese immigration laws and its trade tariffs, had effectively barred the first two options.[26] No one seemed prepared to consider options such as population control, which had been so effective in the Tokugawa period.

Another simpler justification was that of Ishiwara Kanji, of Manchurian Incident fame. He wanted a Japanese military occupation and reorganisation of Asia to enable its resources to be used by Japan in preparation for a Final War to gain world domination.[27] This war was to be between Japan and the United States. Ishiwara was influenced in this by the medieval Buddhist monk Nichiren's belief in a great final war to end all wars. He also took a philosophical position to the effect that war, with its destruction, paved the way for reconstruction and was hence part of the march of civilisation. However, despite the veneer of philosophy, in his view of life all things were subordinated to military considerations—a simple militarism.[28]

Ishiwara himself was not particularly liked as a person and was never greatly trusted by his colleagues.[29] These factors tended to limit his personal influence. Neverthless there was growing sympathy for his views on the importance to Japan of acquiring Asian resources for a future showdown with the United States. And as the 1930s progressed, his idea of using military action to take control of Asia came to prevail over less aggressive Pan-Asianist views.

One such 'softer' view was that of the Sinologist Tachibana Shiraki (1881–1945). Tachibana believed that Japan, as the most suitably qualified nation, should establish not military but cultural and political leadership in Asia. This would create a cultural-political Asian entity that could counterbalance the dominance of the already-established western cultural-political entity. Unfortunately, other than suggesting Confucianism and the Imperial Way as universal guiding principles for this Asian entity, Tachibana did not propose any specific means of organising this. His silence on these matters made it easier for the militarists to prevail.

5.4 PREPARATIONS FOR WAR

It was true that Japan could benefit greatly from the resources of the mainland, especially natural resources in which Japan itself was poorly endowed. However, as the desire for mainland resources took on an increasingly aggressive military tone, rather ironically Japan's economy was entering a recovery phase. In the early 1930s Japan had taken the bold and unprecedented 'Keynesian' step of using government deficit spending to trigger reflation and stop the recession.[30] It had also taken the yen off the international gold standard, which led to a depreciation of around 50 per cent and a consequent increase in Japan's now much cheaper exports. By 1936 Japan had become the world's largest exporter of cotton piece goods. It was one of the first major nations to emerge from the world depression. In fact, for the rest of the 1930s Japan's average annual economic growth was 5 per cent,[31] and between 1929 and 1937 its GDP grew by more than 50 per cent.[32]

This economic upturn indicated that Japan in the 1930s had alternatives to military expansionism.[33] The question was whether it wished to pursue them. Alternatively, it might use a stronger economy to make a stronger military, in the spirit of the Meiji slogan 'rich nation, strong army'.

One problem was that although the economy seemed healthy at a national level, the benefits were not flowing through to enough people. The majority of people were still rural dwellers employed in agriculture, but rural incomes were the slowest to recover. By the mid-1930s they were still only around half of what they had been in the mid-1920s.[34] Despite improved productivity agriculture was simply not as efficient as manufacturing, for its proportion of the workforce was more than double its proportion of the GDP. Within manufacturing, despite the export success of cotton piece goods, textile manufacturing was steadily losing ground to heavier manufacturing industries such as machinery.[35] The fact that textile mills were often based in regional towns added to rural woes.

Urban workers were often little better off, owing to the increasing dualisation of industry. From the early 1930s the government deliberately followed a policy of industrial rationalisation that authorised cartels in important industries. This greatly helped the already rich and powerful *zaibatsu* to grow even more rich and powerful. By 1937 the two major *zaibatsu* alone, Mitsui and Mitsubishi, held between them almost one-seventh of all capital in commerce and industry.[36] The average wage for workers in a large *zaibatsu* (more than 5,000 workers) was more than double that of workers in small companies (fewer than thirty workers).[37]

The link between government and the *zaibatsu* was not always one of unbounded trust. Many in the government felt the established *zaibatsu* had too much influence, were corrupt and decadent, and were difficult to control. They preferred not to rationalise to such an extent that only a few established *zaibatsu* dominated to the exclusion of all other large companies.[38] This was a major reason why the government promoted the 'new *zaibatsu*' such as Nissan and Toyota, which were particularly active in areas such as vehicle production.

These companies in key industries were helped by a raft of laws from the mid-1930s, partly inspired by German example. These forced out foreign competitors by restrictions on foreign exchange and requirements for Japanese managerial control before licences could be issued. Ford was a particular threat, and the provisions of the 1936 Automobile Manufacturing Industry Law were backdated to ensure its new 1935 Yokohama plant became effectively illegal. The same law gave assistance such as tax exemptions to companies who produced military vehicles, thus bringing those companies under government control. Similar laws were passed in industries such as petroleum, steel, machine tools, shipbuilding, and aircraft.

As the government tightened its control over industry, so too did the military tighten its control over the government. After the attempted coup of 26 February 1936 a new cabinet was formed under Hirota Kōki (1878–1948). Hirota was only in office for a few months but was very sympathetic to the military's aims. He greatly increased the military budget, promoted the orientation of heavy industry towards a war effort, and reinstituted a former principle that only admirals and generals on active duty could serve as army and navy ministers.

In November that year, uneasy once again about Soviet intentions in Asia, Japan signed the Anti-Comintern Pact with Germany. Italy joined shortly afterwards. The pact was basically an agreement to assist each other, by exchange of information, against the perceived common enemy, the Soviet Union.

The next year Japan effectively went to war against China, following the Marco Polo Bridge Incident of 7 July 1937. The incident started when legally stationed Japanese troops on manoeuvres near Peking (Beijing) claimed to have been fired on by the Chinese. The situation, which may well have been deliberately provoked by the Japanese,[39] led to a localised clash of arms. Within a month it escalated further into all-out war, even though this was never formally declared.

Even if the initial clash had been accidental, there was no attempt by the Japanese government or the emperor to prevent the escalation.[40] Far from it, new prime minister Konoe Fumimaro (1891–1945) actively promoted a belligerent attitude towards China.[41] China for its part, under a revitalised Chiang Kai-shek, was in no mood to back down either.

Fighting spread to Shanghai in August, with the city falling in November. The Japanese then moved on to the capital, Nanking (Nanjing), which fell in December after only a few days of fighting. The collapse of the city was followed by widespread murder, rape, torture, and looting by Japanese troops in one of the world's most infamous atrocities. Chinese casualties will never be known exactly, and have been placed as high as 340,000 by the Chinese and as low as 30,000 by the Japanese. What is certain that many tens of thousands were killed, many of them civilians.

Some of the atrocities in Nanking were filmed.[42] There has been remorseful public testimony by Japanese troops personally involved in the massacre.[43] No less a figure than Prince Mikasa (b.1915), the emperor's younger brother who was stationed in Nanking, acknowledged in an interview with a popular newspaper many years later that a massacre took place.[44] Nevertheless, even today the Nanking Massacre is still denied by some Japanese, including those in high office. So too is the whole idea of Japan ever having been aggressive.

To the surprise of the Japanese, the Chinese did not capitulate after Nanking. Something of a stalemate eventuated, with Japan making a few gains but little substantial progress. Japan's leaders started to worry that the China campaign might prove protracted and weaken Japan, exposing it to the Soviet Union. Such fears were not entirely groundless. The Soviets had openly expressed their support for China. There were also increasingly serious military clashes between the Soviet Union and Japan in the late 1930s, and the Japanese were coming out second best.[45] The Japanese were further alarmed when Germany signed a non-aggression pact with the Soviet Union in August 1939, in breach of the spirit of Japan's own Anti-Comintern Pact with Germany.

Japan felt betrayed by Germany. Their faith in this former idol had been set back anyway by Hitler's open proclamation of the superiority of the Aryan race and his description of the Japanese as a 'second-class people'.[46] Not a few Japanese feared that Germany might yet turn on Japan as a 'Yellow Peril', and even that some of the other western powers, such as the United States, might join Germany in such a cause. They were never to rid themselves of such doubts.[47]

Nevertheless, German successes in the early stages of World War Two, which started the following month of September 1939, suggested to Japan that a pro-Axis (Germany and Italy) policy would be beneficial. As a result Japan signed the Tripartite Pact in September 1940. The main points of the pact included an agreement to come to each other's aid should there be any attack by a power not currently involved in the war in Europe or the Sino-Japanese conflict. This meant, of course, the United States.

Japan's interests in Asia were also recognised. These centred on the vision of a Greater East Asia Co-prosperity Sphere (*Dai Tōa Kyōei-Ken*), led by Japan. It was an ill-defined vision, but the more idealistic versions of it even included countries such as Australia and New Zealand.

The Tripartite Pact gave Japan confidence to extend its activities on the Asian mainland. Almost at the same moment the pact was being signed in Berlin, Japanese troops moved into the north of French Indochina. There was little resistance from an incapacitated France. The United States responded by limiting exports to Japan of items such as aviation fuel, steel, and scrap iron, but refrained from military action.

There was considerable public indignation and alarm in the United States over Japan's actions in Asia, just as over Germany's actions in Europe and the signing of the Tripartite Pact, but in general the American people supported the official government policy of non-intervention.[48]

In June the following year of 1941 Germany reneged on its non-aggression pact and attacked the Soviets. At least with the Soviets now engaged with Germany, Japan felt reassured that its northern acquisitions in Manchuria would be safe. It could turn its attention to the south. In particular, Japan wanted to secure a base from which it could move into Malaya and the Dutch East Indies, rich in resources. On 22 July 1941 it moved further south in Indochina, even though it realised this would probably provoke a reaction from the United States.

The official American response was to freeze Japanese assets in America and impose a comprehensive export embargo on American goods to Japan. These goods included the vital commodity, oil. Japan depended on imports for more than 90 per cent of its oil, and more than three-quarters of this imported oil came from the United States.[49]

Unofficially, President Franklin Roosevelt immediately agreed to an idealistic plan for the covert bombing of Japan. The plan had been proposed some seven months earlier by Claire Chennault, leader of a volunteer group of Chinese-based American pilots known as the Flying Tigers. The group were employed as mercenaries by the Chinese government in their fight against Japan. Chennault was keen to make pre-emptive strategic bombing raids on Japan itself. He had approached the American government for covert support, and had received some financial backing for his group but not approval for his plan. Then in May 1941 Roosevelt's adviser, Lauchlin Currie, visited China and on his return revived the plan. Roosevelt and some of his senior staff, along with the British, were enthusiastic in spirit but felt it impractical. However, on 23 July—the day after the Japanese southward move in Indochina—Roosevelt and top military officials such as Admirals Hart and Turner put their signatures to Document JB 355 (Serial 691), titled *Aircraft Requirements of the Chinese Government*.[50] Among other things, this authorised the use of 66 Lockheed-Hudson and Douglas DB-7 bombers (other planes to be made available later) for the following clearly stated purpose:

Destruction of Japanese factories in order to cripple production of munitions and essential articles for maintenance of economic structure of Japan.

As it happened, there was a delay in securing the planes, and other events were to overtake the plan before any bombing raids were attempted.

That may have been for the best, for JB 355 was operationally almost doomed from the start. At some 2,000 km from their bases in China these slow bombers would have been outside the range of protection by their fighter escorts, and would almost certainly have been promptly destroyed by Japan's state-of-the-art Mitsubishi Zero fighters. One can only attribute this moment of seeming folly, when experienced military men and political leaders agreed to such an improbable plan, to sheer frustration at Japan's behaviour. Certainly, leading figures such as Secretary of State Cordell Hull and Roosevelt himself were on record more than once around this time expressing their anger at the Japanese and their wish somehow to teach them a lesson.[51]

The oil embargo was far more effective than JB 355 would have been. It left Japan with very limited oil reserves. Obviously, this was an untenable situation. As early as 3 September the nation's leaders decided to go to war with the United States if the situation regarding oil could not be resolved by early October. (The deadline was later extended to 30 November.)

At the same time, an attack on Pearl Harbor, which had been proposed in January that year by Admiral Yamamoto Isoroku (1884–1943), was finally approved, and rehearsed at Kagoshima Bay in southern Kyūshū. There were some in Japan who hoped that diplomacy might still prevail, such as Prime Minister Konoe (despite his belligerence towards China), but Hull in particular remained adamant that Japan should drastically change its policy before any concessions could be made. He wanted the Japanese not just to withdraw from Indochina, but from China as well. Konoe resigned in October, to be replaced as prime minister by army minister General Tōjō Hideki (1884–1948).

Japan made its final concession in late November, agreeing to withdraw from southern Indochina but not from China. Hull did not accept. Japan did not expect him to. Under the command of Admiral Nagumo Chūichi (1887–1944), its fleet was already setting sail from the Kuriles towards Hawaii. It was a large fleet on deadly business, comprising six aircraft carriers with more than 400 planes between them, two battleships, three cruisers, nine destroyers, and more than a score of submarines.

Emperor Hirohito gave his formal approval for war on 1 December, claiming later that 'As a constitutional monarch in a constitutional political system, I had no choice but to sanction the decision by the Tōjō cabinet to begin the war.'[52] However, more importantly, he also said that 'I probably would have tried to veto the decision for war *if at the time I had foreseen the future*' (my italics).[53] That is, it was not that he felt totally unable to intervene, but that he was unwilling to try, because he thought at the time that the outcome of the war would be favourable to Japan.

Hirohito had for some time believed it was possible to strike a decisive blow against the Americans and then move to a peace policy.[54] In this he shared a view with the majority. Only the most fanatical in Japan believed they could defeat America totally. Nor was it a traditional Japanese practice to confront directly a more powerful enemy and risk a humiliating defeat. But there was a widespread fatalistic acceptance that some sort of showdown with America was necessary, and most thought they had a very good chance of winning an honourable draw, as they had with Russia. That is, they could fight the more powerful foe to a point where it grew weary and was prepared to discuss terms of peace, terms which would leave Japan in a better position than it was in during 1941.[55] Or so they thought.

5.5 THE PACIFIC WAR

The first Japanese strike in the Pacific War was not against America at Pearl Harbor; it was against the British in Malaya. About 90 minutes before Pearl Harbor, some 5,000 Japanese troops successfully attacked a British force in Kota Bharu, in the Kelantan Sultanate.[56]

The Japanese realised that in any event war against America almost certainly meant war against Britain too. They needed the resources of Malaya as soon as possible for their war effort, and they knew they had little to fear from Britain. Some months earlier, in a rare display of German assistance to Japan, a German U-boat commander had passed on to them a captured top-secret report from the British Chiefs of Staff to the War Cabinet.[57] The report stated that Singapore and other British territories in southeast Asia were considered indefensible against Japanese attack and would receive little if any military reinforcements. This knowledge not only gave the Japanese the reassurance to attack British positions, it also dispelled any reservations they might have had about committing so many resources to the attack on Pearl Harbor and American positions.

The attack on Pearl Harbor came just before 8 o'clock on the morning of 7 December (local time). The first strike was a wave of 183 bombers. A second wave of 167 bombers hit about an hour later. The American forces there were completely unprepared. They suffered over 4,500 casualties (of whom about three-quarters were killed or missing presumed killed). America also lost four battleships, about 180 aircraft, and three destroyers. In addition, heavy damage was sustained by four more battleships, some eighty planes, and three light cruisers. On the Japanese side, losses amounted to just five submarines, twenty-nine aircraft, and around sixty men.

Though considerable, the damage at Pearl Harbor could and should have been worse. Admiral Nagumo was criticised by a number of his colleagues for making only two air strikes, and for failing to destroy large stocks of oil, machine shops and other repair facilities, aircraft hangars, and numerous undamaged or only partly damaged vessels and aircraft.[58] Militarily, the attack was not really as successful as it should have been. It was as if the Japanese could somehow not believe their luck in being able to inflict the very considerable damage that they did, and withdrew prematurely.

The attack was not a model of operational efficiency but it was of course enough to bring America immediately into the war, with a vengeance. Non-interventionism was effectively neutralised by public outrage at what was seen as a sneaky and dishonourable attack.

The fact that the Japanese struck before formal notification of intent was for many the clear proof of this sneakiness. The Japanese claimed this was due not to deliberate omission on their part but to diplomatic bungling by Japanese embassy staff in Washington, which resulted in the notification arriving one hour after the attack instead of half an hour before it. This has become a matter of some controversy, but in fact the whole issue is rendered academic by the overlooked attack on Kelantan. Even if the notification had arrived on time, half an hour before Pearl Harbor, it would still have come an hour after Kelantan, which was similarly unannounced. In other words, despite official Japanese denials, there is little doubt Pearl Harbor was a deliberate attack without due formal warning—a matter viewed with shame by many of Japan's own top military men, including its leading fighter pilot Sakai Saburō.[59] On the other hand, this 'surprise attack' should not really have been any surprise at all to anybody in view of Japan's earlier tactics against China and Russia.

Regardless of Japan's failure to give formal notification, the question of whether American leaders were actually caught by surprise is a matter of much greater controversy. At one extreme there are those who believe Pearl Harbor was a conspiracy by Roosevelt and colleagues, who knew all about the impending attack but allowed it—or even encouraged it—to happen, sacrificing American lives in order to bring America into the war against Japan's allies Germany. At the other extreme are those who simply feel America was caught napping through complacency. Evidence can be produced for and against both views, and a definitive picture may never emerge.[60]

Certainly, it is beyond dispute that there were many warning signs of the attack, including code intercepts, radar signals, sightings, and intelligence given to America not only by its own agents but also by other nations such as the Dutch. The key question is how much these warnings were actually recognised as such at the time. These were the days when a naval attaché at the US Embassy in Tōkyō, who might be expected to know a thing or two about Japan and its military capacity, was talking of 'licking the Japs in 24 hours'.[61] Many in the navy were talking of wanting to 'knock off the little brown brother any time' before getting down to the Battle of the Atlantic.[62] Such attitudes were not conducive to taking the Japanese military threat seriously enough to pay close attention to all the incoming signs. There was undoubtedly complacency.

On the other hand, it was another certainty that those who were spoiling for a fight, which included some of America's leaders, had their wishes granted by Pearl Harbor. The Japanese might have thrown a harder punch than anyone ever imagined, but at least the fight had started. Whatever the background, the fact remains it was effective in overcoming non-interventionist sentiment and bringing America into the war against Germany, thereby helping Britain, as Churchill very much wanted.[63] Roosevelt himself later told Churchill and Stalin that if it had not been for the Japanese attack he would have had great difficulty in getting the American people into the war.[64] But was this an expression of satisfaction at a goal accomplished, or merely a statement of fact? This is typical of the ambivalent nature of much of the material involved in the unending and labyrinthine controversy of Pearl Harbor—a controversy that, though fascinating and relevant to those interested in Japan, must remain primarily a concern for historians of American policy.

From the Japanese point of view, the fact was that they were now at war with America. Despite the operational criticism of the attack on Pearl Harbor there was much rejoicing in Japan, including in the Imperial Palace.[65] The happy mood was to continue with a sequence of Japanese successes during the very early stages of the Pacific War.

Just a few hours after Pearl Harbor, American air power was severely damaged by an attack on its air fleet, which was grounded in the Philippines and was another sitting target. Within a week or so Thailand was

occupied, yielding diplomatically. The small British naval fleet off
Malaya was badly crippled, allowing Japanese military advances in the
area. Guam fell on 11 December, with a number of other Pacific islands
falling in the following two months. Hong Kong was captured on 25
December. Borneo surrendered on 19 January. On 15 February, in one
of the worst and most demoralising moments in British military history, Singapore surrendered unconditionally following an unexpected
land-based assault. It had been considered by most Britons to be
impregnable and held some 70,000 combatants—more than twice as
many as the Japanese troops attacking it. By the end of February Sumat-
ra, Timor, and Bali had also fallen. Batavia surrendered on 6 March.
Rangoon, in Burma, fell on 8 March, and Java on 9 March. In the Philippines, Manila fell on 2 January 1942, though Bataan held out till early
April and Corregidor Island held out till 7 May. In March General
Douglas MacArthur (1880–1964), the American Commander of Far
East Forces, had left his base in the Philippines for Australia under
orders from Washington. His famous words 'I shall return' became a
rallying cry for Allied forces in the Pacific region.

Initial successes by Japan were in part due to the Allies being occupied in Europe, but in large part also due to the sheer intensity of their
attacks. This was something for which the Allies were not really prepared. Winston Churchill's comment on the fall of Singapore, that 'The
violence, fury, skill, and might of Japan far exceeded anything we had
been led to expect',[66] was shared by many. Westerners had seriously
underestimated Japan. This included Japan's western allies. Hitler
was greatly disturbed by the ease with which the *untermenschen* ('inferior people') Japanese defeated white troops in Singapore in particular.[67]

Japanese intensity was, as the Japanese themselves saw it, spiritually
based.[68] They felt their strength of spirit was greater than that of soft
westerners weakened by materialism and egoism. It included a determination to fight to the death. In one specific illustration, a successful
Allied counter-attack in the Aleutian Islands in May 1943, Japan suffered 2,351 men killed while only 28 surrendered.[69] This ratio of deaths
to surrenders, in the order of 84:1, was not uncommon for the Japanese.
It was even surpassed in some cases, such as North Burma where the
ratio was 120:1.[70] Moreover, the majority of Japanese taken prisoner
were either wounded, unconscious, or otherwise incapacitated at the
time.[71] This contrasts dramatically with the general Allied ratio of 1
death to 4 surrenders[72]—a difference of several hundred-fold, though
boosted by mass Allied surrenders such as at Singapore.

Not all Japanese were prepared to fight to the death, as later oral accounts in particular show.[73] Some did surrender, especially in the later stages of the war, though by that point many found it difficult to do so, for few prisoners were being taken on either side.[74] On the whole, though, most thought it better to die than surrender. Many, of course, were indoctrinated to believe that the sacrifice of one's life for the nation was the ultimate service to the emperor-god, the very aim of one's existence and the ultimate purification. Oral accounts again show the extent of this death wish, which on occasion caused severe anguish to those thwarted in their attempt to die for the cause.[75] To the very end the Allies were never sure that the Japanese race as a whole would not destroy themselves rather than surrender, in a mass death wish known as *ichioku gyokusai* ('the self-destruction of the jewel-like hundred million').[76] Most Japanese believed such fighting to the death for a cause to be in the honourable samurai tradition, but few realised how idealised their view of that tradition was.

At a less glorious level, many Japanese were also given to believe that if captured they would be brutally tortured by the enemy, and that death would be less painless. Even those who were not swayed by indoctrination or by warnings of torture still often preferred death, for they believed surrender would bring shame and victimisation for themselves and their families later, back in Japan.[77] Most of those who did end up alive and captured preferred their families to think them dead in action—in contrast to Allied PoWs, who invariably asked for their families to be informed of the fact that they were still alive.[78]

The idealised belief that a true and perfect warrior fought to the death lay behind the brutality of the treatment meted out to those who failed to do so. Japanese abuse of Allied PoWs is well known. The death rate was around 30 per cent for Allied PoWs in Japanese camps as opposed to less than 5 per cent in German and Italian camps.[79] However, the Japanese treated their own men with almost equal brutality if they were felt to have acted with dishonour, or were somehow otherwise sullied or impure.[80] Those assigned to duties in PoW camps were usually in this category, for a true warrior would have nothing to do with 'disqualified human beings' such as captives. Their own distress and self-loathing at being assigned such duties may partly explain some of the extremes of their behaviour towards their captives.

Brutality to Allied captives was made worse by the anger and distrust that had been brewing towards the west during the previous few decades. There was also a growing feeling of contempt towards westerners, who had set themselves up as superior and would not recognise

Japanese as equals, yet were now proving the weaker in battle. The Japanese readiness to rank things also applied to races, and many did not need indoctrination by the *Kokutai no Hongi* or similar to convince themselves that Japan was the superior nation. As a race they were pure, and they were perfect. Lesser and/or impure beings rarely merited respect—even if they were not captives, as many of the occupied Asian nations found out.

And of course, there were always the sadists, who positively revelled in the opportunity of war to maim, kill, torture, and prove their manliness. All the warring nations had their sadists, and Japan was certainly no exception. On occasion it even seems to have encouraged such behaviour as a means of hardening its troops.[81]

Ironically, the very intensity of Japanese fighting and the very ease of their early victories worked against them. Their easy victories gave them a false sense of invincibility, and displaced earlier thoughts of a quick blow and then a move for peace. Their brutality roused the fighting spirit of the Allies, and also made it unlikely the Allies would accept any offer of cessation of hostilities on terms favourable to Japan.

Japanese invincibility was dented as early as 18 April 1942, in the Doolittle Raid. This was a bombing strike on Tōkyō by sixteen US B-25s launched from carriers well off the Japanese coast, led by Colonel James Doolittle. This time it was Japan's turn to be caught by surprise. The B-25s struck before anyone in Japan realised what was happening, and to the concern and embarrassment of the Japanese not one of the planes was hit by anti-aircraft fire. All flew on to land in China, where eight of the pilots were captured by Japanese forces. Three were executed as terrorists, leading Germany to protest to its ally Japan that these executions set an undesirable precedent.[82] Others suffered vivisection as human guinea pigs in the course of Japanese experiments in chemical and biological warfare.[83]

A more serious blow to Japanese morale came less than a month later, with the Battle of the Coral Sea on 7–8 May 1942. This thwarted Japanese plans to invade Port Moresby in New Guinea. Japan also lost one of its carriers and suffered serious damage to another. America actually suffered greater damage, but the battle marked the first time the Japanese had been stopped in the Pacific.

A very major blow—in fact a decisive turning-point in the war—came the following month, in the Battle of Midway of 4–6 June. Japan had been planning to occupy the island of Midway, some 1,500 km west of Hawaii, as a strategic base. However, its plans were discovered by Allied intelligence. Unlike the case with Pearl Harbor, this time the intelligence was put to effective use. The Japanese fleet, again under Nagumo, lost four of its carriers. It also lost over 2,000 crewmen, and a heavy cruiser.

From that point on, despite a number of victories and advances on the Asian mainland, Japan's fortunes declined, starting in the Pacific. Plans to occupy New Caledonia, Fiji, and Samoa were abandoned, as was any idea of occupying Australia and New Zealand. Their troops were forced out of New Guinea and Guadalcanal by early 1943. Guadalcanal cost them 25,000 men. The Americans lost just 1,500.

During 1943 Japanese resources were stretched. They had to replace their direct control over a number of Asian countries with more indirect control. Occupied nations such as Burma and the Philippines were granted nominal independence. Japan attempted to keep unity within its Asian interests, and primacy for itself, by focusing on its claimed role as liberator from western imperialism. This resulted in the Great East Asia Declaration, made on 6 November 1943 in Tōkyō by the puppet rulers of Manchuria, China, Thailand, Burma, the Philippines, and 'Free India'. The declaration attacked western imperialism and reaffirmed Asian co-operation.[84] Many of the people of these nations may initially have welcomed the Japanese as liberators. However, in reality they were by this stage extremely disillusioned by Japanese harshness. Japanese occupation often left the local civilians deprived of food and other resources and forced to work as labourers, sometimes being transported to Japan itself.

Japanese people themselves were also subject to restrictions on resources and to harsh labour mobilisation laws. All unmarried women under 25 years of age were mobilised for agricultural or industrial labour from September 1943.[85] The scarcity of food in Japan also became severe that year, and by the end of it rations were supplying only 1,405 calories per day, barely half the standard intake.[86]

During 1944 Japan made renewed efforts, largely born of desperation. At home there was a marked increase in the production of war machinery. More than 28,000 aircraft were produced that year as opposed to a mere 5,000 in 1941.[87] But this was still nowhere near the production of the United States or many of the other Allies. In the period 1941–4 Japan produced 58,822 aircraft, whereas in the same period Britain produced 96,400 and the United States 261,826.[88] However technically advanced Japanese planes might be, there were simply not enough of them.

Overseas, there were a number of Japanese successes in China during the year. However, it proved impossible to neutralise the American airbase in Szechwan, which meant America could continue to use it to bomb targets in Japan with its long-range B-29s. America did so with increasing frequency, and met with little resistance. An especially serious blow to Japan was the loss of Saipan in the Marianas in July, after very heavy fighting. This too was now able to be used as a bombing base against Tōkyō. Defence of the homeland thus now became an urgent priority.

The loss of Saipan was a devastating blow for Tōjō himself, since he had reassured his colleagues just a few months earlier that it was impregnable. He was replaced both as prime minister—General Koiso Kuniaki (1880–1950) taking over—and as chief of army staff. Faith in Tōjō and the Japanese war effort as a whole was seriously affected. Many senior military figures, who were also mindful of Germany's declining fortunes, returned to the prewar realisation that a Japanese victory was out of the question. Not a few felt it would be wise to try for peace on the best terms they could obtain. These would certainly be less favourable than had been hoped for in 1941 but would at least bring an end to hostilities. There was a misguided belief that the Soviet Union might act on Japan's behalf in this matter. In reality, a year earlier in 1943 the Soviets had pledged to join the Allies against Japan once Germany was defeated. Neverthless, with thoughts of possible Soviet help in mind, the Koiso cabinet decided to fight on. There was also some hope that a compromise could be reached if the Japanese defence of their homeland was tenacious enough to wear down the advancing Allies, who might agree to peace terms rather than lose personnel.

One tenacious defensive measure taken later that year was the systematic use of suicide *kamikaze* pilots.[89] Formally known as the *Shinpū Tokubetsu Kōgekitai*, or 'Divine Wind' Special Attack Force, the pilots were named after the 'divine wind' (*kamikaze* or *shinpū*) that had protected Japan from the Mongol invasions in the thirteenth century. Though regular aircraft were sometimes used, the 'suicide planes' were usually just bombs fitted with wings and crude steering mechanisms. They were unable to deviate from their intended target, and anyway had no fuel for a return trip. They were known by the Allies as '*baka* bombs' ('idiot bombs'), and their pilots were often teenagers with just a few weeks' training.

The *kamikaze* were first used on 25 October 1944, in the Battle of Leyte in the Philippines. MacArthur was carrying out his promise to return and landed at Leyte on the 20th of that month. The ensuing Battle of Leyte Gulf on 23–26 October was the biggest naval engagement in world history. It resulted in the effective destruction of the Japanese navy. Although Japanese troops remained in various parts of the islands till the end of the war—and in some cases beyond—their control was slowly but surely eroded. Corregidor was retaken by February 1945 and Manila by mid-March.

The retaking of Manila was a particular tragedy for the native residents. The 20,000 trapped Japanese troops, who were almost all to fight to the death, went berserk as the Americans pressed their attack. Though it is a relatively little-known atrocity, scenes of rape and pillage and murder not unlike Nanking occurred. An estimated 100,000 citizens were killed in the month prior to the recapture of the city.[90] Japanese civilians in the Philippines also suffered at the hands of Japanese troops in those final months of the war. In May 1945, retreating Japanese soldiers murdered some twenty children of Japanese civilians accompanying their unit, so the children's crying would not give the unit's position away.[91]

May 1945 also saw the retaking of Rangoon by the British, following the recapture of Mandalay in March. Anti-Japanese resolve among the Allies was further heightened at this point by the discovery of the full horror of the brutal forced labour conditions of the notorious Burma Railway. This was a project carried out by the Japanese between October 1942 and November 1943 with the intent of securing supplies from Thailand. It had caused the deaths of some 60,000 workers, including local labourers and around 15,000 British and Australian PoWs.

In the early months of 1945 the Americans increased their bombing raids on Japan using their long-range B-29s, mostly on low-level night sorties. These raids were greatly facilitated by the capture of Iwojima (Iōjima) in the Bonin (Ogasawara) island group early in March, which provided a convenient base midway between Saipan and Japan. The Japanese really had no answer to these raids. Out of a total of 31,387 sorties between June 1944 and the end of the war in August 1945, only seventy-four B-29s were lost—a loss rate of less than a quarter of 1 per cent.[92] The single biggest raid was on Tōkyō on 10 March, resulting in almost 100,000 deaths. Most of the major cities in Japan, with the exception of allegedly spared 'cultural sites' such as Kyōto and Nara,[93] typically suffered some 40–50 per cent damage to their facilities. It is estimated that at least 13 million Japanese were homeless by the end of May.[94]

On 1 April the invasion of Okinawa began. This was part of Japan itself. Four days later Prime Minister Koiso resigned, to be replaced by the aged Admiral Suzuki Kantarō (1867–1948). The following month, on 8 May, Germany was defeated, and the Allies were free to concentrate on Japan. Things looked very ominous for the Japanese.

Okinawa was lost on 21 June, after almost three months of fierce fighting. 110,000 Japanese troops and an estimated 150,000 civilians died. On the American side, about 13,000 were killed and a further 40,000 injured. These were the highest American casualty figures in the entire war, and suggested the Japanese defence was indeed going to be tenacious. The battle for Okinawa also involved the desperate use of some 2,000 *kamikaze* pilots, and large numbers of panicked mass suicides by civilians who had been taught to believe the American invaders were inhuman monsters. They preferred to throw themselves from the clifftops rather than face life under such a foe.[95]

Defeat was now imminent. However, though Suzuki himself was not particularly committed to a continuation of war, the prevailing mood of the military (especially the army) was to fight to the last. To surrender, it was felt, would be to dishonour those who had given their lives in battle.[96] There was by now a strong fatalism to it all.

On 17 July President Truman—Roosevelt having died in April—met with Stalin and Churchill at Potsdam, Germany, for a two-week discussion of the war situation. Chiang Kai-shek participated by telephone. That month the United States successfully tested an atomic bomb, and Truman waited for the results of the test before deciding on a statement to issue to Japan. This was the Potsdam Declaration, issued on 26 July.[97] Stalin's name did not appear at this stage since the Soviet Union was yet to declare war against Japan, but the Soviets formally endorsed the Declaration later. The Declaration called for Japan to surrender unconditionally or face 'prompt and utter destruction'. It also spoke of an occupation, the purging of military leaders, the establishment of a new democratic political order, and the recognition of Japanese sovereignty but only within the territorial borders established at the beginning of the Meiji period. It made no specific mention of the emperor.

Japan did not accept the Declaration.[98] The Allies were keen to avoid the heavy losses that would surely follow if they pressed on with an attack on the Japanese mainland, known in the plans as Operation Olympic. The Americans were very probably also keen to bring hostilities to a speedy conclusion to minimise gains by the Soviets, who were on the verge of entering the war.[99] They may even have wanted to impress the Soviets with their new atomic technology, or simply just wanted to test it out on a real target.[100] It is also remotely possible they overestimated Japan's development of its own atomic weapons, and wanted to ensure a first strike.[101] In any event, the decision was made to use the new atomic bomb on Japan.

On 6 August an atomic bomb was dropped on Hiroshima. It was the first time such a weapon had been used in the history of the world. It caused around 90,000 deaths immediately or shortly afterwards.[102] Possibly as many again died from the bomb's effects in subsequent years. More than 80 per cent of the city's buildings were destroyed. The lack of a prompt positive response by the Japanese resulted in a second bomb being dropped on 9 August, this time on Nagasaki. This resulted in a further 50,000 fatalities immediately or shortly afterwards, and more than 30,000 in later years.

The day before Nagasaki the Soviet Union declared war on Japan, and attacked Manchuria almost immediately. This was another ominous blow.

Unless it was prepared to see its own total destruction as a nation, Japan now had no realistic alternative but to accept the terms of the Potsdam Declaration. A top-level meeting was convened the evening of the 9th. Some did prefer destruction to surrender, others wanted to fight on for a while in the hope of better terms, others were ready to give in. Hirohito was prepared to accept the Declaration provided the imperial institution could be retained intact. The Americans, informed of this via Swiss and Swedish go-betweens, refused to give an unqualified assurance, but did allow for the emperor to rule subject to the Supreme Commander of the Allied Powers and the will of the Japanese people.

At another meeting on the 14th, to discuss the American response, there was again indecision. Following a request from Suzuki, Hirohito cast the decisive vote, remarking that Japan would have to 'bear the unbearable'.[103]

His decision was not well received by all as the news leaked out. A number of lower-ranking military officers tried unsuccessfully to prevent the emperor from recording his 'surrender speech' for broadcasting to the nation on the following day. Some 500 military personnel were to choose suicide rather than openly defy the emperor. These included several top military leaders such as Vice-Admiral Onishi Takijirō (1891–1945), the man who had conceived the idea of *kamikaze* pilots. Onishi was one of a number who wanted to obtain better surrender terms by a dogged defence of the homeland.

On the 15th the emperor's speech was broadcast over the radio to his people, to advise them of the unfortunate situation. It was the first ever imperial radio broadcast and the first time the vast majority of his subjects had ever heard him speak. His refined and archaic court language was so removed from everyday speech that many simply did not understand what he was saying, and had to rely on the interpretation of others. Even those who did understand the language did not always understand his meaning, for his terms were vague and did not explicitly refer to 'defeat' and 'surrender'. Instead he referred to the 'war situation having developed not necessarily to Japan's advantage', and made it seem as though Japan had decided to stop fighting in order to save humankind from the threat of destruction by the west, not because Japan was defeated.[104]

Eventually, however, the message came across—Japan had lost the war. The formal signing of the Instrument of Surrender took place some weeks later, on 2 September, on board the USS *Missouri* in Tōkyō Bay. It followed an imperial edict earlier that day formally authorising the signing of the surrender and commanding Japanese subjects to honour it.[105]

In its fourteen years of warfare, starting with the Manchurian Incident in 1931, Japan had suffered almost 3 million military casualties and more than half a million civilian casualties. The majority of all casualties occurred in the four years of the Pacific War. All the sacrifice had been in vain for Japan, which suffered its first defeat in a war (as opposed to an individual battle) and was now to suffer its first foreign occupation in the history of the Yamato state. There are some in Japan and elsewhere who claim the defeat was somehow unfair due to the use of atomic bombs, but such a view simply masks the reality that even in terms of conventional warfare Japan was thoroughly beaten.[106]

In a letter to his son Akihito dated 9 September 1945, Hirohito attributed defeat to an underestimation of Britain and America, to too much reliance on spirit as opposed to science, and to arrogant military leaders who only knew how to go forward.[107]

Japan had become a major world power but its ambitions had grown too great. Sōseki had been right. The frog had inflated itself till it burst. The proud Japan of Meiji was now in a humiliated position under Hirohito. In one sense it was lucky to be in any position at all, for not a few among the Allies wanted to see the total destruction of the nation.[108] Even the humanitarian Roosevelt, it seems, had entertained thoughts of effectively breeding the Japanese race out of existence.[109]

Hirohito may rightly have blamed an excess of Japanese spirit for its fall. But it would now take an enormous strength of spirit for the nation to rise again to become a respected power.

REVIEW OF PART FIVE

The fragile democracy that started to appear in the late Meiji period had a brief heyday during the Taishō period. However, it was soon displaced by the ever-present authoritarianism, authoritarianism of an increasingly aggressive military nature. Japan was confident after its successes in Meiji, when it had so rapidly achieved world-power status, and had even acquired colonies of its own through military strength. It continued down that same road with such ambitious intensity that it ended up in confrontation with the Allied western nations—much as it traditionally disliked engaging a more powerful foe.

There were undoubtedly certain external factors partly prompting Japan's behaviour. One particular stimulus was westerners' rejection on racist grounds of the Japanese as real equals. The imperialist policies of the western powers themselves also gave Japan the message that seizing territory was how world powers behaved.

Nevertheless, a major motive for their ambitious course of expansionist action was a basic Japanese belief in their own destiny as a superior race. This was strengthened by indoctrination, and was reflected in the ideas underlying the *Kokutai no Hongi*, the pan-Asianist 'liberation' of Asia from the western imperialists, *musubi*, and so forth.

The military grew increasingly impatient to demonstrate Japanese superiority. Overseas, they deliberately tried to provoke incidents, and at times succeeded. At home, they interfered in politics, not hesitating to assassinate where necessary. They also helped turn an improving economy towards a controlled war effort. And they controlled the emperor, obtaining his 'authorisation' usually by his omission to speak out against their behaviour.

Not content with its gains in Asia, Japan was prepared to take on the greatest of all powers, the United States and Britain. It hoped these would be occupied by the war in Europe, allowing it to make greater gains before moving towards a peace proposal. A quick decisive blow would also teach the arrogant powers a lesson.

However, Japan's own successes counted against it. The ease of its early victories—victories it attributed to its spiritual superiority—made it want to continue the war instead of going ahead with its idea of proposing peace and 'quitting while ahead'. That same ease had turned its frustration towards westerners into contempt, which in combination with its ideas of its own superiority resulted in acts of brutality that also hardened western resolve against it. This would have made any early move for peace difficult anyway.

The war Japan was now almost fatalistically locked into soon turned against it. Overblown ambitions rapidly deflated, finally shrinking to a hope that a tenacious defence of the homeland would persuade the Allies to allow it a reasonably generous conditional surrender. This was not to be. America had developed atomic weaponry, which would cost far fewer Allied lives than an invasion of Japan. Japan was warned, but hesitated. When it became the world's first nuclear victim, it realised the pointlessness of continued resistance, and capitulated unconditionally. Its ambitions were now in tatters.

The main developments in this fateful period for Japan are summarised in Table 5.1.

Table 5.1   Key developments from end Meiji to end World War Two

Development	Time
Fragile 'Taishō democracy' and militaristic authoritarianism coexist	1912–mid-1920s
Economic woes	1920s
Japan given racial snubs by west	early–mid-1920s
New emperor proves to be weak	mid-1920s
Military asserts itself at home and abroad, provoking incidents	from late 1920s
Japanese army establishes colony of Manchuria	early 1930s
Japan turns its back on most of the west	early 1930s
Party politics ends, military virtually unchecked, assassinations commonplace	from early 1930s
Economy improves, but problems remain through dualism and poor distribution of wealth to rural areas	from early 1930s
Economy gears towards war effort	from early–mid-1930s
Expansionist ideologies prevail, including indoctrination through 'emperor system'	from mid-1930s
Unofficial aggressive war with China	from mid–late 1930s
Japan enters uneasy alliance with Germany	from mid–late 1930s
Continued Japanese expansion draws reprisals from America	1940–1
Japan engages Allies, hoping for quick gains in Asia then withdrawal	late 1941
Early gains prompt Japan to continue war	late 1941–early 1942
War turns against Japan, but too late to stop	from mid-1942
Ambitions reduced to defence of homeland	from mid-1944
Japan surrenders unconditionally following atomic bombings	mid-1945

Key values and practices of the day were in many ways an intensification of earlier ones. They are summarised in Table 5.2.

Table 5.2   Key values and practices from end Meiji to end World War Two

- suspicion and unease towards foreigners
- suspicion and unease towards freedom and real democracy
- determination to succeed
- strong national pride and nationalistic spirit
- obedience to authority (albeit often under duress)
- reverence for emperor
- control of world-view
- awareness of importance of economy
- lack of obvious concept of evil behaviour
- distinction between formal authority and actual power, but continuing need for legitimisation by former
- revival of hierarchy, this time applied to race
- intensification of concept of purity, especially applied to Japan itself
- idealisation of Japan's samurai past
- tendency to get carried away by emotion over reason
- tendency to become narrowed in vision
- a certain fatalism

If Japan had been able to moderate its ambitions, and also swallow a little pride by enduring the racist rebuffs from the west, the history of the twentieth century may have been different. Hindsight is a wonderful thing.

Part Six

A Phoenix from the Ashes: Postwar Successes and Beyond

6.1   AMERICAN DREAMS FOR A NEW JAPAN

Allied troops began to arrive in Japan in late August 1945, and the Occupation officially started upon the formal surrender on 2 September. The Japanese had feared brutal Allied reprisals, but were greatly reassured by the surrender-acceptance speech from the man who was to head the Occupation, US General Douglas MacArthur. MacArthur stressed the importance of putting aside hatred and of looking to a future of peace. He also expressed his confidence in the Japanese people to rebuild their nation and regain their dignity.[1]

His men did not let him down. There were inevitably a number of cases of brutal treatment,[2] but in general the Occupation troops showed kindness towards their former foe. The Japanese, for their part, were extremely co-operative. As a result, the scale of the Occupation forces was soon able to be reduced from 500,000 to just 150,000.

Obviously, in addition to the immediate and serious practical concerns of food and shelter,[3] the people of Japan were in a state of confusion and anxiety. Their indoctrinated faith in Japan's divine superiority and invincibility was now seriously undermined. So too was their faith in their political and especially military leaders. Many Japanese felt anger, disillusionment, and a sense of betrayal towards those leaders. Some even had negative thoughts about Hirohito, though not so much towards the imperial institution itself.

MacArthur reassured the Japanese not only by his speech, but also by his manner. Now in his mid-sixties, he had been a general since the age of 38—at the time the youngest ever in the history of the United States. He was a man born to lead, a man dignified and self-assured, firm but benevolent, and possessed of an almost messianic conviction of his own

God-given destiny to shape history.[4] He was in some ways reminiscent of the Meiji oligarchs in his mix of democracy and authoritarianism, and certainly in his conviction that he knew best what was good for the people he ruled. To a nation accustomed to being led, he was a welcome new leader. He was hailed by the Japanese as a new shōgun, Japan's American emperor, even a god.[5] His own men used to say tongue-in-cheek that if you got up early enough in the morning you could see him walking on the waters of the Imperial Castle moat, just a short distance from his headquarters.[6]

In theory the Occupation was an Allied exercise and not merely an American affair, let alone a one-man show. MacArthur's formal title was Supreme Commander for the Allied Powers (SCAP). Of those Powers, China and the Soviet Union sent no troops to Japan, but British Commonwealth troops did play a definite if limited part in the Occupation, mostly confined to a zone in western Honshū.[7] The four major Allied powers—the United States, Britain, the Soviet Union, and China—established an Allied Council late in December 1945 in Tōkyō, where they held fortnightly meetings. There was also a Far Eastern Commission of all eleven victor nations, which met in Washington from February 1946 to determine general Occupation policy that was then to be relayed through the Allied Council.

In practice, however, the Occupation was indeed almost entirely an American affair, and MacArthur was very much master of ceremonies. He dismissed the Allied Council as a 'nuisance' and the Far Eastern Commission as 'little more than a debating society'.[8] He wanted to get on with his job, and the plans he and Washington had in mind had anyway mostly been set in motion already.

Both Washington and MacArthur had plans not only for the functional dismantling of a militaristic and totalitarian Japan, but grander visions of the construction of a utopian new nation. Washington had started its planning as early as mid-1942, with considerable input from New Dealers.[9] MacArthur's plans seem to have come later, but fortunately were quite similar to those of his government.

Washington's policies were often drawn up by 'faceless' figures in the State Department such as Hugh Borton and George Blakeslee. Borton in particular, a self-effacing man recognised for his knowledge of Japan but under-recognised for his role in rebuilding the nation, seems to have had a hand in most things relating to Occupation policies.[10] These policies were for the most part relayed in a directive issued to MacArthur in October 1945. This was the *Basic Initial Post Surrender Directive to Supreme Commander for the Allied Powers for the Occupation and*

Control of Japan, more conveniently known as JCS1380/15 (JCS stand-ing for Joint Chiefs of Staff).[11]

The directive outlined an idealised American-style democracy for Japan. The emperor, if retained, was to have a purely symbolic role as figurehead of the nation. There were to be guarantees of civil rights and personal freedoms, if necessary enforced by a new constitution. All adults, including women, were to have the right to vote. The military and the old-style police were to be abolished, and the *zaibatsu* were to be dismantled. All in the military, government, and business who had contributed to the war effort were to be purged from any responsible office. Labor unions were to be encouraged, and the rights of unionists protected.

MacArthur's largely similar ideas were expressed in more grandil-oquent style. In his memoirs, he likened his position to that of Alexan-der the Great, Caesar, and Napoleon, and wrote:[12]

> I had to be an economist, a political scientist, an engineer, a manufac-turing executive, a teacher, even a theologian of sorts. I had to rebuild a nation that had been almost completely destroyed by the war.... Japan had become the world's great laboratory for an experiment in the liberation of a people from totalitarian military rule and for the liberalization of government from within. It was clear that the experi-ment must go far beyond the primary purpose of the Allies—the destruction of Japan's ability to wage another war and the punish-ment of war criminals.
>
> ...I felt the reforms I contemplated were those which would bring Japan abreast of modern progressive thought and action. First destroy the military power. Punish war criminals. Build the structure of representative government. Modernise the constitution. Hold free elections. Enfranchise the women. Release the political prisoners. Liberate the farmers. Establish a free labor movement. Encourage a free economy. Abolish police oppression. Develop a free and respons-ible press. Liberalize education. Decentralize the political power. Separate church from state....

To restore Japanese dignity and morale, he would encourage them not to abandon everything Japanese, but 'to seek a healthy blend between the best of theirs and the best of ours'.[13]

The fact that in most cases MacArthur was basically following orders does not deny his extraordinarily powerful role. JCS1380/15 itself, while giving him broad orders, somewhat paradoxically also confirmed his personal power. It stated clearly to him that 'in addition to the conventional powers of a military occupant of enemy territory, you have the power to take any steps deemed advisable and proper by you to effectuate ... the provisions of the Potsdam Declaration'.[14] On occasion he was to use that personal power.

Demilitarisation was the first step in the ambitious 'joint' MacArthur–Washington programme for building a new Japan. To this end, the army and navy were demobilised within a few months. Japan was stripped of the territory it had gained by military means, effectively returning it to the situation before the start of the Sino-Japanese war of 1894–5. Steps were taken to start repatriation of the 3 million Japanese troops and the similar number of Japanese civilians scattered around Asia. Orders were issued for Japan to pay reparations to victim nations. A number of Japan's ships were given to the Allies, while other war equipment and weapons were destroyed—including, as a priority task and against MacArthur's own wishes, its nuclear particle accelerators.[15] Between 1946 and 1948 some 700,000 individuals were screened and some 200,000 who were felt to have been, in the words of JCS 1380/15, 'active exponents of militant nationalism and aggression', were 'purged' from office. This too, at least in terms of scale, was seemingly against MacArthur's own personal judgement.[16]

Perhaps the most significant of all demilitarisation measures was the insertion into the new constitution, drafted early in 1946 by SCAP staff, of Japan's famous 'no war' clause. This was inserted by MacArthur personally, but was not necessarily initiated by him, for its exact source is still unclear.[17] In full, the article (Article IX) reads:[18]

> Aspiring sincerely to an international peace based on justice and order, the Japanese people forever renounce war as a sovereign right of the nation and the threat or use of force as a means of settling international disputes.
>
> In order to accomplish the aim of the preceding paragraph, land, sea, and air forces, as well as other war potential, will never be maintained. The right of belligerency of the state will not be recognised.

The punishment of war criminals was also part of the general process of demilitarisation. At the Tōkyō War Crimes Trial, held between May 1946 and November 1948 under the newly created Military Tribunal for the Far East (which involved all eleven victor nations), twenty-five men were tried for major (Class A) crimes such as having plotted and brought about the war. In what has sometimes been described as 'victor's justice', all were found guilty in varying degrees. Seven, including General Tōjō and former prime minister Hirota (the only civilian), were sentenced to death and subsequently hanged.[19] A number of other trials were held elsewhere, such as in Singapore, the Philippines, and Hong Kong. In these local trials more than 5,000 Japanese were found guilty of more specific crimes (Classes B and C) such as gross cruelty towards prisoners of war, and some 900 were executed.

From the outset there was a widely held opinion, both in Japan and overseas, that the individuals on trial were to an extent scapegoats.[20] Many who might be considered more culpable were never brought to trial. Among those who escaped trial were the staff of Unit 731, who had conducted numerous biological and chemical warfare experiments on civilians and prisoners of war. The whole business of 731 was hushed up by the Americans, who offered immunity in return for scientific data from the experiments that their own ethics and laws prevented.[21]

The most controversial omission to prosecute was in the case of Hirohito. This even puzzled most Japanese, however much they might have been relieved.[22] There were certainly many in America, Australia, and the other Allied nations who strongly believed that Hirohito should stand trial, with the expectation he would be found guilty and hanged.[23] The American government's position on the emperor was basically one of proceeding with caution. There was no real wish to dismantle the imperial institution itself, for this had a useful role in keeping the nation together, in maintaining national morale, and also in legitimising Occupation policy.[24] The Japan specialists in the State Department were not unaware of the deep-rooted importance to Japanese people of the exercise of power being legitimised by high authority and thus made acceptable. Without such legitimisation, anarchy might prevail, and expose the nation to communism. Moreover, with the emperor in place the organs of national administration would be more easily kept running. This was an important matter, for unlike the case with the occupation of the familiar old foe Germany—which was far less constructive and more destructive—there were few among the Occupation forces in Japan who had the knowledge or confidence to erect a replacement administrative machinery appropriate for these alien people. Japan specialists like Borton were very thin on the ground in Japan itself.

But as regards Hirohito personally, there was less sympathy in government circles. Many would have been happy to see Hirohito out of the way, either by trial and execution or by abdication, and replaced with a new emperor. That might even make things easier for a new beginning. After all, a new era traditionally went hand-in-hand with a new emperor.

Even many Japanese were thinking Hirohito should at least abdicate.[25]

Hirohito's great saviour was MacArthur. They had met in private late in September and MacArthur had been greatly impressed by him. There seems to have been a strong personal affinity between them. In particular, they shared a hatred for communism. MacArthur felt that retaining Hirohito personally, not just the imperial institution, would be the most effective safeguard against anarchy and communism. In his memoirs he was to say that he felt Hirohito was not personally responsible for any wrongdoing.[26] This may have been a generous interpretation of events, perhaps deliberately so.[27] Nevertheless, in a powerful memorandum to the joint chiefs of staff in January 1946 MacArthur made a very strong plea for the retention of an innocent Hirohito, warning of dire consequences for the Occupation plans if this was not accepted.[28] It was. Hirohito survived. Not only did he avoid trial and probable execution, thanks to MacArthur he even managed to avoid having to abdicate.[29]

This may have been what MacArthur wanted, but it was to leave lingering distrust among many about an undesirable type of continuity with prewar Japan. This distrust was to remain to the present day, especially among Asian nations who suffered under Japanese rule but also among progressive-minded Japanese.

Hirohito may have survived, but he could not escape a change of role and image. He had to become a symbol of the people, and win acceptance and respect from those people in the form of affection rather than mindless awe towards a deity incarnate. In line with Washington policy and MacArthur's own views on the dangers of a god-emperor, Hirohito was to be made a mere mortal.[30] This would greatly reduce the danger of a resurgence of the emperor-system indoctrination seen in the *Imperial Rescript on Education* and the *Kokutai no Hongi*. In that sense his change of status was a further measure against the possibility of any revival of militarism. As a related measure, state Shintō would be dismantled. Shintō would be declared a religion, and religion would be legally separated from the state. It would no longer be a national duty for Japanese to revere their god-emperor.

The *Shintō Directive* that disestablished state Shintō was issued by SCAP staff in December 1945. The same month, SCAP staff also drafted the rescript popularly known as the *Declaration of Humanity* (*Ningen Sengen*), which Hirohito broadcast on 1 January 1946. The official line was that it came from Hirohito himself, but this is demonstrably questionable. In fact, when he saw the draft Hirohito was quite upset at having to renounce his divine descent, and subtly but significantly managed to change this to a renunciation rather of his status as a living god.[31] Realising democracy was now being forced on the nation, he also ensured that the rescript started with a restatement of the *Charter Oath* of 1868, thereby stressing the continuity between monarchy and democracy since the Restoration. In any event, the final version of the *Declaration* broadcast in January included key phrases such as 'the false conception that the Emperor is divine and that the Japanese people are superior to other races and fated to rule the world'.[32] MacArthur and Washington were greatly pleased.

Hirohito's humanisation, and his role as a symbol of the people, were also to be formally reinforced in the constitution a few months later. This changed his role from that of absolute monarch to that of 'symbol of the state and of the unity of the people, deriving his position from the will of the people with whom resides sovereign power'.

From this point on Hirohito, now an emperor of the people, was made to go on meet-the-people tours, despite his obvious discomfort. His personal image of an avuncular 'harmless old man' in ill-fitting suits was designed by SCAP staff to help his acceptability both at home and abroad.[33] Popular books and articles soon appeared stressing his private life and human qualities, and his scholarly achievements as a naturalist. They showed him as a peace-loving, cultured intellectual whose thoughts were always with the people—a human emperor who had been misrepresented by the military and other evil types.[34] Emphasis was placed on his courage in speaking out to end the war. His failure to abdicate was made into a point of honour, for he was personally seeing through the 'unbearable' consequences of the Potsdam Declaration that he himself had decided to accept. In other words, he was manipulated by public relations specialists even more than his grandfather Meiji had been.

The new constitution was arguably the greatest achievement of the Occupation, not just for its humanisation of Hirohito. It stands unchanged to this day as a symbol of the democratisation of the nation—at least on the outside—despite many murmurings about Article IX in particular. It was drafted early in February 1946 by a young and very inexperienced team of SCAP staff plus a few civilians. They worked with a control document from Washington numbered SWNCC 228.[35] Under pressure from MacArthur, who had despaired of the Japanese themselves coming up with a suitable draft,[36] they did the job in less than a week. Their youth and inexperience in state-building made them not unlike the Meiji oligarchs. None of the team knew much about either

Japan or constitutions. Even the man charged with responsibility for carrying out the task, team leader Colonel Charles Kades, admitted to having 'zero' knowledge about Japan.[37] This lack of knowledge meant that the input of the chief author of the control document, Hugh Borton of the State Department,[38] became all the more important. It also meant that the Japanese themselves were able to make—as in many SCAP directives—a degree of informal input in the final product.[39]

Such informal Japanese input was deliberately exaggerated by SCAP, and the constitution was officially said to have been drawn up by the Japanese themselves. This fooled few people. The American origin of the constitution continues to be a source of some controversy. Nakasone Yasuhiro, a well-known nationalistic prime minister from the 1980s, does not necessarily disagree with the content of the constitution. However, he argues that true democracy cannot be imposed by an external power, but should come from within. That is, for better or for worse, the Japanese should have been allowed to produce their own constitution.[40] The willingness of the Occupation authorities to, if necessary, *force* freedom on the Japanese is one of the paradoxes of the constitution and the Occupation. But it is at the same time convenient, for it allows Japan to claim it is a democracy when in practice this is open to question—another case of difference between outer form and actual substance.[41]

The new parliament was to be elected democratically, but just like the Meiji oligarchs, MacArthur wanted democracy on his terms. In the April 1946 elections[42] the incumbent prime minister Shidehara Kijūrō lost out. He was due to be replaced by Hatoyama Ichirō, who headed the newly formed Japan Liberal Party (*Nihon Jiyūtō*), of *Seiyūkai* lineage. However, Hatoyama had been involved in a number of illiberal activities before the war and was not favoured by SCAP. He was purged from office on the eve of forming his cabinet. In his stead, the presidency of the party, and hence the prime ministership, passed to Yoshida Shigeru.

When the new constitutional draft was put before the new parliament for formal approval, the section on women's rights seems to have caused particularly lively debate. This section had become for SCAP a symbol of the new democracy, despite its extraordinary and almost cavalier background—entrusted to a Russian-American 'slip of a girl' (in the words of one Occupation official) and hurried past the Japanese representatives on the draft steering committee without real debate.[43] It was supported by the thirty-nine newly elected women members of parliament—out of a then total of 466 Lower House seats—but opposed by most male politicians. Among the public, it was not just males who

opposed it, but many women too, largely but not entirely due to Confucianist indoctrination that was to linger for many decades more.[44] In any
event, protests were to no avail. The emperor made his support clear.
The new constitution, complete with its guarantee of equal rights for
women, was finally approved after appropriate guidance and reflection.
It was promulgated in November 1946, becoming effective in May 1947.

In most cases the constitution simply formally endorsed policies that
had been put in place already by the Occupation through various directives. Other constitutional provisions were to be embodied in laws shortly
afterwards. Its key points included:

- the emperor made a symbol of the people;
- sovereignty vested in the people;
- war renounced along with maintenance of armed forces;
- equality of the sexes;
- guarantee of human rights in general, notably the 'right to life, liberty,
  and the pursuit of happiness';
- guarantee of freedom of assembly, thought, belief (including religion), and expression;
- right to vote given to all adults over 20;
- separation of church and state;
- guarantee of workers' rights to organise and bargain collectively,
  and of minimum labour standards;
- establishment of free and equal education;
- abolition of the peerage;
- establishment of an independent judiciary;
- provision for revision of constitution (by two-thirds majority in both
  houses and majority public support in a referendum).

A particularly important pre-constitution directive was the *Civil Liber-
ties Directive* of October 1945. This ordered the release of all political
prisoners—including the dreaded communists. It also gave early provision for freedom of assembly, leading to a proliferation of political parties. These had been officially banned in Japan since 1941, when all
parties had been merged into the Imperial Rule Assistance Association,
but in practice they had been strongly discouraged for more than a decade. They now returned with a vengeance—at least numerically, with literally hundreds formed, but the great majority had few members.
Oddities included the Great Japan Charcoal Production Party.[45] Less of
an oddity was the Communist Party, which had suffered severe repression in prewar Japan but now re-formed on the very day of the directive.

A clear illustration of the Occupation paradox of forcing democracy on the Japanese was that, while it was guaranteeing freedom of speech, SCAP was itself practising quite rigorous censorship.[46] At the same time that SCAP was positively insisting films should show human freedoms and dignity, such as enlightened women and kissing in love scenes,[47] it was also banning certain books and movies. Erskine Caldwell's *Tobacco Road*, which showed the darker side of American society, was one example of a banned book, while samurai movies were among the 236 films condemned by SCAP as feudalistic and militaristic.[48] All references to SCAP's involvement in government reforms were also banned.[49]

School textbooks were among the targets of SCAP censorship, for MacArthur too knew the value of these as tools of indoctrination. He ordered the content of all texts and instruction to be revised along democratic lines. Texts such as *Kokutai no Hongi* were replaced with American texts such as the *History of the War*, compiled by SCAP staff.[50] Unsuitable persons were removed from the area of education in October 1945, in an early display of purging. The American 6–3–3–4 system (6 years elementary, 3 years junior high, 3 years senior high, and 4 years tertiary) was introduced. To avoid excessive centralisation, regional authorities were empowered to appoint their own school board officials by election. To remove prewar elitism, four-year universities were greatly increased in number and based on the general American model.

Reforms covered the economy too. A land reform bill of 1946 allowed farmers to own as much land as they could farm themselves—usually around 3 hectares—and to rent out a small amount of land in their village of residence. Rents were controlled, tenants' rights enforced, and various monitoring mechanisms set up. The government itself bought up land from absentee landowners and redistributed it to the farmers themselves. As a result of these various measures, tenancy was reduced from almost 50 per cent to around 10 per cent.[51]

Another major economic reform, seen as being in the interests of both demilitarisation and democratisation, was the move to dissolve the *zaibatsu*. At the end of the war the 'Big Four'—Mitsui, Mitsubishi, Sumitomo, and Yasuda—controlled between them 25 per cent of Japan's paid-up capital, and six lesser *zaibatsu* a further 11 per cent. These ten were the principal targets for reform.[52] Measures taken from late 1945 included dissolving *zaibatsu* holding companies, banning *zaibatsu* family members from working in their own companies, preventing *zaibatsu* from making claims on the government for wartime purchases, removing excess wartime profits, and distributing *zaibatsu* stock on a wider basis. In April 1947 the Anti-Monopoly Law was passed, and some 325 companies in the industrial and service sectors were potentially targeted as having excessive concentrations of power.[53]

In the area of labour,[54] a series of laws between December 1945 and April 1947 carried through the provisions of the constitution, but with some restrictions such as on the right to strike where public welfare was endangered. As a result of these new rights and freedoms, labour union membership increased dramatically from a prewar (1936) high of some 420,000 to about 7 million by mid-1948. The rate of union membership of the workforce was to peak in 1949 at 56 per cent.

However, it was also in the area of labour that one of the most serious incidents of the Occupation occurred. This was the banning by Mac-Arthur of a general strike planned for 1 February 1947.

Communists played a major part in events. Among other things it was a communist, Ii Yashiro, who was the main leader of the planned strike. MacArthur, along with many Japanese government leaders such as Yoshida Shigeru, had been worried from the outset about releasing communists from imprisonment. Those released included the influential Tokuda Kyūichi. He was soon joined by another powerful figure, Nosaka Sanzō, who returned from China early in 1946. The poor state of the economy immediately after the war was already a potential source of unrest, and there were a number of large demonstrations and strikes in 1946. The communists seemed able to use this to their advantage. They did not enjoy much success in the formal political arena, but waged their campaign rather in the workplace.

Though membership of the Communist Party itself was small, it was growing,[55] and the same applied to support for communism among the general public. In December 1945 circulation of the communist daily newspaper *Akahata* ('Red Flag') was 90,000, but by February 1946 this had risen to 250,000.[56] The communists themselves were also disproportionately vocal and active. They expressed open defiance of the emperor and criticism of the government. They occupied leading positions in many unions, and seemed to be deliberately agitating and using strikes and other disputes for political purposes.[57] There were soon fears, both in Japan and overseas, that Japan was—in a phrase popularised by Yoshida—being 'submerged in a sea of red flags'.[58] Yoshida also inflamed the situation by calling communist union leaders 'bandits'.[59]

The planned general strike would have involved almost 3 million public servants and many millions more from the private sector. MacArthur was reluctant to intervene but felt he could not permit such massive disruption and defiance. Just hours before the strike, after discussions with Ii and others had failed, he banned it.

Again in a manner reminiscent of the Meiji oligarchs, MacArthur immediately balanced this act of authoritarianism with an act of democracy.[60] He called for another general election to let the public express their feelings. This was held in April, and to his relief the communists, who had been expecting to increase their seats from 5 to at least 20, actually lost support. They emerged with only 4 seats.

They were not the only losers. The public was not entirely happy with Yoshida, who was widely seen as having too much in common with the prewar types who had led Japan to disaster. His cabinet fell, to be replaced by a coalition led by the Socialist Party under the Christian Katayama Tetsu. The Socialist Party was another party to have suffered prewar bans, though it had not been treated with quite the same harshness as the Communist Party. The other coalition members included the newly formed Democratic Party (*Minshutō*), of *Minseitō* descent. MacArthur too was not always at ease with Yoshida, and gave considerable support to Katayama's cabinet. Among other things he openly expressed his satisfaction at seeing a Christian prime minister in Japan.

By mid-1947, then, most of the Occupation's plans for the demilitarisation and democratisation of Japan were set in place, both formally and informally. The process had been smoother than many had expected, though the activities of the communists and the need to ban the general strike were unfortunate. Public peace of mind was also still less than perfect, and the economy was still very weak. Utopia still seemed attainable, but it did seem to have a few clouds on its horizon.

6.2   COLD WAR REALITIES RESHAPE THE DREAMS

The banning of the general strike was an opportunity for reflection, for both government and public, both American and Japanese. Ever since the Occupation started the Japanese government had been uneasy about the pace and intensity of democractic reforms. Yoshida referred to an 'excess of democracy'.[61] The public too, having been carried away by the first flushes of reform, were now starting to think along the same lines.[62] Certainly, they preferred freedom to repression, but there had to be a balance between freedom and control. One could not allow freedom to become abused and end up as anarchy. Democracy was a powerful, dangerous beast. It could bring blessings, but it needed to be handled carefully and kept under control.

The American government was also alarmed, and so too was the American public. During 1947 there was open criticism in the American media of Occupation policy, of bungling the job, of promoting too much democracy and not enough economic recovery. Those who were not New Dealers were particularly quick to criticise—including within SCAP headquarters.[63]

1947 was also the year in which the term 'Cold War' was coined, to refer to the ideological, economic, and political division between the free world and the communist world. Fear of a major confrontation with the communists underlay much of the change in American mood about Japan and indeed the world. Korea was already divided into communist versus non-communist zones, and Berlin was just about to be. In China, Chiang Kai-shek's forces were on the verge of being driven into Taiwan by the communists under Mao. Eastern Europe was coming increasingly under communist control. It was important that Japan stayed a bulwark of the free world.

But the free world could not exist just as an idea. It needed power and substance. In the postwar world, where all-out military confrontation with its fear of nuclear consequences was to be avoided where possible, this meant primarily economic power. Japan in 1947 was from being an economic power. Production was still not even half its prewar levels, and inflation was running at over 200 per cent per annum. It needed fixing, and MacArthur was perhaps not the man for this particular job.

Early in 1948 Washington sent George Kennan of the State Department on a fact-finding mission to Japan. Kennan had for some time been stressing the need to contain communist expansion. He concluded that the Occupation reforms to date were 'paving the way for a Communist takeover'. He recommended instead that 'The regime of control by SCAP over the Japanese government should be relaxed.... The emphasis should be shifted from reform to economic recovery'.[64] Recommendations by other troubleshooters, such as Under-Secretary of the Army William Draper (an investment banker), were similar.[65] As a result, American policy for Japan from 1948 switched to an emphasis on economic recovery. This meant stopping certain existing policies, and introducing certain new ones.[66]

Purges of business leaders were stopped, for it seemed foolish to remove capable people. Of the 200,000 individuals who were purged during the Occupation, only 3,000 were from business, and even then mostly only partially or temporarily.

The dismantling of the *zaibatsu* was stopped, for their economic effectiveness was recognised. The definition of 'excessive concentration' in the anti-trust legislation was changed subtly but significantly from 'concentration preventing effective competition from market new-comers' to 'concentration disadvantageous to efficient production'.[67] The postwar *zaibatsu* were known as *keiretsu kigyō*, or 'aligned companies'. The payment of reparations to victim nations was also stopped.[68] These had been intended mostly to be in the form of industrial machinery rather than money, in view of Japan's struggling economy. Machinery that had already been seized by the Occupation forces for this purpose, mostly from the *zaibatsu*, was now largely returned to Japanese industry. However, it was not returned to the *zaibatsu*. They were investing in more modern equipment. Instead, it was given to smaller companies, who would normally never have been able to acquire such equipment, even if it was becoming dated.

Labour laws were toughened to prevent industrial disruption. New legislation in 1948 denied workers in public operations the right to strike, and restricted direct political action by workers' organisations.

MacArthur himself had envisaged some of these measures. He personally had from the outset been reluctant to carry out purges in the business world, or to pay reparations. His deliberate stalling in these matters in the early years of the Occupation made the new policy more effective than it might otherwise have been. Nevertheless, he was considered in need of ongoing economic advice. Early in 1949 President Truman sent out the financial expert Joseph Dodge as the official SCAP economic adviser, a job he was to hold till the end of the Occupation.

By this stage Yoshida was back as prime minister. Katayama had resigned in February 1948 after less than a year in office, due to internal dissent within the Socialist Party—a problem that was to plague it for its entire existence to the present day. He was replaced by Ashida Hitoshi, the leader of the Democratic Party, but this cabinet fell after just a few months, largely owing to corruption scandals. Yoshida returned in October, and was confirmed by a sound victory for his newly formed and conservative Democratic Liberal Party (*Minshu Jiyūtō*) in the subsequent general election of January 1949.

His new party had been formed in 1948 from a merger of the Japan Liberal Party (*Nihon Jiyūtō*) and Democratic Party dissidents, bringing together the lineages of both major prewar parties, the *Seiyūkai* and the *Minseitō* respectively. The party was conservative, and despite reservations about Yoshida's prewar style its banner of stability was clearly what an anxious public wanted. Conservatives were to govern Japan right through to the present day (with the exception of a very brief hiccup in the mid-1990s). Yoshida himself, the government figure most associated with the Occupation, was to remain in the prime minister's office till 1954. The man who disliked an 'excess of democracy' clearly struck a chord with the public.

As if to confirm Cold War fears of communism, the communists in Japan had to started to renew their activities after the setback of 1947. They were starting to regain influence and popularity. In the same 1949 elections that gave a vote of confidence to Yoshida's conservative government they sharply increased their Diet seats from four to thirty-five. Something needed to be done. From late 1949 through 1950, some 12,000 communists were removed from office in the so-called Red Purge.[69] However, their proportion of Diet seats was to remain typically in the order of 5 per cent through to the present day.

The Yoshida government was ordered to stabilise the economy and balance the budget, a task to be overseen by Dodge. Under Dodge's direction inflation was greatly reduced, the exchange rate stabilised, and government subsidies cut back. His austere approach was effective, and in 1949 Japan was able to present a balanced budget. By June 1950 real wages were some 30 per cent ahead of 1936 levels.[70] However, his measures also caused hardship and antipathy among many employers and workers. Bankruptcies and unemployment rose.

The greatest boost for Japan's economy, however, came from another external source. In June 1950 communist North Korean troops crossed south of the 38th Parallel, the recognised dividing line between the zones on the Korean Peninsula, and the Korean War started. Yoshida termed this a 'gift of the gods'.[71] The greatest economic benefit was 'special procurements' (*tokuju*) from the US army as it fought in Korea. The value of these procurements was to total some 2–4 billion US dollars over the three-year period of the war, equivalent to about a third of all Japan's foreign income during that time. In effect, it doubled Japan's disposable income, permitting double the amount of imports. It also enabled key industries dependent on imported raw material to double their scale of production.[72] By the end of the Korean War, pre-Pacific War production levels were regained.

The Korean War had a number of other major consequences. One of these was the rearmament of Japanese forces. The bulk of the Occupation troops were to be on duty in Korea, so to maintain security in Japan MacArthur ordered the formation of a National Police Reserve of 75,000 men in July 1950. In order not to breach Article IX of the constitution this was designated a self-defence unit, but rearmament nevertheless caused considerable controversy. To clarify its defensive nature the unit was renamed the National Safety Forces in 1952, and finally given its present title of Self-Defence Forces (*Jieitai*) in 1954. At this point it contained some 165,000 personnel.

Another major consequence of the Korean War was the dismissal of MacArthur. He had responsibility for commanding US forces in Korea, and by his own account seems to have effectively won the war—in conventional terms—within a matter of months.[73] He retook Seoul by late September and captured Pyongyang by late October, which he believed symbolised the defeat of North Korea. He could not understand the lack of follow-up by Washington to his victories, and the fact that instead restrictions as to further action were placed on him. When Chinese communist reinforcements entered North Korea without warning, he was denied permission to take action against them. Washington was now waging a new type of warfare—so-called 'limited warfare'. MacArthur could not understand this 'meeting of naked force with appeasement' and the failure to preserve a 'will to win'.[74] He openly criticised Washington and Truman. Eventually the gap between their ways of thinking became so great that, on 11 April 1951, Truman relieved him of his duties both in Korea and Japan. He was given a hero's send-off from Japan, and a hero's welcome on his return to America.

With MacArthur's dismissal a short but intense era came to an end. His replacement, General Matthew Ridgway, lacked his charisma and vision, but anyway seems to have been appointed simply in a caretaker capacity. There was certainly little memorable about Ridgway's time in office. Even his name is barely remembered. Among other 'non-happenings', he did not even meet Hirohito during his term as SCAP.[75] The Occupation, certainly in the minds of the Japanese, was eternally linked with the great presence of MacArthur—a figure who loomed so large that his very dismissal was, as many have observed, perhaps the greatest of all lessons in democracy that the Japanese were taught during the Occupation.

A further major consequence of the Korean War was that it hastened the need for a peace treaty to be signed with Japan and the Occupation to be formally ended. Among other things this would free America from the continued burden of formal responsibility for Japan. Vague discussions regarding a peace treaty had been continuing for a number of years, at least since early 1947, but it was not till the Korean War that matters were really started in motion. It was complex and took time. Eventually, a Peace Conference was held in San Francisco early in September 1951, at which Japan and forty-eight nations signed a peace treaty (8 September).[76] MacArthur had worked on the treaty with Secretary of State John Foster Dulles, but was not invited to attend.[77]

The San Francisco Treaty confirmed Japan's loss of its former colonies, including Taiwan and Korea. Southern Sakhalin and the nearby Kurile Islands were given to the Soviet Union, though there was to be a fierce dispute—which still continues today—as to what islands exactly constitute the Kuriles. At the other end of the country, the Ryūkyū Islands were placed in an indefinite American trusteeship (eventually being formally returned to Japan in 1972). So too were the Bonin (Ogasawara) Islands a thousand kilometres out in the Pacific from Tōkyō (returned in 1968). Under the terms of the treaty Japan agreed to pay reparations after all, but this was softened by a rider that this was to depend on its economy. In the end it paid very little, despite its subsequent massive economic growth. In general, the treaty was very favourable to Japan. It came into effect on 28 April 1952, thereby bringing an end to the Occupation.

However, it did not bring about an end to the presence of American troops. America may well have wanted to shelve full and formal responsibility for Japan, but it was certainly not willing to leave it vulnerable to the communists. Neither were many Japanese leaders themselves. Just hours after the peace treaty was signed, Japan and the United States signed a joint security treaty that indefinitely guaranteed the maintaining of American military bases in Japan, mostly in Okinawa. This not only helped Japan in terms of military security. It also brought major economic benefits, in particular through the fact that Japan did not have to spend anywhere near as much on its own defence as did most nations. From this point on, right through to the present, it was to spend annually no more than 1 per cent of its GNP on defence, whereas 6–7 per cent is the approximate peacetime norm for most nations.

The general public were less enthusiastic about the continued American presence, and it was later to lead to a number of political and social problems. However, its economic benefit was beyond question. This was a major—if incidental—factor in setting Japan on the road to becoming an economic superpower.

The Occupation was of literally epoch-making significance. It had from the outset been faced with a number of difficulties. It had to be authoritative without being too authoritarian. It had to be both deconstructive and constructive. It had to maintain Japanese morale by preserving some Japanese ways but removing others. It had to nurture democracy without being felt to be 'undemocratically' imposing it. It even had to change course midway. And it had to do all this from a basis of very limited knowledge. To occupy an alien nation in order to build it anew, especially with all these difficulties, was no small task. Yet on the whole it seems to have been largely successful. In no small part this was due to Japanese willingness to learn and to rebuild the nation once again into a respected power. It was also helped by the fact that American government policy underlying the Occupation meant it was not primarily a punitive affair that left Japan crippled and whimpering on its knees. It was an important constructive phase in the nation's modern history that left it in a healthy position to continue along the road to recovery of its position as a major world power.

6.3   BECOMING NUMBER ONE

Japan did not waste the economic opportunity it had been given by America. The government had played a guiding role in the economy since the Meiji period, and it continued to do so. Economic growth was far too important to leave to market forces and private interests.

The Ministry of International Trade and Industry (MITI), which was created in 1949 out of the former Ministry of Commerce and Industry, played a particularly important part. One of its key functions was 'administrative guidance' (*gyōsei shidō*). MITI officials met regularly with the captains of industry to work out broad policies agreeable to the triad of government, the bureaucracy, and big business. These policies covered investment and development in targeted sectors of expected future growth, the protection of key industries, and rationalisation of industries in sectors no longer considered worth pursuing.

Though the actual technical effectiveness of MITI's role has been exaggerated,[78] it was nonetheless symbolically important. It indicated an ongoing close relationship between government and industry, and a willingness by industry leaders to listen to government opinion and to consider national interests. This was not unlike the situation in the Meiji period. Though most governments to some extent plan their economy and hope to guide it, in terms of degree Japan's economy was particularly strongly characterised by the predominance of planning over pure market forces. In economists' terms it was plan-rational rather than market-rational, controlled rather than laissez-faire.

During the 1950s the agreed priority was the development of heavy industry, particularly iron and steel and including products such as ships and heavy machinery. The catchphrase was '*jū-kō-chō-dai*' ('heavy, thick, long, big'). It was to be followed in the 1960s by a new focus on lighter, more knowledge- and technology-intensive industries such as electrical goods and cameras. The catchphrase now was '*kei-haku-tan-shō*' ('light, thin, short, small'). This does not mean, of course, that heavy industry disappeared overnight. Far from it, shipbuilding in particular continued to grow. Vehicle production, combining steel and technology, also accelerated during the 1960s.

In terms of employment of the labour force, secondary industries— mostly manufacturing but also including construction—rose from 22 per cent in 1950 to 35 per cent in 1970.[79] By contrast, primary indus- tries—notably agriculture—fell from 48 per cent in 1950 to around 18 per cent in 1970. Clearly, there was a focus on increased manufacturing, but the rise of tertiary (service) industries should not be overlooked. These have always been important in Japan's economy, and in fact during this period they occupied more of the labour force than sec- ondary industries, rising from 30 per cent in 1950 to 48 per cent in 1970.

Consumer patterns too had their catchphrases. There were the 'Three Treasures' of the 1950s —radio, motorbike, and sewing machine. The treasures were updated and redefined in the early 1960s to mean refrigerator, TV, and washing machine. The late 1960s was the age of the 'Three Cs'—car, colour TV, and cooler (air-conditioner). The Jap- anese consumer was able to acquire more and more goods because real wages tripled between the mid-1950s and 1973.

The economy, as measured by GNP, grew fairly evenly at around 9 per cent per annum during the 1950s. This rose slightly to around 10 per cent in the early 1960s, and then to more than 13 per cent in the late 1960s and early 1970s. That is, between the end of the Occupation and the worldwide Oil Shock of 1973, Japan's economy grew at an annual average rate of more than 10 per cent. By the time of the Oil Shock it was to be an economic superpower. It was the third largest economy in the world (after the United States and the Soviet Union), the largest pro- ducer of ships, third largest producer of steel, second largest producer of cars (the largest by the end of the 1970s), largest producer of radios and televisions, and so on.

Japan's remarkable postwar economic growth is often referred to as an 'economic miracle'.[80] It does, however, have identifiable causes— several dozen in fact, though it may well be a 'miracle' that they all came together. Some of these have already been discussed, some merit fur- ther discussion, and some are a little technical to be discussed in detail here. America also features in not a few of them. In general, the main causes include (not in any order of priority):

- constructive American/Occupation policies, such as reviving the *zaibatsu*, and abandoning reparation payments (as well as giving seized plant to smaller companies);
- American/Occupation financial advice, as from Joseph Dodge;
- American/Occupation financial aid (in the order of 2 billion dollars during the Occupation);
- American procurements during the Korean War;
- American security provisions for Japan enabling military expenditure to be kept to a fraction of that of most nations;
- American goodwill (at least until the 1970s);
- support and guidance for business from the government and bureaucracy;
- widespread agreement as to the importance of planning rather than relying purely on market forces, and of considering national interests rather than merely company interests;
- frequent use of non-tariff barriers to protect domestic industries from foreign competition;
- the opportunity for major companies to adopt 'state of the art' technology on a large scale due to the wartime destruction of existing equipment and facilities (and in some cases due to the seizure of plant for intended reparation);
- relative stability in the government and bureaucracy;
- a long-term orientation with a focus on survival and market share rather than a profit-centred short-term orientation (aided by the low demands of Japanese shareholders);
- within that broad long-term framework, a pragmatic ability to switch focus and diversify in the short term where necessary;
- low government expenditure on relatively unproductive 'social overheads' such as housing and welfare;
- a high personal savings rate and hence large capital accumulation, arising from a need to compensate for inadequate government welfare provisions combined with personal tax concessions and similar incentives by the government;
- a high debt–equity ratio, supported by Bank of Japan policy (meaning large loans able to be secured for little collateral);
- corporate tax concessions and incentives;
- a policy of purchasing patents rather than acquiring them under licence;
- the tailoring of research and development to practical commercial considerations by entrusting most of it to corporations rather than to neutral academic research institutions or similar;

- a favourable world trade situation that permitted the importing of cheap raw materials and the exporting of manufactured goods to eager markets;
- the shift of considerable labour from the relatively unproductive primary sector (particularly agriculture) into the more productive secondary (manufacturing) and tertiary (service) sectors;
- the promotion of consumerism;
- the diligence of the Japanese worker (somewhat open to question as a permanent national characteristic, but certainly a feature of the postwar period);
- the widespread commitment among Japanese as a whole to rebuilding Japan and regaining a place among the world powers;
- the relatively high retention rate of experienced and generally loyal workers through the so-called 'lifetime employment system' adopted in major corporations (though this has been exaggerated);
- the relative lack of disruption to production through industrial action by workers (though this too has been exaggerated, especially for the years prior to 1960).

Many, including some Japanese themselves, would add to the list an emphasis on exports. In fact, the ratio of Japan's exports to GNP has typically been below that of most nations. It is simply that its GNP grew so very big that in absolute terms its exports seemed to dominate the world. A tendency to compare Japan only with America, which has an exceptionally low export-to-GNP ratio and also has a massive trade imbalance with Japan, adds to misperceptions.

Stability in government provided a helpful setting to economic growth. After 1948, despite frequent shuffling and jockeying behind the scenes, Japan was to be governed by conservatives of essentially the same philosophy right through till the mid-1990s. In particular, it was to be governed from 1955 till 1993 by the Liberal Democratic Party (LDP) (*Jiyū Minshutō*). The formation of the LDP in 1955 was basically a realignment of existing parties, and effectively continued the merging of the prewar *Seiyūkai* and *Minseitō* lineages. There was thus an element of conservative continuity between the postwar and prewar eras.

This continuity was also seen in the triad of government–bureaucracy–business. After the purges were stopped many powerful prewar individuals—even some imprisoned for their role in the war—resumed positions of power. Probably the best known of these was Kishi Nobusuke. He had been the official responsible for the 1936 legislation that drove Ford out of Japan, and later became a member of Tōjō's wartime cabinet. Imprisoned for his wartime activities, he was released in 1948. He was elected to the House of Representatives as a Liberal Party member in 1953, was a major architect of the realignment that led to the formation of the LDP in 1955, and became prime minister in 1957 (till 1960).

Kishi and his younger brother, Satō Eisaku (Kishi having been born into the Satō family but adopted by an uncle), were just two of six prewar bureaucrats who went on to become prime minister after the war. Satō was prime minister from 1964 to 1972. The other four were Yoshida Shigeru (1946–7, then 1948–54), Ikeda Hayato (1960–4), Fukuda Takeo (1976–8), and Ohira Masayoshi (1978–80). That is, for the great majority of the vital first few decades after the war, Japan was governed by prewar bureaucrats.

These prewar bureaucrats and their colleagues did their best to reimplement a number of prewar practices, usually subtly and by stages and not enough to bring serious countermoves from Washington, but enough to make them feel more comfortable. One of their main concerns was education, the tried and trusty ground for implanting suitable thoughts. From the mid-1950s the government reasserted central control over education, deliberately undoing the decentralisation policy of the Occupation.[81] In 1956 elections to regional school boards were abolished and replaced by appointment through mayors and/or prefectural governors. The boards were also made subject to the central Ministry of Education. Two years later the Ministry's curriculum became compulsory, replacing the freedom of choice promoted by the Occupation. This was to pave the way for even tighter central control, leading to the rigorous vetting and censoring of textbooks that still continues to the present day.

The public were ambivalent about these continuities. In a general sense links with the past were reassuring, but at the same time many were worried about the type of links that were being re-established. Yoshida Shigeru talked of losing the war but winning the peace,[82] and many shared, and were inspired by, his sentiments of making the nation once again great. This time it would be in economic terms, not military. In the workplace it was common to find the *mōretsu-gata* ('fiercely determined type'), dedicating their own efforts and achievements to the rebuilding of the nation. This was very similar to the nationalistic achievement-orientation of the Meiji period, but without the militaristic overtones—though there were some who did see it as an aggressive continuation of the war, often in combination with a view that Japan's defeat militarily didn't really count as a proper defeat because of the use of atom bombs.[83] Many of the *mōretsu-gata* were proud to think of themselves as latter-day samurai, true corporate warriors.

On the other hand, it was one thing to work for the good of the nation, but there was a limit to the degree of personal sacrifice people were now willing to make. They had been exposed to American-style democracy and human rights, and while they did not necessarily want a surfeit of all this—for they had learned lessons from the communist agitation of 1946–7—neither did they want a total rejection of it. They were no longer the mindless subjects of the god-emperor, subjects whose very aim in life was to be sacrificed.

A particular source of unease for many was a feeling that not enough of the wealth they generated was being passed on to them. This was particularly so in the 1950s, before wage increases started to make ordinary people feel they were actually making real progress. There were still poor conditions in many workplaces, and low wages. Industrial disputes were commonplace, frequently resulting in violent confrontations and even at times in deaths.

The 1953 strike at Nissan was one example of a serious dispute. It lasted for six months and ended in defeat for the members of the All-Japan Automobile Industry Union. The union was literally dismembered into sundry company-oriented unions. This was the start of the so-called 'enterprise union' that still characterises Japanese labour practices, as opposed to the more common 'trade union' of the west. The enterprise union basically comprises all workers in an enterprise (company) below upper management levels, regardless of occupation—which in most cases is anyway considered by the company to be generalist rather than specialist. The trade union, by contrast, is formed on the basis of specific trade/occupation and includes workers from all (or at least other) companies. Some observers of Japanese management have somehow managed to see enterprise unionism as a symbol of harmony between worker and employer, but it is clearly a means of weakening unions and workers' rights by the age-old tactic of division. Though there are broader 'umbrella associations' of unions, in practice workers usually have nowhere to turn for support if problems cannot be sorted out in-house.

One of the most bitter and historic labour confrontations occurred in 1960, at the Mitsui-owned Miike coalmines in Kyūshū.[84] Unrest here had been brewing for some time over rejected wage claims and planned lay-offs. Its background was the policy of the government–bureaucracy–business triad to replace coal with (imported) oil as Japan's major source of primary energy. Little evidence of concern was shown for the serious consequences this would entail for the mining workforce.

The dispute at Miike soon escalated into a major confrontation between the labour movement as a whole and government-backed big business. The employers openly hired strike-breaking thugs, and one of them fatally stabbed a miner to show they were serious. The government also brought in 10 per cent of the national police force, seemingly to confront the miners rather than the thugs. Certainly, the government very much seemed to favour the employers, and did not exactly convey an impression of neutrality. Eventually, after nine months, the strikers lost their battle, though they gained a few concessions on paper.

Unions were rarely to pose a serious threat again through strike action, especially as they became increasingly converted into harmless 'enterprise unions'. Fortunately wages and conditions were soon to improve anyway, helping mollify worker unrest. Grievances came mostly to be aired in other ways while strikes were tokenised into brief stoppages—sometimes only one hour—at agreed times of the year. Thus the amount of days of production lost through industrial action was to be a mere fraction of that in most other major nations, typically less than a tenth. This was a great boost to economic performance.

Workers, at least white-collar males in major companies, were further mollified by the promise of security in the form of 'lifetime employment'. This has been greatly exaggerated in terms of both its scale and its history. Though selective scanning of earlier history can reveal some antecedents in the Meiji period and even the Tokugawa period, it is essentially a postwar practice. Moreover, it has only ever applied at most to a third of the workforce. Nevertheless it became a sort of ideal for society at large. Study hard, get good results, get employed by a top company, and get security for life—not to mention a salary typically a third higher than in a small company, for the dual structure of industry continues to this day.

Another source of public unease was the possibility of a revival of militarism, despite the constitutional restrictions on this. Some Japanese were not averse to renewed military activity,[85] but the great majority were, and felt continuing anxiety about the presence of American troops and the possibility that Japan might be dragged into an American war with the Soviets. Matters came to a head in 1960, with the scheduled renewal of the security treaty with the United States. The authoritarianism being shown by the government in the Miike Dispute at the time did not help ease tensions. Nor did growing Cold War tensions worldwide, and a much-publicised remark a few years earlier by president-to-be Richard Nixon that Japan's constitutional anti-war clause was a mistake.[86]

In negotiations with America Kishi had obtained what he saw as a concession. Japan was now to be consulted before America used its Japan-based troops. Many others saw this rather as increasing the likelihood of Japan becoming embroiled in armed conflict, because it now effectively made Japan seem a willing participant in any American action. There was great opposition to the proposed ratification of renewal, including a series of riots and physical confrontations between parliamentarians in the Diet. At a midnight session in May Kishi succeeded in getting Diet approval for the renewal, catching the opposition unawares. Even greater unrest followed, including a partial takeover of the Diet building in mid-June. President Eisenhower had planned to visit Japan later that month but his trip was cancelled as a result of the unrest. Kishi resigned a few days later, being replaced as prime minister by Ikeda Hayato. Ikeda promised never to repeat the Diet bulldozing tactic of Kishi, and he also partly assuaged the public with a promise of doubling incomes before the 1960s were out.

Protesters against the treaty renewal included many left-wingers, and this provoked a right-wing reaction. One victim of this was Asanuma Inejirō, chairman of the Japan Socialist Party. Asanuma, who among other things had made a number of anti-American pronouncements in recent times, was fatally stabbed by a fanatical right-wing youth during a televised speech in October.[87] Most of Japan and much of the world saw in naked and frightening detail the deadly penetration of the 18-inch blade.

It came to symbolise a turbulent year. The year was itself a symbol of unrest and the seeming fragility of western-style democracy—not unlike the fragility of the Taishō period half a century earlier. Unrest in the workplace was eventually quietened, but the public continued to feel uneasy for some time. Students in particular staged increasingly violent demonstrations over the next few years. Extremists in the left-wing *Zengakuren* (a nationwide student federation) deliberately adopted a policy of violent confrontation, including the use of weapons such as firebombs, and caused the closure of many campuses.[88] Some of their anger continued to be over the treaty renewal, for America's entry into the Vietnam War in 1961 made the threat of Japan's involvement even greater. They were also angered by the increasing expense and increasingly controlled nature of education in Japan, as well as corruption among university officials. Later in the 1960s the most extreme among the students helped form the infamous terrorist organisation the Red Army (*Sekigun*).

But again like the Taishō period, there was both lightness and darkness during the 1960s. Amidst all the unrest and authoritarianism, there
were definite milestones in Japan's re-recognition by the world. In 1961
the *Shinkansen* (Bullet Train) started operating, at the time the most
technologically advanced train in the world. In contrast to the dark symbol of the assassin's blade, it was a bright symbol of a new era of prosperity and technology, and was a great source of pride to the Japanese.
They were able to show it off to the many foreigners who visited Japan
for the 1964 Tōkyō Olympics. Staging the Olympics clinched the real
readmittance of Japan to the international community, which had been
formally staged in 1956 when it was admitted to the United Nations. In
the same year of 1964 travel restrictions were greatly eased, and Japanese started travelling overseas in numbers. The restrictions had been
in place informally since the war partly because of foreign exchange factors but also in deference to lingering anti-Japanese feeling abroad.
Then at the end of the decade, in 1970, the World Exposition was held in
Osaka, and again Japan was able proudly to display its prosperity and
major nation status.

The most important factor in its acceptance, however, was undoubtedly its economic growth. Ikeda's promise in 1960 to double incomes
within ten years was met ahead of time. Incomes doubled by 1967. The
following year Japan's GNP overtook that of West Germany to make it
the second biggest in the free world after the United States.

The re-emergence of Japan as a major power was obviously noted
overseas. Books started to appear around the world analysing its route
to success, not only in terms of economics but in terms of state management, education, and other more general terms. Among other acknow-
ledgements of its status, it featured prominently in world scenarios
projected by 'think-tank' specialists in international affairs. A well-
known early example was Herman Kahn's popular 1971 work *The
Emerging Japanese Superstate*, which sang Japan's praises. Such works
tended to downplay the negative effects of intense economic growth,
such as massive pollution problems.

The Japanese, too, proudly wrote works that sought to explain their
success, both to themselves and to the world. They usually followed a
line of argument that Japan was somehow unique and special, and they
claimed national characteristics such as loyalty, harmony, and group-
orientation. These works were considered a genre in their own right,
known as *Nihonjinron* ('Theories about the Japanese'). Two very well-
known examples were Nakane Chie's 1967 work *Tate-shakai no Ningen
Kankei: Tan'itsu-shakai no Riron* ('Personal Relations in a Vertical

Society: A Theory of Homogeneous Society'), which appeared in English in 1970 as *Japanese Society*, and Doi Takeo's *Amae no Kōzō* ('The Anatomy of Dependence') of 1971, which appeared in English in 1973.[89] Both claimed, with questionable evidence, that Japanese interpersonal relations were unique and stronger than in other societies. Some *Nihonjinron* works, usually implicitly but sometimes explicitly, went a step further and raised once again the spectre of racial purity and superiority, causing alarm among Asian nations in particular.

The praise at home and abroad continued during the 1970s, a decade that was the high point in world respect for Japan as an economic superpower. It was not always unqualified praise, for there were a number of obvious problems, but on balance it was the praise that prevailed over the criticism. One of the greatest of all accolades came in 1979 in the form of Ezra Vogel's work *Japan As Number One*. Vogel praised in particular Japan's economic performance and its apparent skills in state management and national co-ordination. Not surprisingly, the book immediately became one of the bestselling works ever in Japan as the Japanese flocked to the bookstores to lap up this praise from a Harvard professor.[90] His sub-title *Lessons for America* was especially satisfying, for it showed that the pupil had learned so well it was now able to teach the master.

In many regards this was true. In a world now dominated by business, westerners keen to learn the secrets of Japan's success looked enviously towards its management practices in particular. A massive body of literature appeared on the topic,[91] much of it superficial. Not all bandwagon authors realised the recency of practices such as lifetime employment. Even fewer realised that some of the practices associated with Japanese managers were in fact learned from the west—it was just that Japan had made them more effective. These included quality control, which was introduced into Japan in the 1950s by the American engineer W. Edwards Deming, and the use of suggestion-boxes to encourage employee participation, which had been practised by companies such as America's Eastman Kodak as early as the 1890s.[92] To some extent there was even western influence detectable in the practice of lifetime employment, and its companion practice of paternalistic care of an employee's personal life as well as professional.[93]

On the negative side, Japan continued to ignore its underdeveloped infrastructure, preferring to plough its wealth back into further growth instead of improved housing and roads. When it did build, it often seemed to do so not on the basis of proper planning but rather with consideration to providing benefits to the owners of certain land or construction companies. In the background was a network of cosy relations between big business, the underworld, and the government. Corruption scandals in government and big business have long been commonplace in Japan, and the Ministry of Construction has a particularly bad record.

Ironically, when a broad national plan for infrastructural development was finally proposed, it came from a man forever associated with scandal, Tanaka Kakuei. In July 1972, as he became prime minister, Tanaka promoted his master plan 'Rebuilding the Japanese Archipelago'. Among other things he envisaged the elimination of regional inequities, by relocating industries away from their concentration in the Pacific coastal belt to the interior and the Japan Sea coast. The plan was greeted with some cynicism, for his own constituency of Niigata happened to be one of the Japan Sea regions designated for development and Tanaka had a long record of pork-barrel politics, but at least it was a plan.

The plan was never to come to reality. Not only was Tanaka forced from office just two years later following some particularly serious scandals,[94] but also the Oil Shock hit in 1973. Arab oil-producing nations suddenly increased the price of oil five-fold. Most countries were hit badly, and experienced double-digit inflation and severe reduction in economic growth over the next few years. Japan used oil for more than three-quarters of its primary energy, and was virtually 100 per cent dependent on imported oil, 90 per cent of it from the Middle East (this having displaced American oil). Being proportionately so dependent on Arab oil, it was hit particularly badly. In 1974 it experienced negative growth for the first time since the war. That year the wholesale price index leapt 31 per cent, and the consumer price index 24 per cent.[95]

Under the guidance of the Ministry of International Trade and Industry, Japan immediately put in place measures to reduce its reliance on oil. It improved efficiency, especially in energy-saving techniques. It rationalised industries, transferring some of them overseas, and it increased emphasis on the development of low energy-consumptive industries, particularly service and 'high-tech' industries. Over the next ten years or so it was able to reduce its overall dependence on oil by about a quarter, and by diversifying its suppliers it also reduced its relative dependence on Middle Eastern oil by a further fifth.

Despite—or perhaps because of—its vulnerability, Japan recovered faster than other economies. In 1975 it was able to record growth of 4 per cent. Apart from a small slump following a second and lesser oil shock in 1979, it was to maintain this average well beyond the 1970s. This rapid recovery was another source of respect from the west, and seemed to suggest Japan the economic superpower was invincible.

Other evidence of Japanese efficiency was seen in the way that pollution had been successfully tackled in the 1970s, as Vogel pointed out. Government and business had only started to address the problem seriously after massive law-suits from victims of pollution-related diseases, which threatened to become a national embarrassment.[96] Nevertheless, once they set their mind to it, results were fast and effective. It was impressive. The phoenix had not only risen from the ashes, it had soared, and was staying aloft.

Around the same time as the Oil Shock, America had also given Japan a shock or two. These were known as the Nixon Shocks. In July 1971, without any prior consultation with Japan, Nixon announced his plan to visit the People's Republic of China. It was the start of a US–PRC *rapprochement* that caused great difficulty for Japan's own foreign policy. Japan had followed the American line and favoured Taiwan to this point. It now had to make rapid and sometimes embarrassing adjustments. Then just a month later, again with no consultation, Nixon announced his New Economic Program. This included a 10 per cent surcharge on many of the goods Japan exported to the United States (about a third of its total exports went to the US). It also meant an abandoning of the gold standard, in effect forcing the Japanese yen to be taken off the fixed exchange rate that had applied since the war. The yen's value increased greatly, making its exports more expensive. But Nixon was still not finished sending cold messages to Japan. In the summer of 1973, fearing a shortage of soybeans in the domestic market, he abruptly embargoed soybean exports. This badly hit Japan, where American soybeans were an important commodity.[97]

The Nixon Shocks were not as damaging as the Oil Shock, but they were disturbing to the Japanese. They clearly signalled a cooling in American attitudes and goodwill towards Japan. Nevertheless, Japan rode them all out, and by the end of the 1970s many Japanese were starting to wonder if they needed American goodwill anyway. After all, Japan was now the master, and if America turned its back on Japan then it would be America's loss, not Japan's. Hadn't a Harvard professor told them so?

6.4   A SUPERPOWER ADRIFT

Japan's economy continued to grow at around 4 per cent during the early 1980s. Its trade surplus with America, which had started to develop since the late 1970s, became massive, typically in the order of US$40–50 billion. Japanese products were everywhere.

There had been some criticism of Japan's seemingly narrow focus on economic growth during the 1970s, but in general the praise had predominated. The balance was now tipping the other way. Backlashes were starting to become serious, not just in America. The Japanese were increasingly criticised as 'economic animals' who lacked any values other than making money. There were anti-Japanese protests in which Japanese products were destroyed by sledgehammers. Books were appearing that openly denounced the ethics of certain Japanese trade practices.[98]

Some of the criticism was justified. The Japanese were at times undoubtedly guilty of 'dumping' (selling below cost in a targeted market) or erecting non-tariff barriers (disadvantaging imports by non-economic practices such as time-consuming testing). However, the criticism was expressed in increasingly emotional language. It was almost like war brewing—an economic war that was threatening to get out of hand.

To try to remedy the situation a meeting was convened in 1985 in New York's Plaza Hotel, attended by the financial leaders of the United States, Britain, France, Germany, and Japan. In the so-called Plaza Accord they agreed effectively to devalue the dollar relative to the yen. The yen duly rose, in what is known as *endaka* ('high yen'). One result was an increased transfer of Japanese business operations overseas so as to make use of cheaper labour. However, contrary to American expectations, American goods did not make significantly greater inroads into Japan. Japanese goods—now often produced abroad—continued to loom large in the American market.

The Japanese now tried, with some 'success', to stimulate domestic demand by releasing cheap capital. Loans were made available at remarkably low interest. Prices of land in particular, which was used as collateral against loans, were allowed to escalate to absurd levels. The land in the immediate vicinity of the Imperial Palace theoretically had the same price tag in 1988 as all of California. Japan's total land assets at the time were equivalent to no less than 60 per cent of the entire land value of the planet—200 times the 0.3 per cent of the planet it occupies in geographical terms.[99] Stockmarket prices also became grossly inflated, with some companies worth more on paper than the entire GNP of many countries. This was the infamous Bubble Economy.

Japan had become the second largest economy in the free world in the late 1960s. However, it was during the Bubble Economy of the late

1980s that, in terms of per capita income, the Japanese became officially the wealthiest people in the world—at least on paper.

The money inevitably flowed overseas. Japan seemed to be buying up the world. By this stage it was the largest net overseas investor nation in the world. It controlled 4 per cent of the American economy, and Japanese companies even bought up bastions of America such as the Rockefeller Center and Columbia Film Studios.

Equally inevitably, this stirred up anti-Japanese feelings even more. The Japanese called this 'Japan bashing', and felt it all unfair. To their way of thinking they were simply playing the western economic game of capitalism, and they were winning. Westerners were just poor losers, beaten at their own game by a better team.

The rising tensions between Japan and the west during the 1980s had two main interrelated causes. One was criticism from the west, which was in part justified, but was also in part—as the Japanese claimed—an emotional expression of frustration at being bettered.[100] The other was that Japanese national pride crossed the line into nationalistic arrogance, then went even further into nationalistic chauvinism.

One early indication of this intensification of attitude was in 1982, when the Ministry of Education tried to substitute, in the school texts which it vetted, the word 'advance' (*shinshutsu*) for 'invasion' (*shinnyū*) to describe Japan's prewar actions on the Asian mainland. It also tried to delete or tone down references to Japanese atrocities. This caused outrage among Asian nations, and not a few Japanese.[101]

Japanese neo-nationalism became an increasing concern to the international community, particularly because it seemed to be endorsed by leading government figures. In August 1985 Prime Minister Nakasone Yasuhiro, a former military officer noted for his old-style nationalistic views (including his wish to revise Article IX of the constitution), broke with postwar convention and paid homage to Japanese war dead at Yasukuni Shrine not in a private and personal capacity, as had previous prime ministers, but in his official role as head of government. This clearly suggested a revived link between religion and the state—banned by the constitution—and aroused fears about the revival of State Shintō. Around the same time he also made a number of comments to the effect that Japan, being peopled by a pure race, was more successful than multiracial societies. His most famous speech in this regard was in September 1986, at a gathering of young LDP leaders, when he remarked that Japanese were smarter than Americans, because intellectual levels in America were lowered by blacks and Hispanics.[102]

As a result of strong western reaction Nakasone had to apologise for his speech. Yet he had made his speech just weeks after international criticism had forced him to sack Education Minister Fujio Masayuki for publicly playing down the Nanking atrocity, and for also stating that Japan's 1910 annexation of Korea was partly Korea's responsibility because it had agreed to a merger.[103] It was as though Fujio's fate had taught Nakasone—and others who made similar remarks—nothing.

But Nakasone was openly called soft and a Reagan yes-man by the Diet member and novelist Ishihara Shintarō, who in 1989 co-wrote a controversial book entitled *The Japan That Can Say 'No': Why Japan Will Be First Among Equals*.[104] The book expressed strong resentment at complaints and requests (for technological co-operation) from a second-rate America, and also clearly showed a strong nationalistic belief in Japan's supremacy. Japan is the key to the future, the book proclaims, and America should get wise to this and stop expecting Japan to play second fiddle. Japan should take a firmer line against America, and stop dancing to its tune.

Partly a response to Japan bashing, it was an inflammatory piece of writing that appealed, not unlike the *Kokutai no Hongi* of 1937, to basic emotion rather than intellect. Among other things it repeated a some-times heard accusation that America had used atom bombs on Japan and not on Germany for racist reasons.[105] This overlooked the not unimportant fact that the atom bomb was not successfully tested till July 1945, two months after Germany had already surrendered. Indeed, the book saw American racism as the source of all problems. Then, quite obviously becoming carried away by its own strongly nationalistic line, it suggested that the recent economic success of Asian nations was not unconnected with the fact that they were once occupied—however briefly—by Japan (whereas former western colonies had not achieved such success).[106]

On the other hand, while those such as Ishihara met western criticism with defiance, others in the government tried to take a more conciliatory and constructive approach. They promoted Japan's internationalisation (*kokusaika*), making it a catchphrase of the decade. To some extent this was inevitable, as Japan tried to diversify its international relations away from America, and as its people travelled increasingly overseas. A number of positive moves were made, such as the establishment of scholarships for overseas students and exchange programmes for young people in general. However, criticism was soon made that Japan was abusing the spirit of internationalisation. Instead of bringing Japan and the world together, it seemed to be using internationalisation as a vehicle for explaining Japan to the world—or more exactly, why it was different from (and better than) the rest of the world. The newly established and government-backed International Centre for Japanese Studies in Kyōto (Nihon Bunka Kenkyū Sentaa, or Nichibunken), for example, was seeming to produce *Nihonjinron* works that stressed Japan's uniqueness, and in a way favourable to Japan.

Some of the western criticism of Japan struck a chord among the Japanese public. In the same year of 1979 that Vogel praised Japan as Number One, a European Community Commission report referred to the Japanese as 'workaholics' who lived in 'rabbit hutches'.[107] Both these put-down terms deeply hurt the Japanese, particularly because they seemed to contain an element of truth. The Japanese did work some 400 hours more per year than the typical western worker, and they did live in tiny houses, that at around 90 sq m were only half the size of a typical American dwelling.[108]

These unflattering terms, along with others such as 'rich nation, poor people',[109] also brought to the fore broader questions about the quality of life in Japan, questions that were asked increasingly during the 1980s. The Japanese not only worked long hours and lived in cramped houses, they often had an hour's crowded train-ride to get to work, and another hour back. Those in the Tōkyō region could enjoy only a twelfth of the green park space per capita that Londoners did. At least most of the houses in Tōkyō had sewerage, for the national rate of connected sewerage (that is, flush toilets) was still under half. And as land prices rose during the Bubble years, even 'rabbit hutches' became so expensive that an inter-generational mortgage was the only way most people could manage to buy one. At the end of the decade, in 1990, long-time critic Jon Woronoff went on to attack Japan's ultimate accolade, the work by Vogel, by producing *Japan As—Anything But—Number One*, in which he particularly criticised the poor standard of living.

The Japanese public's national pride was greatly hurt by all this. But it was pointless counter-criticising westerners such as Woronoff, for they were right. The problems lay within Japan itself. What had all the sacrifice and hard work been for? There had been similar grievances about the quality of life and the distribution of wealth in the 1950s, but the Japanese had been assuaged by wage increases and material acquisitions. They had, in the famous words of the social commentator Hidaka Rokurō, become a 'controlled society' (*kanri shakai*), in which their meek acceptance of government policies was bought by material affluence.[110] But just how much genuine satisfaction could be obtained from a Gucci handbag or a Cartier watch or designer suits? The public had been promised infrastructural improvements in the early 1970s, but these had been put on hold because of problems such as the Oil Shock. There was now, at the end of the 1980s, no excuse. It was time that the Japanese people received some real benefit from the nation's wealth.

The Japanese public of the late 1980s were further angered by a particularly serious scandal, the Recruit Scandal. The Recruit company, which had started as a recruiting agency but had diversified into various activities including real estate, made use of the easily available finance of the Bubble era to win political favour by massive distribution of funds. More than 150 officials, politicians, and other people in positions of influence received contributions, cheap loans, and, in particular, preflotation shares in the company. These shares increased in value five-fold upon public issue, making a very quick and handsome profit for the recipients in what was known popularly as a 'stock-for-favours' scandal. By mid-1989 some twenty or so members of the Diet (of whom most were in the LDP) had resigned over their involvement with Recruit, including half a dozen cabinet ministers. Resignations included the then prime minister, Takeshita Noboru, and his predecessor Nakasone.

Upper House elections that year resulted in an unprecedented majority for the Japan Socialist Party. This was more a reflection of public frustration towards the incumbent conservative government than it was a serious vote for the socialists. It was the Lower House that really mattered, not the Upper House, and so the LDP stayed in control of the country, but it had received a sharp warning.

That same year of 1989 also brought an end to an era, for Hirohito died in January. There was hope that under his son, Akihito, there might be some change of direction that might finally benefit the public. The new era was given the name Heisei, literally meaning 'Achieving Full Peace'.[111] This had very positive connotations, suggesting that some of the problems lingering from the war—some would say Hirohito himself had been one—were now to be overcome. The hard work of rebuilding the war-torn nation was, perhaps, at an end, and the public could enjoy the fruits of their labours. Unfortunately the new period got off to a bad start with the breaking of the Recruit Scandal and Ishihara's provocative book.

As Japan entered the 1990s, foreign anger mounted towards it, while in Japan itself public anger mounted towards the government. A crisis was looming.

Perhaps fortunately for Japan—at least for its international relations—at that moment the Bubble burst, and its economy collapsed.

Price escalation in Japan had become so out of hand that, from late 1989, the Bank of Japan was forced to increase interest rates stiffly—choosing to burst the bubble rather than to wait for it to collapse by itself.[112] 1990 and 1991 saw Japan plunging into a recession which, after stabilising, was to stay with it through the 1990s. Land prices fell rapidly by more than a third. Stock market prices plummeted from their December 1989 high by more than 60 per cent. Bankruptcies and bad debts abounded. Unemployment increased. Overall, economic growth slumped, remaining virtually flat and rarely over 1 per cent. The government and business occasionally interpreted this and that event as a sign of imminent recovery, but this did not eventuate. In one of the quarters of 1997 the economy even experienced an annualised shrinkage of as much as 11 per cent.

Among other consequences of the recession, Japan's much vaunted and much exaggerated lifetime employment system, which was dependent on continued high growth, effectively collapsed. A total of 60,000 managers—supposedly in the most secure of positions—were dismissed in just the two years 1992–3.[113] Over the next few years more than one in ten managers were either dismissed or demoted. Worried managers flocked in droves to join rapidly growing independent unions whose existence had once hardly been noticed.[114] Law suits were lodged by not a few of those dismissed or demoted. A major setback for Japanese managerial and economic expertise came in 1996, when for the first time a major Japanese corporation was obliged to have a westerner take over as president at its headquarters in Japan—the Scot Henry Wallace (a former Ford employee) filling the top position at Mazda on a rescue mission.[115]

Lifetime employment had been a bastion of the *Nihonjinron*-style of thinking about 'uniquely' Japanese familialism, group loyalty, harmony and so forth. Its collapse greatly undermined such thinking.

The bursting of the Bubble quickly lessened tensions with the west. Most western economists had felt the Bubble was inevitably going to burst, though it had lasted longer than expected and was starting to cast doubt on their predictions. Its bursting gave reassurance to the world that economic laws did work after all, and could not be flouted by a real Japanese 'economic miracle'. It also meant the end of fears of Japan buying up the entire world. Perhaps even more importantly, in a broader sense it deflated Japanese arrogance. The Pacific War had deflated their sense of superiority in military terms, and the Bubble and its ensuing recession now did the same in economic terms. It was not exactly a loss for Japan, for it still remained a very mighty economic superpower, but it did show that it was not invincible.

The Japanese public were less reassured. In fact, they were devastated. They were angry enough already about Japan's wealth not being used to improve the quality of life for ordinary Japanese. The collapse of the economy now meant that real improvements would be postponed yet again. Even more importantly, it threatened to undo much of the hard work and sacrifice they had offered in the cause of the nation.

At the same time, yet more scandals involving politicians were coming to light. In 1992 another major one broke, the Sagawa Kyūbin Scandal. Once again large numbers of politicians and officials were seen to have received large sums of money in return for favours, this time to the Sagawa Company (a parcel delivery service). Once again leading figures such as Takeshita and Nakasone were involved. The involvement of the underworld was also apparent.

Public anger was so great over the combination of economic collapse, continuing poor quality of life, and continuing corruption in the government that in October that year a major in the Self-Defence Forces, Yanai Shinsaku, even publicly mooted the idea of a military coup.[116] There was great public sympathy for his claim that politicians were feathering their nests while the nation suffered, and that corruption had to be stopped. There was less sympathy, however, for his idea of letting the military take things into their own hands. Most Japanese very much wanted to avoid that, for Japan had been down that road before and paid the price for it. Yanai was dismissed.

Yanai was not the only one to be dismissed. So too was the LDP, in July the following year. In June 1993 a vote of no confidence was moved against Miyazawa Kiichi, the prime minister since November 1991. As finance minister in 1989 Miyazawa had resigned over the Recruit Scandal. On his return to politics he had tried to placate the public by promising to make Japan a 'lifestyle superpower'. This was clearly not happening. The vote against him led to a snap election the following month. In the election the LDP failed to gain a majority in the all-important Lower House, winning only 223 of the 511 seats.[117]

The public had had enough, and the 38-year unbroken regime of the LDP was brought to an end. The change of emperor had not brought about any great improvement. Perhaps a change of government would.

The change of government, however, was not in fact so very great. Conservatives still ruled. Miyazawa's successor as prime minister, Hosokawa Morihiro, was a former LDP man and grandson of the immediate prewar prime minister Prince Konoe. Hosokawa headed an alliance of some seven parties, many of which had been formed in haste just prior to the election. He did manage to initiate legislation that brought significant changes to the electoral system,[118] but he too was soon forced to resign through involvement in scandal.

The years that followed saw an intense flurry of political activity reminiscent of the 1890s. Parties formed and unformed, allegiances shifted, intrigues abounded. In the nine years between late 1987 and early 1996 Japan had as many prime ministers. The one constant factor was the continuing control of the nation by conservatives. Even the Socialist Murayama Tomiichi, who was prime minister of a new alliance between June 1994 and January 1996, was very obviously under the thumb of conservatives.[119] The Socialist Party—which changed its name in the early 1990s to the Social Democratic Party of Japan—abandoned most of its policies, allied with its arch-rivals the LDP, and lost much of its credibility and far more than the ground it had gained in the late 1980s. In fact, it was to lose seats in just about every election and, after yet another name change (dropping 'of Japan'), it was virtually to disappear from existence by the late 1990s. By late 1996 the LDP was back formally in power, without even the need for coalition partners. In 1991 Nakasone had said that the public had no one to turn to but the LDP. It would seem that his comment is even more appropriate in the late 1990s.

To the surprise of many observers, the Japanese public of the late 1990s have lapsed into a form of political complacency. They had expressed their anger in the Upper House elections of 1989 and the Lower House elections of 1993. In local elections in 1995 they had also chosen two former comedians to be governors of Tōkyō and Osaka, which seemed to be some sort of political statement.[120] The Kōbe earthquake of January 1995, which killed over 5,000 people, had also been the cue for further venting of public anger towards the government and business, over matters such as corrupt building practices that had weakened structures in the first place[121] and the lack of prompt and effective response to the disaster. Since then, however, apathy has prevailed. The October 1996 Lower House elections, which saw the LDP back in power, also saw a record low voter turnout (59 per cent).

It is as though the disillusioned public have accepted—with a fatalism not unknown in Japanese history—that certain things simply are not going to change, at least not without some sort of major external stimulus. Serious scandals, for example, have continued to abound right through to the late 1990s, on an almost monthly basis. In fact, in one sense they have become worse, for whereas corruption was once believed to be found only in government and business and not in the bureaucracy, this belief has now been shown to be naive. Moreover, recent scandals have not only involved those in power making money for themselves, they have involved the public as victims. A third of Japan's AIDS victims are now known to have caught the disease as a result of untreated blood knowingly being allowed by the relevant authorities to be used in transfusions. Small-time investors are now known to have been made to suffer greater losses than they might normally have in order to minimise losses made by important investor-clients.

Beneath the political apathy, the Japanese public of the late 1990s are anxious. This anxiety seems to have displaced the anger of the early 1990s. There is a general anxiety caused by the recession, which has gone beyond expectations and continues in the late 1990s to produce new shocks as major financial institutions go bankrupt. Other major causes of anxiety include the shock of the Kōbe earthquake in 1995 and the notorious subway gas attacks by the AUM Shinrikyō group later that year. These events brought out a latent sense of vulnerability in the Japanese. In addition, government White Papers repeatedly show public concerns over rising crime, the disintegration of families, financial insecurity, the ageing of society, the deteriorating ethics and morals of young people, and the nature of education.

The government too shares many of these concerns. It has introduced new laws to allow for nursing care insurance for the elderly. It has promised to reform education so as to lessen examination pressure and allow for more creativity. It has started a policy of financial deregulation in an attempt to restore health to the economy. Just how effective these measures will be remains to be seen.

Internationally, anger towards Japan may well have been defused but negative feelings have certainly not disappeared. In particular, Asian nations are dismayed and disturbed by Japan's failure to take appropriate opportunities to address its prewar and wartime behaviour. The death of Hirohito in 1989 and the 50th anniversary of the end of the war in 1995 provided such opportunities. Not only were these opportunities passed up, the situation was aggravated. The Diet produced a watered-down formal statement on the war which expressed the usual regret but did not make a proper apology. It was widely seen as an insult to victim nations. In the mid and late 1990s Japanese politicians continued to make statements that denied or downplayed Japanese atrocities, and at times even the very idea that Japan was ever aggressive. In 1996 Prime Minister Hashimoto Ryūtarō even repeated Nakasone's 'official' visit to honour the war-dead at Yasukuni Shrine. Around the same time the government effectively brushed aside complaints by so-called 'comfort women'—those who had been forced into sexual service of Japanese troops—by consigning their claims to a private fund.

This sort of attitude has not been helpful to Japan's re-acceptance by Asia, and in broader terms still jeopardises its relations with the world at large. Many Asian nations have respected Japan for its economic achievements, and even modelled themselves on it. But they have certainly not respected its unwillingness to face up to the abuses of the past.[122] Their faith in Japan's economic leadership has been set back by Japan's economic collapse (and their own economic difficulties in recent times), but has not been extinguished. However, the balance between respect and disrespect is shifting. If Japan does not face reality soon, feelings towards it will become very much weighted towards the negative.

As Japan faces the new millennium it has continuing problems both at home and abroad. It seems to have no real master plan to tackle its problems at home, and it seems not to know—or not to want to know—how to be part of the world. There is no vision, no sense of direction, no sense of purpose. The images used of it have changed. The soaring phoenix or risen sun have become the rudderless ship. It is indeed as though the helm of the ship of state has become inoperative. Some have said this is because it has run out of models.[123] It no longer has some specific target that it can 'catch up and overtake'. It has no channel for its national energies.

This would seem to be largely true. The old-style 'successism' of the Meiji period and the immediate postwar period cannot be easily revived in the present day. Japan cannot strengthen its military and go out and build an empire by force. It cannot revive the emperor system. It cannot expect its people to make personal sacrifices like the 'determined types' of the 1950s in order to help economic growth. Indeed, it will find it difficult to get its people to make any sacrifices at all in a nation dominated by disillusionment and a time dominated by postmodern values.

But it can, perhaps, draw on some of its national characteristics and past patterns of success. In particular, it can draw on its people's national pride and willingness to work for national interests. It can draw on its people's high regard for learning and achievement. It can draw on its pragmatic ability to mix elements old and new, foreign and domestic. It can set its sights once again on blending self-help and national help and becoming a superpower. This time, however, it needs to be a superpower in tune with the present age, along the lines of Miyazawa's promised 'lifestyle superpower'. In this it can once again learn where appropriate from models around the world, and improve on them. But this time it must also seek to share its achievements with the world, not simply to use them as proof of its own supremacy.

Becoming a postmodern lifestyle superpower will be a great challenge for Japan, for many values of the present age are not easily reconciled with Japan's traditional strengths, such as authoritarian guidance of the nation, sacrifice, and hard work. But the Japanese have long relished a challenge and responded positively to it. Working towards a goal once promised them will make the challenge all the more appealing.

REVIEW OF PART SIX

The Occupation of defeated Japan was essentially an American affair. Based initially on twin aims of demilitarisation and democratisation, it was constructive rather than destructive. For MacArthur and some in Washington, it was a chance to build a Utopia. Demilitarisation policies included demobilising the military, breaking up the *zaibatsu* that had contributed to the war effort, purging unsuitable figures from positions of influence, and punishing war criminals. Thanks to the personal protection of MacArthur, Hirohito was not tried as a war criminal nor even forced to abdicate. Instead, he played an important part in MacArthur's policies of democratisation. He became humanised and the symbol of the nation, and also gave legitimacy to Occupation reforms. The ultimate demilitarisation policy was the renunciation of war, which was to be enshrined in a new constitution.

The new constitution, drawn up by young Americans with some but limited input from the Japanese, embodied most of the Occupation's democratic reforms. It confirmed Hirohito's new role, vested sovereignty of the nation in its people, affirmed human rights and equality of the sexes, separated church and state, affirmed various freedoms such as of speech and assembly, and provided for progressive reforms in labour and education. In addition, party politics returned. Progressive land reforms greatly reduced tenancy, and made more people owners of the land they worked.

However, many in America and Japan felt the reforms were too liberal, especially in view of rising Cold War tensions. In particular, there was concern about rising communism. A planned general strike for February 1947, which MacArthur had to ban at the last moment, was a symbol of labour unrest and the communist threat. A continuing weak economy increased that threat of communist takeover.

Washington appeared to lose faith in MacArthur during 1947, and sent a number of advisers who took a harder line. The key aim now was to strengthen Japan's economy and make it a Far Eastern bastion of the free world. The dissolution of the *zaibatsu* was stopped, along with the purges. Japan also avoided paying any significant reparations to victim nations. Labour laws, only just introduced, were toughened. Through strict financial policies under the guidance of specialist American advisers, inflation was reduced and the economy started to recover. A major boost to economic recovery came through American procurements for the Korean War, which started in 1950.

The Korean War also led to MacArthur's dismissal over a policy disagreement with President Truman, and to the signing of a peace treaty and the end of the Occupation. At the same time that the peace treaty was signed, America and Japan signed a security treaty that allowed for American troops to be stationed in Japan. Since America effectively took responsibility for Japan's security—despite the formation of a Self-Defence Force—Japan had very little defence expenditure, which further helped its economy.

During the 1950s the conservative Japanese government deliberately undid some of the Occupation reforms. Education in particular saw the reintroduction of centralisation and tight government control. However, it did not undo the Occupation's recent economic policies, but built upon them, combining them with its own tradition of government guidance over the economy. Economic performance was further helped by traditional attitudes such as a willingness to learn and to work hard for the interests of the nation. Some were even determined to refight the war, but this time in the economic arena.

Through these and a variety of other economic factors—a mixture of self-help and American help, of authoritarianism and democracy, of cultural predispositions and economic mechanisms—Japan was able to achieve rapid economic growth over the next two decades. In the late 1960s it became the third largest economy in the world after America and the Soviet Union.

Progress was not always smooth. Industrialisation had caused serious pollution. Labour unrest had continued in the 1950s, culminating in a major confrontation at Miike in 1960 between the labour movement on the one hand and government and business on the other. The government-business combination won. It was from this point that many of the policies of so-called Japanese-style management were put in place, notably enterprise unions and 'lifetime employment'. Fortunately, improvements in the economy led to wage increases and material acquisitions that helped placate the workforce.

Japan's economy continued to grow during the 1970s despite the Oil Shock. It also cleaned up its pollution problems. It seemed invincible. Pride in Japan's achievements led to the production of self-congratulatory *Nihonjinron* literature that tended to stress Japan's uniqueness, with strong overtones of innate supremacy. Many westerners seemed to agree, and furiously started studying aspects of Japan such as its management style in order to improve their own nations/companies. A major accolade came in 1979 when a Harvard professor wrote a best-selling book that referred to Japan as Number One and also to the lessons it could teach America. The pupil had now become the master.

Unfortunately, Japan's success led in the 1980s to arrogance among many Japanese and to envy and frustration among many westerners. Japanese neo-nationalism, defiance, and clear sense of racial supremacy—exacerbated by comments even at prime ministerial level—alarmed the world, and Asia in particular. For its part the Japanese government-business combination seemed locked into a continued path of economic expansion, even though many of the public were starting to grow angry over the lack of infrastructural reform. Japan was Number One as an economic superpower, but its people often lived in Third World conditions. International attempts to address Japan's economic domination by causing the upvaluing of the yen and the release of cheap capital in fact made matters worse, as Japanese 'Bubble money' now bought up property around the world. In the late 1980s, Japan's establishment was the target of anger among westerners, Asians, and many of its own public, especially when the public learned of major scandals that saw politicians lining their own pockets. The accession of a new emperor in 1989 brought no change, adding to frustrations.

The situation was reaching crisis point when, perhaps fortunately, the economy collapsed from around 1990. It took with it many of the pillars of *Nihonjinron* arrogance. For example, dismissals of managers showed how exaggerated claims of innate harmony and loyalty had been. This economic downturn deflated tensions with the west, but made the Japanese public even more upset, for it now seemed that infrastructural reform would be postponed yet again. All their hard work and sacrifice to make Japan an economic superpower now seemed in jeopardy.

Public frustration over this, combined with ongoing government scandals, led to a historic toppling of the LDP in 1993, and other expressions of public anger. However, as a result of the continuing economic recession, combined with other events such as the Kōbe earthquake of 1995 and the AUM gas attacks of the same year, as well as broader concerns such as the ageing of society, public anger seems to have been displaced by public anxiety. With an almost fatalistic resignation the public of the late 1990s have become politically apathetic. The LDP are back in power, and scandals continue. No one in power seems to have any real vision or sense of direction or purpose.

As Japan faces the new millennium, it is vital that it revives a sense of purpose, and taps once again into appropriate traditional strengths such as its people's determination to achieve and willingness to learn. Taking on the challenge of making Japan a 'lifestyle superpower' in tune with the present age would seem one way of achieving this, and of continuing to earn the respect of the world. But among other things, this will entail making proper peace with Asian nations by facing up to Japanese behaviour of the past.

Key developments of the period are summarised in Table 6.1.

Table 6.1   Key developments from end World War Two to late 1990s

Development	Time
Occupation aims for demilitarised and democratised Utopia	1945–7
Occupation changes course in view of Cold War, aims at strengthening Japan's economy as a free world bastion	1947/8–52
Post-Occupation conservatives make Occupation reforms more Japanese, but build on its economic foundations	1952 on
High-speed guided growth, unease at home assuaged by material gains	early 50s–early 70s
Recognition abroad and pride at home over economic achievements, despite problems with infrastructure	late 60s–late 70s
Growth slower but continuing	mid-70s–mid-80s
National pride turns to nationalistic arrogance, western respect turns to anger, public also angry over poor lifestyle and corruption	1980s
Japan dominates world with Bubble economy, situation at home and abroad nears crisis	late 1980s
Economy collapses, pride/arrogance deflated, tensions with west reduced	early 90s
Recession continues, corruption continues, public anger vented politically	early–mid-90s
Recession continues, corruption continues, Japan's direction uncertain, public anger displaced by public anxiety and political apathy, relations with Asia over past still tense	mid–late 90s

Key values and practices of the period are summarised in Table 6.2. Most of them are once again continuations of past values.

Table 6.2   Key values and practices from end World War Two to late 1990s

---

- determination to succeed
- continuing national pride and nationalistic spirit
- willingness to learn from stronger powers
- resilience
- single-mindedness of purpose
- suspicion and unease towards unrestrained democracy
- obedience to authority (albeit often under duress)
- awareness of importance of economy
- awareness of importance of education to shape world-view
- pragmatic ability to mix old and new, native and foreign
- importance of legitimisation of power by high authority
- partial revival of sense of Japanese racial supremacy
- lack of enthusiasm for socialism
- preference for conservatism
- tendency to get carried away by emotion over reason
- tendency for vision and focus to become too narrow
- partial revival of fatalism
- relatively easy-going morality (despite occasional anger at excesses)

Through a mix of good fortune, good tactics, and traditional strengths, Japan became one of the world's greatest ever economic superpowers. Its challenge now is to earn recognition as a superpower in a broader sense, in tune with the internationalised, postmodernised values of the present day. It must join the world, not seek to dominate it.

Conclusion: Lessons for Aspiring Superpowers

The term 'miracle' has been applied by westerners more than once to Japan's modern history. It has been used to describe its achievements in Meiji, when in just half a century it developed from an obscure and isolated land of paddy fields to a major imperial power. It was used again just a few decades later, to describe the nation's even more rapid postwar rise from the ashes of defeat to become by some measures the wealthiest on the planet, and by any measures a huge economic superpower.

However, true miracles have no logical explanation. Japan's achievements do. Pure chance has certainly played its part, but more often than not Japan's achievements have come about through its response to circumstance. That is, in a sense Japan helps make its own luck, capitalising on good fortune and overcoming adversity. In general its pattern of response to circumstance has been based on values and practices rooted in history.

Paradoxically, though a tendency to fall back on traditional values might seem to constrain Japan's variety of response, one of its key traditional values is pragmatism. This entails responding to the particulars of a situation on a flexible and practical case-by-case basis as opposed to being shackled by some abstract set of principles that predetermine a course of action. Japan has had certain constraining codes of principle, such as the much exaggerated and idealised 'way of the warrior', but in general the Japanese—including many warriors in practice—have preferred pragmatism over rigid idealism. This gives them a certain freedom of movement at individual level, and at a national level minimises internal conflict between idealists and allows the nation to present a relatively united front. Ever since its earliest days in the Yamato period there has been almost no religious conflict in Japan, and very little in the way of moral censure. Instead there has been a lot of give-and-take on matters that often divide westerners, a mutual tolerance which among other things has made it easier for individuals in Japan to work together.

There have occasionally been forces that seem to be opposed to pragmatism, such as intolerance, absolutes, and ideals, but these have not dominated its history. The Tokugawa regime, for example, showed great intolerance towards those who defied its policies of orthodoxy, but this was generally confined to outward form. If outward behaviour met acceptable standards, there was scope permitted for considerable freedom at a less formal level. It was, again paradoxically, a type of intolerance prepared to compromise in practice under certain circumstances. Absolutes such as reverence for the emperor in Meiji and prewar Japan have been the exception rather than the rule. In general things are seen as relative, and it is subtle shades of grey that usually prevail over simplistic black and white. For example, the absolute nature of the Christian God is one major reason why the religion has not taken root in Japan, though it is tolerated. Christians have their causes to fight for and their idealised goals to aim for, and so too—like everyone—do the Japanese, pragmatists though they be. However, in Japan's case there has almost always been great scope for compromise and flexibility on the way to achieving those aims and winning those causes.

In particular, there has been a readiness to try out different things, mixing old and new, native and foreign, till the best mix is achieved. Moreover, the Japanese seem to have a great ability to 'Japanise' the new and foreign to make them more easily blended with tradition and more acceptable. The Meiji state-builders exemplified this, mixing new foreign elements such as democracy and western technology with old methods of Tokugawa authoritarianism and even older practices in state creation from the Yamato-Nara era, which in some cases were in turn adapted from Chinese practices. The Tokugawa shōgunate had itself drawn on earlier policies by Hideyoshi and Nobunaga, who had in turn borrowed some of their ideas from Ashikaga Yoshimitsu.

Learning from others is one of Japan's great strengths. At a national level this is particularly so when those others seem to have something stronger or better than Japan does. It has adopted, adapted, and frequently improved, making the strengths of a potential competitor or foe into its own strengths. This is not just a case of 'know thy enemy': it is a case of knowing what makes thy enemy a threat and then using their own strengths against them. More than 1,000 years ago Japan learned much from China, to the point where it was no longer a vassal nation but considered itself a superior one. It repeated the process to some extent in the sixteenth century, learning the use of firearms from the west. In the Meiji period it furiously studied western imperial powers till it became one itself. After the war it learned much from America—admittedly with little choice to start with—but went on beyond its compulsory lessons to the point where it reversed roles and became recognised as the master.

The enthusiasm to learn from others is part of a broader respect for the power of learning and education in general. This has always been the case, but particularly obviously since the Tokugawa period. If you are educated, you can achieve things better than if you are not. This is beneficial both to the individual and the nation. From the state's point of view, it is true you also become potentially more difficult to control and co-ordinate, but this can be overcome by controlling knowledge itself, so that what you learn is 'safe'. The Meiji and early Shōwa governments showed clearly that they recognised the importance of controlling education, and the government since late Shōwa has displayed a not dissimilar awareness.

Education as a means of achieving success is a reflection of a general wish to achieve. This dates particularly from the Meiji period, when successism that combined both individual and national interests was greatly encouraged. However, an achievement-orientation is also seen earlier, in, for example, the dynamics of Tokugawa merchants, the material drive of the Tokugawa peasant, or earlier still in the often ruthless ambitions of sundry medieval warlords. Amongst the nation's leaders, it is seen as early as the Yamato period.

Fortunately for Japan, its rulers have not found it too difficult to merge individual and national interests, for the national cause has always been a strong one. Ever since Japan was founded there has been a clear wish to make the nation strong and respected—at least respected by China, for awareness of the wider world was relatively limited till the arrival of Europeans in the mid-sixteenth century. Europeans' arrival stimulated further a sense of national identity, aided by insularity and a strong insider–outsider mentality (which was itself reinforced by Tokugawa policies that made strangers a source of possible punishment). The return of westerners in the mid-nineteenth century brought forth a much stronger and more widespread type of nationalism, with the public at large committed to making their nation great and powerful. Indoctrination helped, but the buds of nationalism were there already in most of the public, brought to flower by a sense of crisis. The sense of national crisis soon turned to a sense of national pride. The fact that national pride returned so quickly after Japan's setback by defeat in the war is testimony not only to the depth of national spirit but also to the Japanese quality of resilience.

Japan's rulers have also benefited from having a public relatively willing to tone down individual interests for some greater cause. Japan's groupism has been much exaggerated, but it is true that there has been a greater awareness shown in Japan than in many nations of the strength of the group. It is no good having a team of strong horses if they do not actually work as a team, and end up all pulling in different directions, as so often seems to happen in the west. Moreover, every team needs a leader, a co-ordinator, and this too is something the Japanese have recognised. There have been cases in Japan, especially in times of crisis, of extremely powerful and dominant leaders, but in general their preference is for one who can bring a team together, a skilled pragmatist who can compromise here and balance interests there, often keeping a low profile, and get the job done. This has been helped by Japan's preference for a distinction between formal authority and actual power. It is often the faceless people behind the scenes who make most of the decisions, benefiting from a greater freedom of movement than that permitted to those formally in authority.

For these various reasons western-style democracy and concepts of individual rights have only ever had limited appeal in Japan. Of course the Japanese, like anyone, have preferred freedom to repression, but they have shown a greater readiness than most westerners to accept limits. The survival of the group means the survival of at least the majority of its individual members. It is in the interests of each individual to preserve the group—one main reason why harmony has become such an ideal. But the group can be destroyed if any one individual is allowed too much freedom. This will necessarily impinge on the freedoms of the others, and destroy the balance that holds the group together. The western world has the same sort of idea in theory, as seen for example in Rousseau's 'social contract', but in practice—as if to convince itself of the wonders of democracy and equality—it often seems to prioritise the interests of minorities, especially if they are seen as somehow disadvantaged. Japan has never done that. The only 'minority' it has ever really respected is the numerically minor ruling elite.

This does not all mean that Japan has never had its moments of naked self-interest. The medieval samurai is a classic example of this. But it does mean that over time it has found muted—or better still, guided— self-interest to be better. The self-interest of the medieval period was harshly suppressed, at least in terms of its naked expression, by the Tokugawa regime. This was a particularly important period for the Japanese, who became accustomed to obeying authority and to the idea of real collective responsibility (though in theory this had been the legal norm for many centuries before). Open pursuit of self-interest was revived during the subsequent Meiji period, but harnessed by the government for the good of the nation, to achieve the best mix of democracy and authoritarianism. Of course the degree of authoritarianism was not to the liking of some Japanese, especially during the prewar years, but in general there has been acceptance of the fact that one can have a surfeit of democracy. There was genuine widespread sympathy for Yoshida Shigeru when he expressed such a comment about the early Occupation reforms. There has been a genuine willingness among the Japanese public to allow the nation's leaders a larger and more intrusive role than in many western nations—though that is being put to the test in the 1990s.

Confucianism, with its ideals of harmony and order and 'knowing one's place', has played a significant part in shaping Japanese attitudes. It seems a basic part of human nature—at least in the male-dominated historical world—to be ambitious and competitive and enjoy status. Confucius knew this, and so do the Japanese. Throughout their history they have valued hierarchy and ranking. They are of the view rather that it is enforced equality among unequal beings that is unnatural and a source of unhappiness and frustration. It can dampen ambition and undermine achievement, and it is not helpful to the nation to have weak people treated as the equal of strong people. The Japanese have long recognised inequalities openly, rather than trying to mask them and pretending they do not exist. This was one reason Darwinism appealed so much. At a national level, they are quite happy to take on the rest of the world to prove themselves the fittest, the nation who should top the hierarchy. If they lose out, then they will learn from whichever nation bested them and keep trying till eventually they make Number One—for they feel that that is 'their place'.

Within the nation, however, hierarchical competition could easily promote an unhealthy type of individualism, so competition is waged in safer, more guided ways, particularly in education. Unlike the situation so frequently encountered in the western world, those who top the class in school are not put down as 'nerds' or elitists—they are genuinely respected. A hard worker is similarly respected. There is almost none of the mentality often found in the west of trying to get away with as little as possible. A shirker is treated with contempt. It is in such terms of winning respect, both by peers and superiors, that the hierarchical competition is usually waged within Japan, and ranking of a type not always detected by westerners is conferred. It is a type of hierarchy that strengthens the group rather than weakens it.

Japan's main strengths, then, may be summarised as:

- pragmatism—especially flexibility and an ability to compromise and adapt;

- a respect for the power of learning, particularly learning the strengths of others;
- a respect for ambition and achievement, including hard work;
- a strong sense of nationalism;
- an appreciation of the strength of the group;
- an awareness of the importance of having limits on individual rights and freedoms;
- an acceptance of authority;
- an acceptance of hierarchy and inequality among individuals.

Of course, playing to national strengths is not always an easy game. Strengths are often two-edged swords, and at the same time potential weaknesses. Proper balance and fine-tuning are important. For example, national pride can very easily become nationalistic arrogance and chauvinism. Achievement-orientation can become ruthlessness, or a single-mindedness of purpose that can in turn become a narrowness of vision and an inability to know when to stop. Acceptance of authority and of limits on individual rights can lead to totalitarianism. Acceptance of hierarchy can lead to abuse of 'inferiors'. A readiness to learn can be abused by indoctrination. Learning from others can become a problem when there seem to be no others left to learn from. Pragmatism can lead to a loss of sense of direction, and in a moral sense to an unhealthy tolerance of corruption. Focus on the group can lead to a lack of responsibility at individual level.

Japan has discovered all of these negative potentials at some point or other, particularly during the war and to a lesser extent again in the 1980s and 90s. It has other weaknesses too, such as a sense of fatalism that can on the one hand suddenly undermine achievement-orientation and on the other permit ideas of racial supremacy—provided it is ultimately Japan's—as somehow ordained by destiny. Its lack of an obvious sense of evil may well have helped its pragmatic approach to life but it has also made it easier for 'undesirability' to be judged in other terms. These 'other terms' have, at a fairly harmless level, often simply meant breach of the rules, but a deeper level they have at times meant impurity. This has in the past combined with Japan's high degree of homogeneity to produce a belief that Japanese are pure, while the rest of the world is impure.

Japan has had its problems, certainly, but what nation has not? It is having a particularly problem-plagued time at the moment as it struggles to re-orient itself as a different style of superpower, one that has no other obvious models to learn from—at least not of the traditional type.

In the present day, many of its traditional strengths may not be appropriate, though some will. A respect for learning, for example, would seem a timeless quality.

Despite the war and the recent dent in its image as an economic superpower, Japan has earned an indelible place in history for its remarkable achievements. Vogel may have overstated the case, but there are still many lessons that the world can learn from this extraordinary nation—from its mistakes, as well as its successes.

Notes

1 FROM THE STONE AGE TO STATEHOOD

1. For example, the Tsuchigumo people, or 'earth spiders', in Chapter 52 of the *Kojiki*.
2. Philippi 68, p. 17.
3. These three episodes are from the *Kojiki*, Chapters 22, 21, and 79 respectively.
4. See Okamura (92, p. 50) regarding claims of a million years, Katayama (96, p. 19) regarding claims of 500,000 years, and Pearson (92, p. 38) regarding claims of 200,000 years.
5. Pearson 92, p. 64.
6. See Bowles 83, p. 34, Pearson 92, p. 273, and Farris 85, p. 43 and p. 47, regarding life expectancy.
7. Pearson 92, p. 35. For a discussion of the development of the discipline see Barnes 90.
8. Until a very recent find of 15,000-year-old pottery at Shinonouchi in Nagano, the oldest pottery was dated at 10,000 BC, and this marked the start-date of the period. Ceramic figurines—as opposed to vessels—of twice this age have been found in eastern Europe.
   Opinion is divided as to whether Jōmon pottery is a local Japanese invention (for example Kidder 93, p. 56), or was introduced from the mainland from a source yet to be discovered (for example Aikens and Higuchi 82, p. 114 and p. 182).
9. Such is the view of Morimoto Tetsurō, an expert on comparative civilisation. He is opposed by scholars such as Sahara Makoto, curator of the National Museum of History. See the report in the *Japan Times*, Weekly International Edition, 10–16 November 1997.
10. Tsukada 86. See also Barnes 93a, pp. 89–91.
11. *Japan Times*, Weekly International Edition, 15–21 September 1997.
12. Higuchi 86, p. 123. Rice-grains have been found in Kyūshū dating back to about 1,250 BC, but the earliest evidence of actual cultivation is around 1,000 BC.
13. Katayama 96, p. 22.
14. See Okazaki 93, p. 271, and Barnes 93a, pp. 168–70.
15. To try to reflect the changes over time it is often broken into sub-periods. However, new discoveries mean that divisions between sub-periods become blurred and new sub-periods are added, producing a confusing picture. For example, 'Middle Jōmon', which refers to approximately 3,500 BC–2,000 BC, was coined when the Jōmon period was deemed to start around 7,000 BC but is now very far removed from the actual middle of the period. To avoid confusion I deliberately omit reference to sub-periods.
16. Regarding population see Kidder 93, pp. 63–8, Kidder 83, p. 74, and Farris 85, p. 3.

17. Kidder 93, pp. 70–6.
18. See Pearson 92, p. 28, regarding views on egalitarianism, and pp. 81–2 regarding hierarchy.
19. Pearson 92, p. 63.
20. For a bewildering range of heights, see Pearson 92, p. 152, Kidder 77, p. 32, Barnes 93a, p. 77, and Katayama 96, pp. 22–3. Katayama also believes that skeletal heights increased during the period by some 2 cm through micro-evolution.
21. Between 1900 and 1993 heights of 20-year-olds increased dramatically from 160.9 to 171.4 cm for males and from 147.9 to 158.4 cm for females. (See *Asahi Shimbun Japan Almanac 1997*, p. 218.) Presumably this reflects greatly improved diet, health, and general living conditions.
22. See Ossenberger 86 and Dodo 86, and also Katayama 96 and Pearson 92 (p. 63).
23. Interestingly, despite their northern associations, it seems the Ainu and the particular Jōmon stock they represent can be linked back to an ancient Mongoloid stock originally from *southern* China/*southeast* Asia. (See Ossenberger 86, pp. 211–12, and also Dodo 86, pp. 157–8, and Katayama 96, p. 24.)
24. See the *Japan Times*, Weekly International Edition, 7–13 April and 19–25 May 1997 regarding legal and governmental recognition.
25. See Bowles 83, p. 34, Pearson 92, pp. 129–31, Bleed 83, p. 160, and Katayama 96, pp. 23–8 for brief discussion of these differing views. See also Hanihara 91. As an example of divided opinion, Aikens and Higuchi (82, p. 180) comment that continental immigrants were few in number, while Pearson (92, p. 131) remarks that a considerable population probably arrived. It was once felt possible that there was no real immigration at all and that gradual evolution could explain differences between Jōmon and Yayoi (for example H. Suzuki 69). However, recent genetic research—in addition to obvious physical differences—confirms that immigration took place. (See Katayama 96, pp. 23–8.)

    There is also some disagreement on the exact route the immigrants took within Japan, but wider acceptance as to the route by which they arrived in the country, which is felt to be via Korea. However, it is not clear whether the point of origin was Korea itself or China.
26. Higuchi 86, p. 123. Some experts (for example Pearson 92, p. 131) now believe rice cultivation to have begun in earnest around 400 BC, and start the Yayoi period from this earlier date.
27. Barnes 93a (p. 185), Kidder 83 and 93, and Pearson 92. For detailed discussion of cultural development in Hokkaidō during the ancient historical periods see Aikens and Higuchi 82.
28. The above description draws particularly on the *Wei Chih* account discussed later in the text, but also on Kidder 93, pp. 97–8.
29. Kidder 93, p. 106.
30. Wa was originally written with a character used by the Chinese with the uncomplimentary meaning of 'land of dwarfs', and possibly pronounced Wo rather than Wa. The character now used for Wa means 'harmony', and is also able to be read in Japanese as 'Yamato'. See entry 7153 (p. 1062) in *Mathews' Chinese–English Dictionary*.

31. Okazaki 93, p. 275. Lo-lang was established in 108 BC.
32. A summary translation of the relevant parts of the *Wei Chih* is given in Tsunoda et al., 64, vol. 1, pp. 4–7.
33. From the *Wei Chih*. See Tsunoda 64, vol. 1, p. 6.
34. The *Hou Han Shu* (History of the Later Han), compiled ca 445, refers to a tributary mission from the King of Na (Nu), a kingdom in northwest Kyūshū, at this time. See Okazaki 93, p. 280, and particularly the translation of the relevant part of the *Hou Han Shou* in Tsunoda 64, vol. 1, p. 7. An inscribed seal given to the envoys of AD 57 by the Chinese emperor was discovered in 1784 in Fukuoka Prefecture, and is generally accepted by scholars as genuine.
35. For discussion of the controversy see, for example, Kidder 93, pp. 97–9, Okazaki 93, pp. 283–4, and Ledyard 83a. For a recent overview, see Edwards 96. (Edwards himself favours Nara.) The recent discovery of a major Yayoi power base at Yoshinogari in Saga Prefecture in northwest Kyūshū has added some weight to the Kyūshū theory, but not enough to overturn the general preference for the Nara location. (See translator's note to Okazaki 93, pp. 284–6, and see Sahara 92 for a detailed description of the site.) Himiko's tomb, obviously, has not yet been discovered.
36. Higuchi 86, p. 122.
37. Aikens and Higuchi 82, p. 334.
38. Philippi 68, p. 208, and Kidder 93, p. 105.
39. The theory was first proposed in the late 1940s by the historian Egami Namio, and now has a number of variants. It is summarised in Ledyard 83b. Ledyard 75 has advanced one variant of the theory. Critics include Edwards 83, and Aikens and Higuchi 82, p. 336, but Kidder (77, p. 57) appears to give considerable support to it. In recent years Wontack Hong has advanced another variant, in which an invasion was launched by a king of Paekche (one of the kingdoms of Korea), leading to the unification of Yamato Japan by the year 390. See Hong 94, in which he also reviews earlier theories.
   The 'horse-rider' theory is not widely supported, but it has not been totally disproved either. On the one hand there is still no convincing alternative explanation for the abundance of fourth- and fifth-century horse-related items found in Japan, items of foreign manufacture. On the other hand, it is surprising the *Kojiki* and *Nihon Shoki* do not make more mention of horses.
40. Aikens and Higuchi 82, p. 335.
41. See, for example, Mushakōji 76, who refers to the approach as '*awase*' (amalgamation or adaptation). See also van Wolferen 89, who argues that the whole Japanese 'system' is based on a meshing of mutually accommodated interests. Kitahara 89 (a psychologist) describes the preferred Japanese attitude towards potential threat—throughout history—as one of 'identification with the aggressor', attempting to incorporate rather than confront any strong point of that threat. On the other hand, Japanese history also shows that when a foe was considered weak, little if any attempt was made to avoid confrontation.

42.   The chiefs of major kin-groups, which were known as *uji*, were given ranks (*kabane*) and assigned 'portfolios', such as taxation, military matters, etc. The *uji* themselves were ranked. Elite *uji* leaders formed a ministerial class known as *omi*, while *muraji* were a lower, more executive class. Actual provision of goods and services was by occupational groups of varying status known as *tomo* or *be*, many of whom were Korean immigrants. Below the *be* at the bottom of the hierarchy were the *nuhi*, or slaves.
43.   Piggott 89.
44.   The following is based on the translation in Keene 68, p. 31.
45.   Although the scholars were Korean they wrote in Chinese (Korean Hangul is a later script). Written Chinese was subsequently adapted over several centuries to form the basis of written Japanese. Physical evidence of Chinese writing can be found in Japan inscribed on imported items as early as the first century AD, and from very early on there were various individuals in Japan who could read and write Chinese. However, it is Paekche scholars of the fifth century who are credited with its systematic introduction.
46.   Though Buddhism originated in India, not China, and was moreover brought into Japan through Korea rather than from China directly, to all intents and purposes it was seen at that time in Japan as something Chinese rather than Indian or Korean. See Reischauer 64, p. 18.
47.   Okazaki 93, pp. 297–312, discusses the Korean kingdoms in detail. Barnes (93b, p. 47) asserts that Kaya was never a Japanese colony.
48.   Politically, Confucius (Kung Fu-tzu, ca 551–479 BC) advocated a paternalistic government in which the sovereign is benevolent and honourable and the subjects are respectful and obedient. His stress on harmony, hierarchy, and proper order made his ideology an appealing one for rulers wanting to maximise stability.
49.   The text is given in Tsunoda 64, vol. 1, pp. 48–9.
50.   Kiley 83 discusses the *ritsuryō* system in detail. See also Oda 92, pp. 14–16, and Haley 91, pp. 29–30.
51.   Kiley 83, p. 322.
52.   Farris 85, p. 8.
53.   For detailed discussion see Farris 85. Immunity against smallpox was to take almost a thousand years.
54.   In his poem 'Leaving a Banquet' he writes that he will leave because his wife will be waiting and his children may be crying. See Katō 81, p. 76.
55.   The following is based on the translation in Bownas and Thwaite 64, pp. 36–7.
56.   Pearson 92, p. 29, and Barnes 93b, p. 45.
57.   Pearson 92, p. 215.
58.   See Amino 92 and Morris-Suzuki 96. It should be appreciated that at the time places such as Hokkaidō and Okinawa were not part of Japan.

2   OF COURTIERS AND WARRIORS

1.   For example, Naniwa (present-day Osaka) in 645 and Fujiwara (south of Nara) in 694.

2. In fact, some of the oldest surviving printed material in the world is found in Buddhist charms printed by the Nara court around 770. See Reischauer and Craig 79, p. 20.
3. Reischauer 88, p. 45.
4. Examinations nowadays have a built-in safeguard by being based heavily on rote learning and multiple-choice format. The present-day system allows for those with merit to succeed, but ensures that they are conformist and unlikely to threaten established elite preferences.
5. Haley 91, pp. 29–30, and Oda 92, p. 15.
6. These were Meishō (r. 1630–43) and Go-Sakuramachi (r. 1762–70). They both reigned in a period when the position of emperor was dominated by the shōgun, or military ruler.
7. Takeuchi 83, p. 163.
8. See Farris 85, Chapters 3 and 4. Irrigation was a particular problem.
9. This and other epidemics are discussed in detail in Farris 85, Chapter 2.
10. Farris 85, p. 68.
11. Torao 93 discusses land and taxation in detail. See also Farris 85, Chapters 3 and 4.
12. Based on the translation in Keene 68, p. 44.
13. Based on the translation in Keene 68, p. 43.
14. Takeuchi 83, p. 164, and also Torao 93, p. 415.
15. See Seidensticker's 1981 translation, p. 418.
16. Reischauer and Craig 79, p. 33.
17. Reischauer and Craig 79, p. 29.
18. E. Satō 74, pp. 95–7.
19. Kiley 74, p. 110.
20. Hurst 76, Chapter 11.
21. See also Morris 79, p. 25, who discusses the 'cultural emancipation' from China.
22. See W. and H. McCullough 80, vol. 1, p. 10. No Heian woman wrote in Chinese, and women were by no means respected for any knowledge of Chinese. Intriguing though this is, the reasons are unfortunately not clear.
23. It is contained in the *Kokinshū* (Old and New Collection) imperial anthology of 905. The translation is my own.
24. N. Suzuki 83, p. 231.
25. Owing to the proliferation of imperial descendants, which caused both financial strain and sometimes difficulties over succession, distant relatives were excluded from the dynastic lineage in a practice known as 'dynastic shedding'. From 814 this practice was extended in Japan even to sons and daughters, in no small part due to the fact that Emperor Saga (r. 809–23) had fifty children. Of these, thirty-three were given the surname Minamoto, and thereafter all 'shed' members of the imperial line were given either the name Minamoto or Taira. Details of this are given in Hurst 83, pp. 176–7.
26. Cholley 78, p. 75.
27. There is much disagreement among experts as to what exactly happened. For example, Cholley (78, p. 75) supports the 'threat' theory. Shinoda (78, pp. 82–3) does not, but admits that Kiyomori's sparing of the children seems inexplicable. Maison and Caiger (72, p. 98) feel that Kiyomori was

simply susceptible to feminine appeal, raising the distinct possibility that Tokiwa may have taken the initiative in offering herself to Kiyomori. In any event, all experts agree that it was a fatal decision by Kiyomori.

28.   The principle of punishment or even execution of an entire family for the actions of an individual member was sanctioned both in the *ritsuryō* (see Kiley 83, p. 328) and in legal conventions dating back to at least the third century (according to the *Wei Chih*). It was to continue till as late as the nineteenth century.

29.   From the *Heike Monogatari* (Tale of the Taira), one of a number of *gunki monogatari* (military tales) popular in the twelfth century. It is available in translation (H. McCullough 88). The material here is from Keene 68, p. 176.

30.   This should not be confused with social responsibility. Throughout history, many Japanese have even taken their own lives (or in modern times resigned) when their position makes them symbolically accountable for the failure of their group, or in similar circumstances when a course of self-punitive action is strongly prescribed by social convention.

31.   See the translation by Sadler 70, p. 7.

32.   From Keene 68, p. 187.

33.   From La Fleur 78, p. 57.

34.   The title had been in use for some centuries on a temporary basis, for generals on campaigns, but Yoritomo was the first to use it permanently.

35.   It is, for example, the major theme of Haley 91. See also Massarella 90, pp. 25–6, and J. Hall 68, p. 41.

36.   Gay 85, p. 49.

37.   Reischauer and Craig 79, p. 46.

38.   See J. Hall 68 for detailed discussion of feudalism and its applicability to Japan.

39.   H. McCullough 71, p. 18.

40.   Butler 78, p. 91.

41.   See Hori 83, on which much of the following account draws.

42.   In terms of cavalry tactics, the Japanese had little or no experience, as their mounted warriors generally fought singly, not in groups. The matter of weaponry raises one of the most intriguing yet ignored questions in Japanese history. Contemporary scroll-paintings indicate unmistakably that the Mongols had cannon, albeit primitive. However, I have been unable to find any explanation of why the Japanese did not attempt to produce their own versions. Most histories simply state that firearms (a term referring to hand-held weapons) were first brought to Japan by the Portuguese in the mid-sixteenth century. Given that the Japanese of that later time immediately developed their own firearms in an early display of the adaptive skills for which they are widely recognised, and given the importance of preparing better for a second Mongol attack, it is mystifying that no attempt appears to have been made to adapt, or even simply imitate, Mongol gunpowder-based weaponry.

43.   Shinoda 83, p. 171.

44.   Collcutt 93, p. 60.

45. Varley 83, p. 192.
46. See Katō 81, p. 301, who comes to the same conclusion.
47. The following draws on H. McCullough 59, p. xx.
48. See Massarella 90, p. 32.
49. Massarella 90, p. 32.
50. Gay 85, p. 58.
51. From the translation in Keene 68, p. 299.
52. For more details see Massarella 90, pp. 23–4, Elisonas 91, p. 302, and Cortazzi 90, p. 130.
53. Cooper 65, p. ix.
54. See Cortazzi 90, p. 121, who also gives a number of other analogies.
55. For example, at Nagashima in 1574. See Elison 83a, p. 63.
56. In his destruction in 1571 of the Tendai Sect's Enryakuji Temple on Mount Hiei (in Kyōto), as many as 10,000 people were encircled and systematically massacred, including not only priests but women and children. See Maison and Caiger 72, p. 143. Contemporary accounts are found in Tsunoda 64, vol. 1, pp. 305–8, and (by a European) in Cooper 65, pp. 98–9. There were also many casualties in his capture in 1580 of the Jōdo Shin Sect's castle stronghold at Ishiyama Honganji in Osaka.
57. Cooper 65, pp. 101–2.
58. Elison 83a, p. 64. Nobunaga did briefly accept high offices from the court in 1577 but resigned from them after only a few months.
59. Nobunaga had bought 500 matchlocks for his troops while still a teenage commander in 1549, just six years after their introduction by the Portuguese. However, despite refinements by Japanese craftsmen, their effective use in battle was for some years impeded by such problems as the delay in loading and firing. A number of other *daimyō*, such as Tanegashima Tokitaka (1528–79) and Katsuyori's father Takeda Shingen (1521–73), were similarly enthusiastic about firearms, but Nobunaga seems to have been the most effective user. The battle is depicted, though with some dramatic licence, in Akira Kurosawa's famous film *Kagemusha*. For a detailed account of the battle, see Turnbull 87, pp. 79–94.

    The mystery still remains why the Japanese did not attempt to produce firearms three centuries earlier, when they saw primitive gunpowder-based weapons being used by the Mongols.
60. A contemporary account of this incident is given in Cooper 65, p. 103.
61. 'Sword Hunt' was a misleading term, since all types of weapons were confiscated. A surprising number of firearms were found. The edict is given in Tsunoda 64, vol. 1, pp. 319–20.
62. The edict is given in Tsunoda 64, vol. 1, pp. 321–2.
63. The captain of the Spanish ship *San Felipe*, which was wrecked on the Shikoku coast late in 1596, had apparently spread a rumour suggesting they were an advance guard, but Hideyoshi's actions still seem extreme. See Massarella 90, pp. 45–6.
64. Cooper 65, pp. 111–13.
65. From 1590, at Hideyoshi's instigation, the size of fiefs was measured in *koku*, a yield of rice equivalent to 182 litres or just over 5 bushels, which was supposed to represent the requirements of one person for one year.

3   THE CLOSED COUNTRY

1. A translation is given in Tsunoda 64, vol. 1, pp. 326–9.
2. See Hearn 1904, p. 193.
3. T. Satō 90, p. 41. See also Hanley and Yamamura 77, pp. 89–90. The Keian Proclamation of 1649, issued under Ieyasu's grandson Iemitsu (shōgun 1623–51), is a good example of such prescriptions.
4. The system was a slight modification of the Chinese system, particularly with regard to the primacy of the warrior.
5. Impurity was defined in theory on religious grounds, especially as Shintō *kegare* (pollution). This concept dated back to before the Nara period and mostly referred to physical dirt or death or serious illness, but in practice also came to include a wide range of 'undesirable things', including, in some cases, simply being an outsider and/or a threat. Menstruation was also included in *kegare*, meaning that women were generally considered unclean—though obviously they were not removed from mainstream society. They were, however, banned entry to sacred places such as Mount Fuji (and in fact are still banned from some mountains even today). This is despite the fact that the paramount Shintō deity, Amaterasu, is female.
6. Adoption between classes was far from unknown, and wealth could also work wonders for status. The distinction between artisan and merchant was always weak, and in the latter part of the period the distinction between peasant and artisan also became blurred, especially as a result of part-time work in both spheres of activity. There was even some blurring between the theoretical extremes of samurai and merchant, especially in the early days when foreign trade was allowed. The shōgunate and most *daimyō* used 'favoured merchants', who in those early days at least were of samurai class despite their merchant activities. Later in the period some merchants were also allowed certain samurai privileges such as wearing swords. In the final days of the period too there were again cases of samurai engaging in merchant activity. And throughout the period there was a degree of blurring of the class distinction between peasant and samurai in that village headmen were also often allowed the samurai privilege of wearing swords.
7. Bolitho 83, p. 53.
8. Nakai and McClain 91, pp. 544–5, and Reischauer and Craig 79, p. 86.
9. See Cooper 65, p. 154.
10. Carletti was actually describing the years 1597–8 but his comments apply equally to punishments a few years later. See Cooper 65, pp. 156–8, and see also Cooper's related note pp. 166–7.
11. See Cooper 65, p. 159.
12. Cooper 65, notes p. 167.
13. See also Cooper 65, notes p. 165.
14. This also relates to the distinction between in-group and out-group, embodied in the Japanese concepts of *uchi* (inside or home) and *soto* (outside) that are considered basic to Japanese group formation and perceptions of belonging and identification. These have been widely discussed by many commentators. See for example Nakane 70, or Bachnik and Quinn 94.

15. Befu 68, p. 314.
16. See Haley 91, esp. pp. 57–62, and Haley 92, pp. 42–3.
17. See Massarella 90, pp. 359–63.
18. See, for example, the various contemporary accounts given in Chapter 22 ('Persecution') of Cooper 65, pp. 383–98 (esp. p. 390).
19. Elison 83b, p. 98.
20. Massarella 90, pp. 343–4.
21. A detailed account of the Dutch and their Deshima base is given in Boxer 68. Another predominantly non-Catholic nation, England, may also have been allowed to continue trade with Japan if the shōgunate had not over-estimated the extent of English Catholicism—possibly being deliberately misled by Dutchmen keen to retain exclusive trade privileges. See Massarella 90, pp. 359–63.
22. The exceptions included some intercourse with Korea, where a *wakan* (Japan House) was located in Pusan. There were a surprisingly large number of Japanese overseas at the time of this ban. Japanese traders (and pirates) operated as far afield as the Indian Ocean and the Arafura Sea just north of Australia. There were also many Japanese actually residing overseas. There was a community of some 3,000 Japanese in the Philippines, there were numerous Japanese in Siam (Thailand), and Japanese residents as far away as Seram (in present-day southeast Indonesia). These people were eventually absorbed into local communities. See Bolitho 93, p. 69, for further illustration of the scale of Japanese overseas activity at the time, and similarly Massarella 90, esp. pp. 135–6. See also Frei 91, esp. pp. 14–15. Frei estimates that some 100,000 Japanese left Japan's shores between 1604 and 1635, of whom some 10,000 may have taken up permanent residence overseas.
23. The seal was popularly called *maru* (circle), which is still used today as a suffix in the name of Japanese ships (rather like the English prefix SS- or HMS-).
24. Morris-Suzuki 96, p. 83.
25. Morris-Suzuki 96, p. 83.
26. Many others followed him, including in modern times. One of the best known was Nitobe Inazō (1862–1933), who tried to explain Japan to the world at the start of the twentieth century and saw *bushidō* as the key national characteristic. See his 1905 work *Bushidō: The Soul of Japan*.
27. See the translation of *Shidō* (The Way of the Samurai) in Tsunoda 64, vol. 1, pp. 389–91, esp. p. 390.
28. The text is believed to be based posthumously on a manuscript by the Confucian scholar Kaibara Ekiken (1631–1714, also Ekken). See the partial translation in Paulson 76, p. 11.
29. Leupp 95, p. 3. See also pp. 47–55 for a detailed discussion of homosexuality among samurai.
30. Leupp 95, p. 95. See also p. 20 regarding Confucian tolerance of homosexuality.
31. The most noted *haiku* poet was Matsuo Bashō (1644–94). *Haiku* and *senryū* are both seventeen-syllable verses, the *haiku* generally focusing on nature, *senryū* on the human world.

32.   Many of the genres of the day, particularly *chōninmono* and *kōshokubon*,
       are represented by the writer Ihara Saikaku (1642–93).
33.   As many commentators have observed, sexuality continues to be
       very much a part of present-day Japanese society, as seen in the large
       amount of pornography and frequency of extra-marital affairs and
       sexual offences. See for example Buruma 85, who among other things
       traces direct links between present pornography and prints of this
       period.
34.   It was not just the chaos that worried the shōgunate. Many samurai, as
       well as merchants and peasants, attended performances and became
       involved with the performers, who were invariably 'outcasts'. This mixing
       of the classes was not seen as desirable.
            For details of the sexual associations of *kabuki*, including sexual frenzy
       during performances, see Leupp 95, pp. 130–1 and pp. 90–2.
35.   For detailed discussion of *geisha*—who were all male till the mid-1700s—
       see Dalby 83, and for Yoshiwara see Seigle 93. The *shamisen* is a three-
       stringed lute-like instrument.
36.   Reischauer and Craig 79, pp. 98–9.
37.   See Hanley and Yamamura 77, esp. pp. 226, 324, and 330–1.
38.   Hanley and Yamamura 77, p. 227.
39.   Reischauer and Craig 79, p. 98.
40.   See Hanley and Yamamura 77, pp. 88–90.
41.   See T. Satō 90, esp. pp. 62–72, for a detailed discussion of technological
       developments.
42.   Most *daimyō* sold surplus domain rice, but others 'cashed' a range of
       goods reflecting increased specialisation, such as sugar-cane from the
       Shimazu family's Satsuma domain in southern Kyūshū. The sophisticated
       mechanisms included, by the eighteenth century, a futures market. See
       Reischauer and Craig 79, pp. 94–5.
43.   Reischauer and Craig 79, pp. 96–7, and Maison and Caiger 72, pp. 176–7.
44.   See Sakudō 90 for a detailed discussion of the development of merchant
       houses.
45.   See Morris-Suzuki 89, pp. 26–30. Morris-Suzuki discusses in her work a
       number of other economic thinkers of the period.
46.   The Confucianist Arai Hakuseki was one of a number of respected figures
       who openly expressed admiration for western science.
47.   See Reischauer and Craig 79, pp. 116–17, for discussion of these various
       attempts. See also Beasley 89a for a fuller discussion of foreign visits in
       general.
48.   Bolitho 89 discusses the famine and its consequences in detail, as also for-
       eign threat at the time.
49.   Jansen 89, p. 309.
50.   Bolitho 89, p. 126.
51.   See his diary extract in Pineau 68, p. 92.
52.   The British merchant company Jardine Matheson, for example, had set
       up a base at Yokohama by the late 1850s. See Williams 72, pp. 85–8.
       Williams' work is just one of a number of anthologies of accounts written
       by and about foreigners in Japan during the 1850s and 1860s (and in a rare
       few cases even earlier, before Perry), providing interesting outsider

insights into a variety of aspects of life in Japan at that time. For another particularly interesting account see Black 1883/1968.

53. In theory the shōgunate refused to accept responsibility for westerners' safety outside designated areas, though in practice it swiftly executed any attackers. There were a number of attacks on foreigners by extreme nationalists, one of the most famous being the murder of the English businessman Charles Richardson in 1862. Richardson was one of a party of four Britons (including one woman) attacked while riding in the hills behind Yokohama. Even official buildings were not immune from attack, with the British Legation in Edo being attacked in 1861 and burned down in 1863.

54. The most outspoken supporter of the poison theory is Donald Calman, who states categorically that Kōmei was assassinated. It seems the respected Japan expert Ernest Satow (1843–1929), who was actually in Japan at the time, was also of that opinion, as are a number of modern doctors. See Calman 92, pp. 90–3. By contrast, Conrad Totman discusses the poison theory but believes that, in terms of available evidence, smallpox was the cause of death. See Totman 80, p. 287, and his related note 41 on p. 521. Jansen (89, p. 353) states without qualification that Kōmei died of smallpox. Mayo (74, p. 158) remarks that his sudden death while recovering from smallpox was mysterious, but does not elaborate.

4 BUILDING A MODERN NATION

1. Jansen 89, p. 365, and Vlastos 89, p. 383.

2. The '*Ee ja nai ka*' ('Who cares?!') phenomenon began with the imminent demise of the shōgunate in late 1867 and continued for some two or three years. It clearly indicated a confused mixture of happiness and anxiety, excitement and disorientation. Mass hysterical behaviour included dancing wildly in the streets, dressing extravagantly or throwing off clothes altogether, indulging in public orgies of sex and drink, giving away money and possessions, performing obscenities for the sake of it, entering people's homes and taking things without permission, and generally abandoning all inhibitions and pretence to rational behaviour. The social psychologist Munesuke Mita (92, pp. 147–53) discusses the phenomenon in some detail, and some footage of a re-enactment is contained in the "Meiji Revolution" section of the *Pacific Century* video series.

3. The text of the Charter Oath is given in Tsunoda 64, vol. 2, pp. 136–7.

4. The main text of the 1868 Constitution is given in Tsunoda 64, vol. 2, pp. 137–9.

5. At this stage there were 77 prefectures (as opposed to 260 domains at the end of the Tokugawa period), but this was reduced to the present number of 47 in 1889. For a discussion of the overall dismantling of the *han* (domains), see Umegaki 86.

6. The tax reform and its consequences are discussed in Yamamura 86.

7. This was one of a number of 'study tours' to learn from the west. The Iwakura Mission, which visited America and Europe, also attempted—

unsuccessfully—to modify the 'unequal treaties' signed by the shōgunate in its final days.

8. See too Morris 75, p. 254.

9. However, the following year the government sent 3,500 men on a punitive expedition to Taiwan, whose aboriginals had killed some shipwrecked fishermen from the Ryūkyū Islands. The expedition was mainly aimed at asserting Japan's claim to the Ryūkyū Islands over that of China by treating the murdered islanders as Japanese nationals, and it was eventually successful in this. It was also an opportunity for former samurai to feel a sense of worth, but was less successful in this regard.

10. Saigō had a fatalistic fascination with death. He was also an extreme patriot opposed to westernisation, and a true old-school samurai in his opposition to commercialisation and industrialisation. See Morris 75, pp. 217–73.

11. The date 1 January 1873, for example, corresponds to 6 December 1872—the 6th day of the 12th month of Meiji 5—in the old lunar calendar. The correlation between the two calendrical systems is very complicated owing to intercalary (extra) months and leap years, and it is advisable to use conversion tables such as those in Tsuchihashi's *Japanese Chronological Tables*.

12. However, the first modern paper was in English, started by foreigners in Nagasaki in 1861.

13. Hirakawa 89, p. 471. The emperor himself almost always wore western clothes.

14. The percentage of men with western haircuts rose from 10 per cent in 1872 to 98 per cent in 1887. The lyrics of a popular song of early Meiji ran 'Tap a cropped head and it plays the tune of civilisation and enlightenment'. See Mita 92, p. 198.

15. See Henshall 89 for detailed discussion of transport developments during Meiji.

16. Shibusawa 58, p. 229.

17. Rickshaws were invented not in ancient China but in Tōkyō in August 1869 by Akiba Taisuke, and rapidly spread from there not only throughout Japan (around 150,000 being in use nationwide within a decade) but through much of Asia. An account of some early western entrepreneurs in both steamships and stagecoaches is given in Henshall 94.

18. *Meiroku Zasshi*, p. 125, note 1.

19. *Meiroku Zasshi*, p. 115.

20. See Shibusawa 58, p. 231.

21. See, for example, the short story "The Girl-Watcher" of 1907, by Tayama Katai (in Tayama Katai 1907/81). Sexual molestation on trains is a major problem in present-day Japan, with more than 90 per cent of regular women travellers becoming victims at some point.

22. As seen in Turgenev's *Rudin* or Goncharov's *Oblomov*. In modern popular terms, the 'superfluous man' is very similar to the Charlie Brown figure who always seems to miss out. In Japanese literature of the day, see the under-achieving protagonist of the novel *Ukigumo* (Drifting Clouds, 1887–9), by Futabatei Shimei (1864–1909).

23. Fukuzawa travelled to America and Europe on several official missions, and was so strongly associated with westernisation that at one stage all

books about the west were, regardless of author, popularly known as 'Fukuzawa books' (*Fukuzawa-bon*). As early as 1858, while still in his early twenties, he founded the institution that was later to become Keiō University, where he promoted his views. In his earlier years he was associated with human rights, but in later years came to apply his self-help views in a more aggressively nationalistic way, advocating Japanese imperialist expansion in Asia. Over time he became increasingly anti-western. He is also noted for his advocacy, from 1881, of a view that Japan should cease to consider itself a part of Asia ('*Datsu-A ron*'). Fukuzawa's life and writings are discussed in detail in Blacker 64.

24. Fukuzawa 1872/1969, p. 1.
25. The term is often incorrectly attributed to Darwin himself. In a 1902 Maruzen Bookstore survey of 78 prominent Japanese men as to their choice of the most influential writing of the nineteenth century, Darwin's *Origin of Species* (1859) had 23 votes, while 'the philosophy of Spencer' had 15.
26. A convenient printing of this letter is given as an appendix in Hearn 1904, pp. 481–4. The letter was first published on 18 January 1904, in *The London Times*, a month after Spencer's death. As he had predicted, it caused an outrage.
27. See Yamaguchi 83, p. 151, for this and other prohibitions imposed on foreigners.
28. See Hirakawa 89, pp. 467–8. Not all foreign advisers, at least early on, were westerners. In 1872 as many as 43 out of 160 foreigners employed by local governments were Chinese. Many were advisers on techniques for firing tea, a major export of early Meiji. (See Morris-Suzuki 94, p. 66.)
29. Hirakawa 89, p. 468.
30. Beauchamp 83, p. 311.
31. Hirakawa 89, p. 469.
32. See Mita 92, pp. 244–7.
33. It was conveniently overlooked that this latter phrase was used to no avail in China.
34. The role of education in the inculcation and harnessing of desired values during Meiji is treated in detail in Mita 92, pp. 224–94, including a detailed analysis of textbooks of the day. Mita also discusses Meiji 'successism' in general. Gluck 85, esp. pp. 102–27, also discusses Meiji education.
35. Tight centralised control of school texts is still a very major issue in present-day Japan.
36. Eight years earlier, in 1882, Yamagata had been responsible for the issuing of an *Imperial Rescript for Soldiers and Sailors*, which was to become a sort of prototype for the 1890 rescript. It had stressed the overriding importance of loyalty to the emperor. The main text of the 1882 rescript is given in Tsunoda 64, vol. 2, pp. 198–200, and the 1890 rescript pp. 139–40.
37. Gluck 85, pp. 38–9, 103, and esp. 151.
38. This is the title of Gluck 85.
39. Cooper 83, p. 308. There were similar suggestions to adopt the English language, and so forth, all in the cause of Japan's acceptance by the west.
40. Uchimura Kanzō (1861–1930) was a prime example of this. He despised the idea of denominations, and was also a strong nationalist who insisted

on the need for a 'Japanese Christianity untainted by western influence'. See Cooper 83, p. 309. The present-day popularity of Christian-style weddings, which now account for almost half of all weddings in Japan, should be seen simply as a particularised social fashion and not confused with genuine Christianity.

41. The liberal Nakae Chōmin (1847–1901) was one. He had studied in France, was much impressed by Rousseau and French and British liberal thought, and promoted popular rights through his prolific writings.

42. *Rikken Kaishintō* was also sometimes translated as the Progressive Party or Progressive Reform Party. From this point on, to the present, Japanese political parties were to form, unform, re-form, and change their name with bewildering frequency (particularly during the 1890s). To avoid confusion I have deliberately tried to avoid unnecessary detail here.

43. For details of political novels see M. Nakamura 68, Chapter 2. Their heroes were mostly successful politicians from world history, and their themes the political processes by which success was achieved. Regarding 'home-grown' constitutions, many village councils produced their own suggested versions of a constitution. See "The Meiji Revolution" in the *Pacific Century* video series, and Gibney 92, pp. 96–7.

44. Itagaki had been one of those thwarted by the overturning of Saigō's 1873 proposal to invade Korea. Okuma was a well-known personal rival of Itō Hirobumi, and was being eclipsed by him.

45. Reischauer and Craig 79, p. 168.

46. The German general staff system had been adopted from 1878. In matters of command the chief of staff was answerable only to the emperor, who was the supreme commander, and not to the government or even the army minister. Drafts for the legal code initially favoured the French model, but this was gradually displaced by the German, which dominated the code finally issued in 1896.

47. These included Albert Mosse (1846–1925) and Karl Hermann Roesler (1834–94).

48. Reischauer and Craig 79, p. 173.

49. Reischauer and Craig 79, p. 173.

50. The text of the constitution and the accompanying oath are given in the *Kōdansha Encyclopedia of Japan*, vol. 3, pp. 7–9.

51. For detailed discussion see Large 92, pp. 7–9.

52. Stockwin 92, p. xii.

53. See Banno 92, p. 9.

54. See Beasley 89b, p. 668.

55. The difficult political situation of the time is described in detail in Banno 92.

56. See, for example, Reischauer and Craig 79, p. 178, and Beasley 89b, p. 669.

57. Gluck 85, p. 67.

58. See Iriye 83.

59. For details see Reischauer and Craig 79, pp. 180–2.

60. Katsura is himself sometimes referred to as a *genrō*, but in practice he was considered a junior by the older *genrō*.

61. Okamoto 83, p. 346.

62. This was the 'Revolution of 1905', not to be confused with the better-known revolution of 1917.
63. Okamoto 83, p. 347. Japan had already decided the previous month that it would seek mediation, and the victory certainly helped its bargaining power.
64. Reischauer and Craig 79, p. 188.
65. Reischauer and Craig 79, p. 183.
66. Hunter 89, pp. 243–4.
67. One extreme case, cited by Morris-Suzuki (94, p. 78), was the Kamaishi iron-works, in which the government invested some 2.2 million yen and which it sold to a local merchant for a mere 12,600 yen—just 0.5 per cent of cost.
68. Francks 92, p. 38.
69. Francks 92, pp. 38–9.
70. Francks 92, pp. 38–9.
71. Crawcour 89, p. 613.
72. See Morris-Suzuki 94, pp. 111–12, and Francks 92, pp. 190–1.
73. Francks 92, pp. 38–9.
74. Francks 92, pp. 189 and 51.
75. One of the more popular models is the 'developmental state' model described by Chalmers Johnson, which he applies in particular to Shōwa Japan but whose origin he sees in the Meiji period. (See Johnson 82, esp. p. 23.) This 'plan-rational' model treats the state as having intervened constructively in the economy, as opposed to leaving it to market forces ('market-rational' or 'laissez-faire'), in order to guide and develop it in a way appropriate to the nation's interests. By contrast, Penelope Francks agrees that the government did not want to rely on market forces alone but feels that the constructiveness of the state's involvement has been exaggerated, and that economic development was not quite as planned as the 'developmental state' model suggests. In her view actual government intervention was a rather hit-and-miss response to circumstances of time and place. (See Francks 92, esp. pp. 255–6.)
76. Among other things, he rarely made public tours after around 1890, even though this was the point from which the new emperor-centred ideology was particularly strongly promoted. His withdrawal from public life was possibly partly because of his rather vulgar and embarrassing personal habits. See Behr 89, p. 14.
77. Tayama Katai 1917/87, pp. 247–51.
78. In the poem 'Kimi Shinitamō Koto Nakare' (You Must Not Die, My Brother).
79. See the partial translation in McClellan 69, p. 37.
80. See Mita 92, Part One, esp. pp. 21–8.
81. Tayama Katai 1917/87, pp. 248–9.

5 THE EXCESSES OF AMBITION

1. Duus 83, p. 198, Reischauer and Craig 79, p. 228, and Storry 63, pp. 160–1.

2. Stanley 83. For a vivid personal insight into this 'Korean hunt' I am indebted to Yoshio Okamoto, of Kōbe, whose father, though a Japanese, was mistaken for a Korean and barely escaped with his life.
3. Stanley 83.
4. Storry 63, p. 153.
5. Frei 91, Chapter 6.
6. R. Daniels 83, p. 164.
7. Kosaka 92, p. 35.
8. It was in later years to be deemed, by countries such as South Africa, an 'honorary' white nation, but such patronising for economic expediency was hardly real acceptance.
9. Large 92, pp. 28–31.
10. Kosaka 92, p. 28, and Forster 81, pp. 59–60.
11. Morris-Suzuki 94, pp. 105–16.
12. Reischauer and Craig 79, p. 206, and see also Hunter 89, p. 93.
13. See Hunter 89, p. 95, and Duus 83, pp. 198–9, for opposed views of the differences between the rural and the urban (the former downplaying them, the latter highlighting them).
14. Hunter 89, p. 97.
15. Reischauer and Craig 79, p. 243.
16. Reischauer 88, p. 97.
17. Reischauer and Craig 79, p. 249, and Hata 88, p. 295.
18. Large 92, p. 49.
19. Duus 88, p. 7.
20. R. Hall 74, p. 9.
21. *Kokutai no Hongi*, p. 55.
22. The fourteen quotations in this paragraph are respectively from pp. 66, 71, 67, 67, 78, 78, 78, 81, 80, 93, 100, 82, 82, and 55 of *Kokutai no Hongi*.
23. R. Hall 74, pp. 8–9.
24. Kawai 38, pp. 69–72.
25. Kawai 38, p. 74.
26. See, for example, the *Addresses to Young Men* given by Hashimoto Kingorō of the nationalistic *Sakurakai* (Cherry Blossom Society). Excerpts are given in Tsunoda 64, vol. 2, pp. 289–91.
27. Li 92, pp. 75–6, and Peattie 83, p. 345.
28. Li 92, pp. 73–6.
29. Peattie 83, pp. 345–6.
30. Hunter 89, p. 124.
31. Dower 92, p. 53.
32. Forster 81, p. 62. Forster also points out that by contrast Australia's GDP grew by only 10 per cent over the same period.
33. Kosaka 92, p. 32.
34. Reischauer and Craig 79, p. 246.
35. Between 1929 and 1937 the proportion of GDP occupied by chemicals, metal, and machinery rose from 30 per cent to 50 per cent. (See Forster 81, p. 62.) Between 1920 and 1940 iron and steel production increased eleven-fold, machinery six-fold, and chemicals also six-fold. (See Hunter 89, p. 124.)
36. Hunter 89, p. 125.

37. Morishima 82, pp. 109–12.
38. Hunter 89, pp. 125–6, and Francks 92, pp. 63–5.
39. The Japanese further claimed one of their number had been killed, but no name was ever given for this supposed casualty. See also Gluck 92, p. 14. By contrast, some commentators, such as Boyle 83, believe the incident was a genuine accident. The Japanese record of engagement with a foe—once they feel such engagement is inevitable—at least suggests the strong possibility of provocation.
40. Kitaoka 92, p. 165.
41. Large 92, pp. 89–92.
42. Some footage appears to have been faked American propaganda, but some of it is authentic. See Dower 86, pp. 45–6.
43. See "Nanjing Testament", in the *Japan Times*, Weekly International Edition, 22–28 August 1994. The article includes first-hand testimony from a soldier who took part in the massacre, Nagatomi Hiromichi. See also Hunter 89, p. 58.
44. The interview with Prince Mikasa appeared in the *Yomiuri* newspaper on 6 July 1994 and was reported in English in the *Japan Times*, Weekly International Edition, 18–24 July 1994.
45. The biggest incident was in May 1939, when Soviet troops assisted Mongolians involved in a skirmish with Japanese forces at Nomonhan, on the Manchurian border. In a clear defeat, the Japanese lost almost 20,000 men.
46. Coox 88, p. 336. See also Dower 86, p. 207.
47. Coox 88, p. 336. For a virtually contemporary and rather bewildered British view of Japan's relationship with Germany under such strained circumstances, see Vansittart 43.
48. Reischauer and Craig 79, p. 260.
49. Hane 86, p. 297.
50. This document was declassified in 1970 but appears to have remained undiscovered in Washington's National Archives till 1991. However, Lauchlin Currie and some of the pilots had already confirmed the top-secret plan. It is discussed in some detail, for example, in Schultz 87, Chapter 1, and was revealed to a wider audience in the ABC News video "Beaten to the Punch", which aired in the United States on 22 November 1991 in the programme *20–20*. The video shows the document itself complete with the signatures of Roosevelt and top military figures, and also contains interviews with Currie and others. The authenticity of the document has been confirmed not only by Currie but by specialists such as Gaddis Smith of Yale University.
51. See, for example, Schultz 87, p. 5, and Rusbridger and Nave 92, p. 121. Winston Churchill himself referred to a comment by Roosevelt in August 1941 that Congress might prevent him *declaring* war, but this would not prevent him from *making* it. This clearly suggests Roosevelt's readiness to act covertly if necessary. See Churchill 51, p. 593.
52. Hirohito made this claim in 1946, defending himself. See Large 92, p. 114.
53. See Large 92, pp. 113–14.
54. Bix 92, p. 354.

55.	See, for example, Dower 86, esp. p. 36 and pp. 259–61, for comment on a widely held Japanese attitude that westerners were soft, lacked commitment to a cause (through their selfishness), and could not endure a long and arduous struggle.

56.	Operational details of this action are given in Barber 94.

57.	For details of the report, its capture, and its effects, see Rusbridger and Nave 92, Chapter 5.

58.	Coox 88, p. 343.

59.	Sakai 94, p. 20.

60.	The literature on Pearl Harbor is extensive, and the interpretations of events are many and varied. At the risk of over-simplifying an issue that should not be treated simplistically, those of a generally revisionist view, which inclines towards a 'conspiracy' or 'cover-up' interpretation or similar and tended to be at its peak just after the war, include John Flynn (44 and 45), George Morgenstern (47), Charles Beard (48), Robert Theobald (54), and Husband Kimmel (55). For a later example of revisionism, see the video "Sacrifice at Pearl Harbor", screened on BBC2's *Timewatch* programme, 5 April 1992. Those who have opposed the revisionists include Samuel Morison (53), Roberta Wohlstetter (62), Gordon Prange (86), and Henry Clausen and Bruce Lee (92).

61.	See Dower 86, p. 109.

62.	See Dower 86, p. 109.

63.	Bartlett 78, pp. 19–20.

64.	Dallek 79, p. 307.

65.	Large 92, pp. 114–15.

66.	See Coox 88, p. 348.

67.	Dower 86, p. 207.

68.	Benedict 47, p. 22, and Dower 86, esp. p. 36 and pp. 259–61.

69.	Coox 88, p. 353.

70.	Benedict 47, pp. 38–9.

71.	Benedict 47, p. 38, and Trefalt 95, esp. p. 116.

72.	Benedict 47, p. 39.

73.	See, for example, the account by Suzuki Murio, entitled "As Long As I Don't Fight, I'll Make It Home", in H. and T. Cook 92, pp. 127–35.

74.	One example of a 'planned and well-disciplined' Japanese surrender was that of 42 Japanese—more than twice the number of their Australian captors—at Womgrer in New Guinea on 3 May 1945. See Thompson 45, pp. 2–3. As Thompson—an interrogator/interpreter—points out, this surrender was still very much the exception.

75.	See, for example, the account by Yokota Yutaka, entitled "Volunteer", in H. and T. Cook 92, pp. 306–13. Yokota was a suicide minisub pilot who was thwarted by problems such as mechanical failures. He comments (p. 309) that 'There's an old expression, "*Bushidō* is the search for a place to die." Well, that was our fervent desire, our long-cherished dream. A place to die for my country. I was happy to have been born a man. A man of Japan.' He is one of many who overestimated the role of death in traditional *bushidō*. He also talks of envy towards those chosen for suicide missions, and of physical beatings for those such as himself who returned, even for reasons beyond their control. His anguish was to continue well after the war.

76. Dower 86, pp. 232–3.
77. Trefalt 95, esp. pp. 118–20. For further discussion of the attitudes of Japanese PoWs, see also Gordon 94 and Carr-Gregg 78.
78. Benedict 47, pp. 38–40, and Trefalt 95, esp. pp. 115–16.
79. Dower 86, p. 48, and for figures and descriptions of the treatment of Allied PoWs of the Japanese see also Daws 94.
80. Benedict 47, Chapter 2, esp. p. 39, and also Utsumi 96, p. 201. The idea of dishonour was also linked with imperfection and impurity. Concern for purity also sometimes led Japanese to treat with callousness and brutality anyone they felt to be impure, Japanese or not. This could be a criminal or even a sick or wounded soldier, as Benedict also points out.
81. A disturbing example is the account by Uno Shintarō, innocuously entitled "Spies and Bandits", in H. and T. Cook 92, pp. 151–8. Uno, a self-confessed master of the art of beheading, prides himself on his ability to kill and torture. He—and some of his superiors—saw this as an important aspect of educating troops (p. 156).
82. Behr 89, pp. 263–4.
83. Williams and Wallace 89, p. 178. These experiments mostly took place at Ping Fan in Manchuria under the now notorious Unit 731 headed by Major (later General) Ishii Shirō (1892–1959). Prisoners of war and enemy civilians, including women and children and from as early as 1932, were used as live experimental subjects, known as *maruta*, or 'logs of wood'. In some cases entire villages were infected with plague germs or similar. Those conducting the experiments included Japanese civilians, who appear to have become inured to the work. An account from one such civilian, Tamura Yoshio, is given in H. and T. Cook 92, pp. 159–67. The most detailed discussion of Unit 731 and its experiments is the work by Williams and Wallace.

    Despite various plans and unsuccessful attempts, neither biological or chemical weapons appear to have actually been used by the Japanese against the Allies during the Pacific War, though there was extensive use of biological weapons against the Chinese. Regular Japanese troops themselves seem to have known little or nothing of these tactics, nor of the experiments, and at least 10,000 of them ended up as accidental victims of their own nation's germ warfare. (Williams and Wallace 89, pp. 69–70.)
84. G. Daniels 93, p. 101.
85. G. Daniels 93, p. 103.
86. T. Nakamura 88, p. 491.
87. G. Daniels 93, p. 103.
88. For these and other details of wartime production, see Hane 86, pp. 331–3.
89. See Morris 75 for a detailed discussion of *kamikaze* pilots.
90. A particularly poignant account of the atrocity given by survivors was released internationally by Reuter in February 1995. My particular source here is the *Waikato Times* of 8 February 1995. It is not clear how many of the estimated 100,000 were killed by the Japanese, and how many by American bombardment.

91.   See the *Japan Times*, Weekly International Edition, 23–29 August
        1993. The incident was later reported to the US Army's war crimes
        branch, who judged it to be 'a heinous act repugnant to the sense of
        all civilized nations'. However, it was referred to the Japanese
        authorities, since laws governing the conduct of war crimes trials at
        that time prevented acts of brutality against one's own nationals from
        being treated as war crimes. The outcome is unclear. Similar acts
        took place in the defence of Okinawa, and no doubt elsewhere. (See
        too the 27 November–3 December 1995 edition of the same
        newspaper.)
92.   Coox 88, p. 369.
93.   Following recent research by the historian Yoshida Morio there is now
        some dispute as to whether these really were spared for cultural reasons,
        as the American government has claimed—a claim officially accepted by
        the Japanese government—or whether they were simply not strategically
        important as targets. For an English language summary of Yoshida's
        views, see the *Japan Times*, Weekly International Edition, 19–25 July
        1993.
94.   Heinrichs 83, p. 276.
95.   There are a number of poignant accounts of these suicides given in
        H. and T. Cook 92. They also reveal the degree of indoctrination of
        hatred and fear towards Americans, which proved to be unfounded
        once the American troops had arrived. Many American 'demons'
        treated the Okinawans better than the (mainland) Japanese had,
        as the survivors themselves remark. This left many Okinawans feel-
        ing betrayed by mainland Japan, feelings that have still not fully
        subsided.
96.   Heinrichs 83, p. 276.
97.   The text of the Potsdam Declaration—also known as the Potsdam Pro-
        clamation—is given in Borton 55, pp. 485–6.
98.   The Suzuki cabinet ended up using the word *mokusatsu* (literally 'kill
        with silence'). This term basically means 'to ignore with contempt',
        but it has been claimed it was used to mean simply 'no comment at
        this stage'—that is, Japan simply wanted more time to consider the
        Declaration, and was not really rejecting it. However, such a view fails
        to take into account other comments made by Suzuki (see Butow 54,
        p. 148) that more clearly indicated Japan's rejection of the Declara-
        tion.
99.   The historian most associated with this view is the American Gar Alpero-
        vitz. See for example his 1965/85 work.
100.   Sayle 95, p. 54. Sayle sees the testing motive as particularly applicable to
        General Leslie Groves, head of the Manhattan Project for the develop-
        ment of the A-bomb.
101.   The whole question of how far Japan was advanced in its own nuclear
        technology is a matter of considerable controversy. Most westerners still
        do not realise the extent of Japanese expertise in this area at the time.
        Two Japanese scientists—Yukawa Hideki and Tomonaga Shinichirō—
        later received Nobel prizes for prewar work in nuclear physics, and a
        number of others had worked with top western scientists. Japan had no

fewer than five nuclear particle accelerators—the only nation other than America to possess them. Destruction of these cyclotrons was one of the very first tasks of the postwar Occupation forces. The matter of a possible nuclear strike by Japan against the Allies has been discussed for some time, but was particularly brought to prominence by Robert Wilcox (85). Most specialists (such as Low 90) feel his claims are greatly exaggerated, and argue that despite its expertise Japan still lacked sufficient relevant knowledge actually to build a bomb, lacked co-ordination, and also lacked uranium. On the other hand, it is known that Germany was supplying uranium ore to Japan. Moreover, recently declassified documents show Japan did in fact have enough uranium compounds to make at least one bomb. It had, for example, more than 500 kg of uranyl nitrate at a navy depot in Tokuyama, Yamaguchi Prefecture. (See the *Japan Times*, Weekly International Edition, 20–26 January 1997.) In any event, while is very unlikely Japan was near nuclear capability in 1945, it is impossible simply to dismiss out of hand a scenario in which American fears about a Japanese strike played at least some part in the American decision to drop their own bomb. An official American report of July 1945 stated that '*Most* of us are certain that the Japanese cannot develop and use this weapon effectively' (my italics). Presumably, *some* were not so certain. See Dower 93c, Note 26 on p. 95. (Dower himself, while referring to the report, is strongly of the view that Japan lacked nuclear capability.)

102.   Clear figures regarding casualties are difficult to ascertain. The usual figure is 140,000, but in 1995 the Hiroshima City authorities gave the number of confirmed dead by the end of 1945 as 87,833. (See the *Japan Times*, Weekly International Edition, 7–13 August 1995.)

There is a substantial amount of literature dealing with the atomic bombings (especially Hiroshima) and their effects on the victims. One of the best-known works available in English is *Kuroi Ame* (Black Rain) of 1966, by the novelist Ibuse Masuji (b.1898). For some very recent and very poignant poetry and comment by a survivor of the Hiroshima bombing, the female poet Hashizume Bun (b.1931), see Hashizume 96.

103.   See Large 92, p. 126.

104.   The text of the emperor's speech is given as an appendix in Behr 89, pp. 407–8.

105.   The text of the Instrument of Surrender is given in Borton 55, pp. 487–8, and the imperial edict p. 489.

106.   For discussion of operational factors in Japan's defeat, such as poor inter-service co-ordination, loss of merchant shipping, poor code security, and so forth, see Coox 88, pp. 377–9.

107.   Behr 89, p. 366.

108.   In a survey conducted in November 1944, 13 per cent of Americans—more than one in eight—wanted the Japanese to be utterly exterminated. (See Cohen 87, p. 27, and Dower 86, pp. 53–5.) Such a view was not confined to the general public, but was also found among the nation's leaders.

109.   Dower 86, p. 150.

6   A PHOENIX FROM THE ASHES

1. A detailed account of the surrender ceremony, including the text of the speech, is given in MacArthur 64, pp. 272–7.
2. For details see Nishi 82, pp. 47–9.
3. For details see Hane 86, pp. 341–3. About one house in five throughout the nation had been destroyed (more than half the houses in the case of Tōkyō and Osaka), and food was in desperately short supply. The Occupation forces provided some food relief, but not in substantial form till early 1946. Many Japanese in late 1945 spent almost their entire energies simply trying to obtain enough food to stay alive. See also "Out of a Firestorm" in the BBC *Nippon* video series.
4. These traits are unmistakably clear from his less than modest memoirs (MacArthur 64) and from the comments of those who knew him well, such as his personal aide Faubion Bowers (see interview in the video "Reinventing Japan" in the *Pacific Century* series). See also Reischauer 88, p. 104, and Dower 93b, p. 165.
5. Cohen 87, pp. 53–4.
6. Storry 63, p. 240. Theodore Cohen—himself an important figure in the Occupation—repeatedly points out that those around MacArthur usually had mixed feelings towards him, respecting him but angered by his self-importance and his failure to acknowledge the achievements of others. See Cohen 87, pp. xix–xx, p. 54, and p. 63.
7. China was busy with domestic troubles. The Soviets demanded their own zone of occupation, in Hokkaidō, and when this was refused, declined to send their troops to serve under a US commander. The British troops were mostly Australian. See Cohen 87, pp. 58–61, for details of the position of the Soviets and other Allies.
8. MacArthur 64, pp. 291–3.
9. Regarding commencement of planning, see Ward 87b, p. 395, and Borton 67, pp. 4–8. See also Ward 87a, pp. 3–4. New Dealers were liberals supportive of the 'New Deal'—the social and economic reforms introduced in America by President Roosevelt during the 1930s to alleviate the effects of the Depression. They were particularly concerned to achieve a more equal distribution of wealth, and labour reforms supportive of unions rather than big business interests. See Cohen 87 for a general discussion of the New Deal aspect of planning for Japan.
10. Borton published a number of works on Japan in the postwar period, but greatly downplayed his own major role. However, examination of important directives and other documents of the day reveals his involvement in the great majority. For an informed comment by a contemporary on the extent of his role, see Cohen 87, p. 18.
11. For details of JCS1380/15, see Gibney 92, p. 182. (Gibney himself was a member of the Occupation.) It should not be confused with the much vaguer and simpler directive issued in August, the *US Initial Post Surrender Policy for Japan*, also known as SWNCC 150/4 (SWNCC standing for State [Dept]-War-Navy Co-ordinating Committee).
12. MacArthur 64, pp. 280–3.
13. MacArthur 64, p. 283.

14. See Cohen 87, p. 11–12.
15. MacArthur 64, pp. 286–7.
16. MacArthur 64, p. 298.
17. Many western commentators attribute it to MacArthur without qualification, while many Japanese nowadays prefer to believe it was of Japanese origin. In fact it is a classic case of 'buck passing', when one might have expected rather a case of 'credit grabbing'. It is beyond dispute that MacArthur pencilled the clause and handed it to the SCAP team working on the new constitution. One of that team, Richard Poole, confirms this, attributing the clause to MacArthur himself (see interview in "Reinventing Japan"). However, in his memoirs (MacArthur 64, pp. 302–4) MacArthur denies it was his own idea and asserts that the initiative came from then Prime Minister Shidehara Kijūrō. Yoshida Shigeru, who succeeded Shidehara as prime minister, recalled in his own memoirs (Yoshida 61, p. 137) his impression that MacArthur had suggested it to Shidehara, not the other way round as MacArthur claimed. As an alternative, Theodore McNelly (McNelly 87, pp. 79–80) raises the possibility that it might have come from Shidehara, but in response to a suggestion by Charles Kades, who was in charge of the team drafting the constitution and who was greatly impressed by the anti-war Kellogg-Briand Pact of 1928. To add to the range of possible sources, Robert Ward (Ward 87a, pp. 23–4) draws attention to a State Department plan for postwar Japan, drawn up on 9 May 1944 by Hugh Borton, which refers to 'the wide consensus which now exists that Japan should not be permitted in the postwar period to retain an army, navy, or air force'. Though this particular Washington plan refers to the 'postwar' period and not a permanent arrangement, and may not have been specifically sent to MacArthur anyway, an early document of August 1945, SWNCC 150/2, does clearly refer to the 'complete and permanent' disarmament of Japan. (See Dower 93b, p. 168, though Dower feels the clause's origin was in Tōkyō not Washington.) Borton himself (Borton 55, Note 5 on pp. 423–4) attributes the 'renunciation of war principle' to MacArthur, and later (Borton 67, p. 16) attributes the idea of disbanding the armed forces to his State Department colleague George Blakeslee. Nor, in a broader sense, should it be forgotten that half a century earlier Japan itself had disbanded the Korean army.
18. The full text of the constitution is given in the *Kōdansha Encyclopedia of Japan*, vol. 2, pp. 9–13, and in the *Asahi Shimbun Japan Almanac* (1997), pp. 284–91.
19. For further details of the Tōkyō Trial see Minear 71 (in full) and 83 (in brief). See also Tsurumi 87, Chapter 2, for more discussion, including evidence of unfair trial procedures.
20. See, for example, Tsurumi 87, p. 16.
21. Williams and Wallace 89, p. 286.
22. Tsurumi 87, p. 16.
23. In an opinion poll conducted in June 1945 77 per cent of American people wanted Hirohito severely punished, and on 18 September that year a joint resolution was introduced into the Senate (and referred to a committee) declaring that Hirohito should be tried as a war criminal. Many leading

figures from among the other Allied nations, such as the prime minister of
New Zealand, and leaders from Australia, the Soviet Union, the Nether-
lands, and China, were also of the view that Hirohito should be tried. (See
for example Bix 95, pp. 320–1, MacArthur 64, p. 288, Behr 89, p. 294 and
p. 332, and Ward 87a, p. 11.)

24. See, for example, Large 92, pp. 136–9, Bix 95, p. 323, and also Borton 67,
pp. 15–16. For a fuller discussion of the American government's views on
both the imperial institution and Hirohito personally see Ward 87a,
pp. 3–18.

25. Contemporary figures who felt he should have abdicated either at once or
at an early stage of the Occupation include the immediate prewar prime
minister Prince Konoe Fumimaro and the immediate postwar (Aug–
Oct 45) prime minister Prince Higashikuni Naruhiko. Later figures who
shared such a view include the novelist Mishima Yukio and the novelist-
cum-politician Ishihara Shintarō—both strong nationalists. Tsurumi
(87, p. 26) discusses ongoing Japanese reservations, and among other
things notes that Hirohito's failure to step down has paved the way for
a belief that governing individuals need not take responsibility for their
decisions.

26. MacArthur 64, p. 301.

27. There is great controversy over Hirohito's war responsibility. Like Pearl
Harbor, it is an issue that should not be over-simplified. Relevant works
range from the critical (such as Bergamini 71, Behr 89, and Bix 92) to the
supportive (such as Mosley 66 and Shillony 73). Many commentators
nowadays hold views similar to those of Stephen Large (92), basically a
balanced but mildly sympathetic position to the effect that Hirohito was a
weak man caught up in circumstances too powerful for him to handle.
That is, he was guilty by omission rather than commission, in failing to
stop the wrongdoings of others. On the other hand, the detailed writings
of Herbert Bix in particular suggest a less sympathetic view might be more
appropriate. Among other things, Bix lists examples of Hirohito's active
involvement in such matters as strategic military planning, as in pressing
for the deployment of army air power in the Guadalcanal campaign (92,
pp. 352–4).

28. For details see Ward 87a, p. 16, and Behr 89, p. 348.

29. Large 92, p. 141, and Nishi 82, pp. 55–6.

30. MacArthur 64, p. 284 and pp. 310–11. See also Ward 87a, p. 7, for a Washington policy recommendation, seemingly initiated by Hugh Borton as
early as May 1944, that Hirohito's divinity should not be supported.

31. Bix 92, pp. 318–21.

32. See Large 92, p. 147.

33. Ward 87a, p. 13, Large 92, p. 152, and esp. Behr 89, pp. 364–5.

34. Bix 95, p. 331.

35. Ward 87a, p. 36.

36. MacArthur 64, p. 300.

37. See the video "Reinventing Japan", which contains revealing interviews
with Kades and a number of other SCAP staff involved in the drafting of
the new constitution.

38. McNelly 87, p. 80.

39.	Ward 87b, p. 400.
40.	See interview in "Reinventing Japan". It is not just Japanese who express such a view. In a book questioning the nature of democracy in modern Japan, Herzog (93, Chapter 1) makes a similar point.
41.	In addition to Herzog 93, for details of undemocratic aspects of modern Japan see McCormack and Sugimoto 86. These include criminal justice practices that clearly violate human rights.
42.	By a directive from SCAP these were carried out in line with the provisions of the draft constitution, even though this was yet to be formally accepted by the parliament that was now being elected. This meant that women voted for the first time.
43.	The proposal regarding women's rights was drawn up by Beate Sirota, a 22-year-old woman who despite her Japanese-sounding name was a Russian-American. She was the only one of the drafting team who had any real experience of Japan, one of the few civilians and one of the few not picked virtually at random. She was chosen for a number of reasons: she had spent her childhood years between 5 and 15 in Japan, she was fluent in Japanese, and she was a woman.

	Of all the remarkable stories of the drafting of the constitution, hers is one of the most remarkable. As she elaborated in "Reinventing Japan" and in a later interview (see the *Japan Times*, Weekly International Edition, 31 July–6 August 1995, pp. 10–11), she put her contribution together after madly dashing around libraries to find any relevant material. It was too detailed, and was heavily cut back by Kades. When put to Japanese representatives for their comments, they were initially unwilling to accept such a dramatic change for women as guaranteeing equality. However, this part of the constitutional draft was only reached after sixteen solid hours of discussion, largely on the role of emperor. Everyone was desperately tired and wanted to finish as soon as possible. She herself had been acting as interpreter for the Japanese during discussions and as a result was seen by them as a kindly disposed helper. They were unaware that it was she herself who had drafted the item that now came before them. She quotes Kades as saying to them that 'Miss Sirota has her heart set on the women's rights, so why don't we pass them?' She adds simply 'And they did.'
44.	It was not until the 1990s that a majority of Japanese women came to disagree with traditional gender roles. See surveys reported in the *Japan Times*, Weekly International Edition, 2–15 January 1995 and 15–21 April 1996. See too Kumagai 96, pp. 100–1. Many women, even quite young ones, still agree with traditional roles. See esp. Iwao 93. As Iwao and other contemporary women commentators show, Japanese women's perception of the female role is a complex issue. Though Confucianism is a major factor, it is not the sole determinant of Japanese women's position in society. Neither is male chauvinism, nor actual lack of opportunity for women regardless of constitutional 'guarantees' of equality. Many women themselves still remain fundamentally unconvinced of women's suitability for certain occupations, usually relating to the exercise of power. In politics, for example, women voters strongly prefer male candidates. In the October 1996 Lower House elections, women represented 10 per cent of

all candidates, but fewer than 5 per cent of those elected were women, despite female turnout exceeding male. Clearly, this is an issue that merits further discussion, in a more specialised context.

45. See the video "Out of a Firestorm".
46. This is covered in some detail in Nishi 82, pp. 90–105. See also Braw 91. In fairness to the Occupation, this is also an illustration of the universal philosophical question of the extent to which tolerance can tolerate intolerance.
47. See the videos "Reinventing Japan" and "Out of a Firestorm".
48. Nishi 82, pp. 103–4.
49. Reischauer and Craig 79, p. 282. This lies behind many of the comments made by Occupation officials attributing everything to the Japanese. Obviously, it was not just the Japanese who differentiated between what was said on the outside and what was actually done on the inside.
50. Nishi 82, p. 166.
51. For full details of land reform see Dore 59.
52. Hadley 83, p. 364. The six lesser *zaibatsu* were Asano, Furukawa, Ayukawa (Aikawa), Okura, Nomura, and Nakajima.
53. Hadley 83, p. 365.
54. The following draws on Cohen 87. Cohen himself oversaw most of the labour reforms.
55. A US government report of April 1946 reported the number as just 6,800 (Nishi 82, p. 95), whereas in March 1947 it was reported by Nosaka Sanzō to be 60,000 (Cohen 87, p. 281). Even allowing for distortion of the figures, the trend of rapid growth is unmistakable, and the concern among the authorities obvious. As Cohen points out by way of comparison, in Russia just prior to the April 1917 revolution there were fewer than 50,000 Bolshevik card holders, in a population double that of Japan's.
56. Nishi 82, p. 95.
57. Cohen 87, p. 261.
58. Yoshida 61, p. 75.
59. See Frost 83, p. 53.
60. See also Frost 83, p. 54.
61. See the video "Reinventing Japan".
62. Cohen 87, pp. 299–300.
63. The remarkable General Charles Willoughby, the German-born aristocrat who now headed SCAP's Intelligence Section, was one such highly placed critic. See Cohen 87, pp. 90–6.
64. See Gibney 92, p. 201.
65. See Cohen 87, Chapters 21–25, for details on Draper, Kennan, and others, and their financial policies.
66. This is popularly termed the 'reverse course', but this is a misleading over-simplification. There were many continuities between pre-1947 and post-1947 Occupation policies. A 'shift of course' is more appropriate terminology.
67. See Frost 83, p. 53.
68. Following protest from a number of Asian nations Japan was in fact to pay very modest reparations to those nations in later years, principally in the form of capital goods produced in Japan from raw materials supplied by

the nations themselves. In effect, however, Japan can be considered to have emerged with an extremely light burden of reparations—another source of lingering discontent towards Japan among Asian nations.

69. For details see Borton 55, pp. 365–6.
70. Cohen 87, p. 458.
71. See Dower 79, p. 316.
72. T. Nakamura 81, p. 42.
73. For details of MacArthur's account of the Korean War and his view of Washington policy, see MacArthur 64, Chapter 9.
74. MacArthur 64, pp. 378–9.
75. They first met in May 1952, after the Occupation had formally ended. See Large 92, p. 157.
76. The Soviet Union, Czechoslovakia, Yugoslavia, Poland, and India did not sign. A number of other nations only signed on condition that the United States also signed special security pacts with them, such as the ANZUS Pact (linking Australia, New Zealand, and the United States). Neither of the two Chinas was invited to the conference, for diplomatic reasons.
77. MacArthur simply states in his memoirs (MacArthur 64, p. 383) that 'I was not invited to attend. Perhaps someone just forgot to remember.'
78. See Weinstein 95, and Beason and Weinstein 96, for detailed illustration of the limits of MITI's success. One well-known and less technical example is the failure of MITI to support Sony in its early days in the 1950s.
79. Figures for industrial structure here and immediately below are taken from *Japan 1995: An International Comparison*, p. 20.
80. Some refer to it as a 'second miracle', the first one being its economic growth during Meiji.
81. See Schoppa 91, Chapter 5, for detailed discussion of the process of recentralisation.
82. See Dower 79, p. 312.
83. See for example Ishihara 76, esp. p. 84, regarding the continuation of the war.
84. Considerable footage of this dispute is included in the video "Inside Japan Inc." in the *Pacific Century* series. For fuller treatment of unrest in the mining industry in general see Allen 94.
85. These included the erratic literary genius Mishima Yukio, who had pre-war-style militaristic and ultranationalistic leanings and even had his own private army dedicated to the service of the emperor. Some years later, in 1970, amidst much publicity, he committed 'warrior's suicide' by ritual disembowelment. This was seemingly out of disgust with what he saw as Japan's present effeteness and lack of integrity towards its cultural heritage. The incident caused considerable embarrassment in Japan and concern overseas.
86. In December 1953. See Borton 55, p. 449.
87. Footage of the assassination is included in the video "Inside Japan Inc." in the *Pacific Century* series.
88. For further details of the *Zengakuren* and student unrest, see Steinhoff 84.
89. For detailed critical discussion of these and other *Nihonjinron* works, including some written by westerners, see Dale 86. See also Taylor 85, esp. Chapter 1.

Just as the *Nihonjinron* works of this time tried to analyse the reasons for Japan's success, there had in fact been works written just after the war that tried to analyse the reasons for Japan's defeat. These earlier, negative works are also termed *Nihonjinron* by some scholars, meaning that one has to be careful of the term. For a discussion of these other types of *Nihonjinron*, see Aoki 94.

90. Western academics were far more reserved about his book—though they obviously bought it too—for it contains a number of very questionable assertions. These include claims of student satisfaction, union happiness, and a wonderful welfare system. His work is often treated nowadays as a western example of *Nihonjinron*, with all the negative connotations that entails.

91. Among recognised works, those supportive of Japanese management practices include Pascale and Athos 82, and Morita 87. By contrast, Sethi, Namiki and Swanson 84 is critical. Whitehill 91 tends towards the supportive but is generally balanced and a useful introduction to the subject.

92. Whitehill 91, pp. 236–7.

93. Though these were largely postwar practices, and were genuinely valued by the Japanese through their stress on security and familialism, there were nevertheless indications of early western influence. In the late Meiji period Japanese study missions overseas had identified as worthy of emulation the 'cradle to grave' family-style personnel policies of companies such as Krupp in Germany and National Cash Register in the United States. See Dore 84, esp. pp. 23–4.

94. He was forced to resign in December 1974 after a number of corrupt deals were disclosed in a popular journal. His name is invariably linked with the Lockheed Scandal, in which he received massive paybacks from Lockheed in return for using his position to place aircraft orders with the company. In fact, though his dealings with Lockheed took place in 1972–3, they were not revealed till 1976, and were not the cause of his resignation. For details of these and other scandals involving Japanese politicians and bureaucrats, see Herzog 93, Chapter 7.

95. T. Nakamura 81, p. 230.

96. For details on pollution diseases, see Ueda 83 and Ui 92. For details of the litigation see Upham 87 and McKean 81. See also Barret and Therivel 91 for broader discussion of environmental attitudes.

97. Reischauer 88, p. 118.

98. See, for example, Wolf 83.

99. See Woronoff 90, p. 223, regarding the comparison with California, and Tada 96 regarding the planetary comparison.

100. When Sony bought up Columbia Studios its president, Morita Akio, was astonished at the intensity of anti-Japanese reaction. He made the very important point that it takes two to make a deal. It was not simply a case of Sony buying, but of Coca-Cola selling. He wondered why there was no criticism of the seller, only the buyer. The answer is obviously that people preferred to see it that way. This is emotion not reason. It also raises once again the unfortunate possibility of racist thinking. When it was discovered that Japan controlled 4 per cent of the American economy

there was a similarly extreme reaction, yet Britain had controlled a similar percentage for some time, evoking no reaction.

101. The leading Japanese opponent of official falsification of Japanese history, and of textbook interference in general, is the historian Ienaga Saburō. Ienaga has been fighting a legendary campaign since the 1960s, and has had some but limited success. His greatest success is perhaps the publicity he has generated. For a useful account of his battles, see NLSSTSS 95.

102. On the effects of this speech see, for example, Russell 91, p. 416. Russell gives a useful account of general Japanese attitudes towards blacks.

103. See the report in the *Far Eastern Economic Review*, 18 September 1986, pp. 14–15.

104. The book *'No' to Ieru Nihon* was written jointly with Sony's president Morita Akio, who—fearing his interests in America might be jeopardised—insisted his name be dropped from the authorised English translation that appeared in 1991. Morita's belief that westerners would not pay real attention to anything written in Japanese was similar to Nakasone's assumption in 1986 that westerners would not pick up his Japanese comments about blacks and Hispanics. They both illustrate a widespread Japanese belief that Japan is somehow set apart from the rest of the world, and is a sort of hallowed ground for Japanese only.

105. Ishihara 89/91, p. 28.

106. Ishihara 89/91, p. 61.

107. See Wilkinson 81, p. 221.

108. Figures available in *Asahi Shimbun Japan Almanac*, annually.

109. Woronoff 85, p. 250.

110. Hidaka 1980/84, esp. p. 9.

111. The official translation is 'Peace and Harmony'. This is not exactly incorrect, but seems to prioritise euphony over precise accuracy.

112. Wood 93, p. 11.

113. See the *Japan Times*, Weekly International Edition, 13–19 June 1994.

114. For example, in a period of less than two years the formerly little-known Tōkyō Managers' Union experienced a 20–fold increase in its membership. See the video "Goodbye Japan Corporation".

115. For details see the report in the *Far Eastern Economic Review*, 25 April 1996, pp. 63–4. Late in 1997 Wallace stepped down to be replaced by another westerner, the American James Miller (another former Ford employee).

116. See Yanai 92.

117. The number of Lower House seats had been increased relative to the 466 of the immediate postwar period.

118. The existing number of 511 Lower House seats, which comprised multiple members (up to six) from 129 constituencies, was changed to 500 seats, comprising single members from 300 constituencies plus 200 seats allocated on the basis of proportional representation. The institution of single-seat constituencies was aimed at reducing the chances of corruption, on the grounds that voters are more likely to decide their choice of a single member on the basis of ideology and policy, as opposed to the case of multiple members where material benefits promised to a

constituency (pork-barrel politics) are more likely to become a factor in their choice. The first election under this new system was held in October 1996. Little seems to have changed in practice.

119. He was promised the prime ministership by Kono Yōhei, president of the LDP, if he brought his party into a once-unlikely alliance with the LDP and others. See the *Japan Times*, Weekly International Edition, 4–10 July 1994. Throughout his term he made comments suggesting he was only ever on borrowed time, and was struggling with his conscience. Numerically, the LDP dominated the alliance.

120. These were respectively Aoshima 'Nasty Gran' Yukio and Yokoyama 'Knock' Isamu.

121. McCormack 96, p. 11. Out of 143 gas tanks in Kōbe built by Mitsubishi Liquid Gas, 114 were found to have been constructed below official standards.

122. The main exception is Malaysia's prime minister, Mahathir Mohamad, who has shown a very positive attitude towards Japan and does not seem overly concerned about the past.

123. For example Gluck 92, esp. p. 19.

References

Abbreviations

CEJ: *Cambridge Encyclopedia of Japan*, 1993, Cambridge University Press
CHJ: *Cambridge History of Japan*, 1989 on, 6 vols., Cambridge University Press
JJS: *Journal of Japanese Studies*
JQ: *Japan Quarterly*
KEJ: *Kōdansha Encyclopedia of Japan*, 1983, 8 vols., Kōdansha, Tōkyō
MN: *Monumenta Nipponica*
NZJEAS: *New Zealand Journal of East Asian Studies*

Aikens, C. and Higuchi, T., 1982, *Prehistory of Japan*, Academic Press, New York and London.

Akazawa, T. and Aikens, C. (eds.), 1986, *Prehistoric Hunter-Gatherers in Japan: New Research Methods*, University of Tōkyō Press.

Allen, M., 1994, *Undermining the Japanese Miracle: Work and Conflict in a Coalmining Community*, Cambridge University Press.

Alperovitz, G., 1985, *Atomic Diplomacy: Hiroshima and Potsdam: The Use of the Atomic Bomb and the American Confrontation with Soviet Power*, Penguin, Harmondsworth.

Amino, Y., 1992, "Deconstructing Japan" (trans. G. McCormack), *East Asian History*, No. 3, Australian National University, Canberra, pp. 121–42.

Aoki, T., 1994, "Anthropology and Japan: Attempts at Writing Culture", *Japan Foundation Newsletter*, 22/3, pp. 1–6.

Asahi Shimbun Japan Almanac, annually, Asahi Shimbun Company, Tōkyō.

Aston, W., 1896/1972, *Nihongi: Chronicles of Japan from the Earliest Times to AD 697* (translation of *Nihongi*), Tuttle, Tōkyō (1972 version).

Bachnik, J. and Quinn, C. (eds.), 1994, *Situated Meaning: Inside and Outside in Japanese Self, Society, and Language*, Princeton University Press.

Banno, J., 1971/92, *The Establishment of the Japanese Constitutional System* (trans. A. Stockwin), Routledge, London (Japanese original 1971).

Barber, L., 1994, "The 'Takumi Detachment' Goes to War: The Japanese Invasion of Kelantan, December 1941", *NZJEAS*, 2/1 (June 1994), pp. 39–49.

Barnes, G., 1990, "The 'Idea of Prehistory' in Japan", *Antiquity* 64.245, pp. 929–40.

Barnes, G., 1993a, *China, Korea, and Japan: The Rise of Civilization in East Asia*, Thames and Hudson, London.

Barnes, G., 1993b, "Early Japan", *CEJ*, pp. 42–8.

Barret, B. and Therivel, R., 1991, *Environmental Policy and Impact Assessment in Japan*, Routledge, London.

Bartlett, B., 1978, *Cover-Up: The Politics of Pearl Harbor, 1941–1946*, Arlington House, New York.

Beard, C., 1948, *President Roosevelt and the Coming of the War, 1941*, Yale University Press.

Beasley, W., 1989a, "The Foreign Threat and the Opening of the Ports", *CHJ*, vol. 5, pp. 259–307.

Beasley, W., 1989b, "Meiji Political Institutions", *CHJ*, vol. 5, pp. 618–73.

Beason, R. and Weinstein, D., 1996, "Growth, Economies of Scale, and Targeting in Japan (1955–1990)", *Review of Economics and Statistics*, pp. 286–95.

"Beaten to the Punch", 1991, ABC News, video aired in the United States, 22 November 1991, in the programme *20–20*.

Beauchamp, E., 1983, "Foreign Employees of the Meiji Period", *KEJ*, vol. 2, pp. 310–11.

Befu, H., 1968, "Village Autonomy and Articulation with the State", in Hall and Jansen 68, q.v., pp. 301–14.

Behr, E., 1989, *Hirohito: Behind the Myth*, Villard Books, New York.

Benedict, R., 1947, *The Chrysanthemum and the Sword: Patterns of Japanese Culture*, Secker and Warburg, London.

Bergamini, D., 1971, *Japan's Imperial Conspiracy*, William Morrow, New York.

Bix, H., 1992, "The Shōwa Emperor's 'Monologue' and the Problem of War Responsibility", *JJS*, 18/2 (Summer 1992), pp. 295–363.

Bix, H., 1995, "Inventing the 'Symbol Monarchy' in Japan, 1945–52", *JJS*, 21/2 (Summer 1995), pp. 319–63.

Black, J., 1883/1968, *Young Japan: Yokohama and Edo, 1858–79*, 2 vols., Oxford University Press.

Blacker, C., 1964, *The Japanese Enlightenment: A Study of the Writings of Fukuzawa Yukichi*, Cambridge University Press.

Bleed, P., 1983, "Prehistory", *KEJ*, vol. 3, pp. 158–60.

Bolitho, H., 1983, "Tokugawa Shōgunate", *KEJ*, vol. 8, pp. 52–6.

Bolitho, H., 1989, "The Tempō Crisis", *CHJ*, vol. 5, pp. 116–67.

Bolitho, H., 1993, "The Tokugawa Period", *CEJ*, pp. 67–77.

Borton, H., 1955, *Japan's Modern Century*, Ronald Press, New York.

Borton, H., 1967, *American Presurrender Planning for Postwar Japan*, Occasional Papers of the East Asian Institute, Columbia University, New York.

Bowles, G., 1983, "Japanese People, Origin of", *KEJ*, vol. 4, pp. 33–5.

Bownas, G. and Thwaite, A., 1964, *The Penguin Book of Japanese Verse*, Penguin, Harmondsworth.

Boxer, C., 1968, *Jan Compagnie in Japan, 1600–1817: An Essay on the Cultural, Artistic and Scientific Influence Exercised by the Hollanders in Japan from the 17th to the 19th Centuries*, Oxford University Press.

Boyle, J., 1983, "Sino-Japanese War of 1937–1945", *KEJ*, vol. 7, pp. 199–202.

Braw, M., 1991, *The Atomic Bomb Suppressed: American Censorship in Occupied Japan*, M. E. Sharpe, New York.

Buruma, I., 1985, *A Japanese Mirror: Heroes and Villains of Japanese Culture*, Penguin, Harmondsworth.

Butler, K., 1978, "Woman of Power Behind the Kamakura Bakufu: Hōjō Masako", in Murakami and Harper 78, q.v., pp. 91–101.

Butow, R., 1954, *Japan's Decision to Surrender*, Stanford University Press.

Calman, D., 1992, *The Nature and Origins of Japanese Imperialism: A Reinterpretation of the Great Crisis of 1873*, Routledge, London.

Carr-Gregg, C., 1978, *Japanese Prisoners of War in Revolt: The Outbreaks at Featherston and Cowra during World War II*, University of Queensland Press.

Cholley, J.-R., 1978, "The Rise and Fall of a Great Military Clan: Taira no Kiyomori", in Murakami and Harper 78, q.v., pp. 72–8.

Churchill, W., 1951, *The Grand Alliance*, Houghton Mifflin, Boston.

Clausen, H. and Lee, B., 1992, *Pearl Harbor: Final Judgement*, Crown, New York.

Cohen, T., 1987, *Remaking Japan: The American Occupation as New Deal*, Free Press, New York.

Collcutt, M., 1993, "The Medieval Age", *CEJ*, pp. 60–3.

Cook, H. and Cook, T., 1992, *Japan at War: An Oral History*, New Press, New York.

Cooper, M., 1965, *They Came to Japan: An Anthology of European Reports on Japan, 1543–1648*, University of California Press.

Cooper, M., 1983, "Christianity", *KEJ*, vol. 1, pp. 306–10.

Coox, A., 1988, "The Pacific War", *CHJ*, vol. 6, pp. 315–82.

Cortazzi, H., 1990, *The Japanese Achievement*, Sidgwick and Jackson, London.

Crawcour, S., 1989, "Economic Change in the Nineteenth Century", *CHJ*, vol. 5, pp. 569–617.

Dalby, L., 1983, *Geisha*, University of California Press.

Dale, P., 1986, *The Myth of Japanese Uniqueness*, Croom Helm, London.

Dallek, R., 1979, *Franklin D. Roosevelt and American Foreign Policy, 1932–1945*, Oxford University Press.

Daniels, G., 1993, "Japan at War", *CEJ*, pp. 95–105.

Daniels, R., 1983, "United States Immigration Acts of 1924, 1952, and 1965", *KEJ*, vol. 8, pp. 164–5.

Daws, G., 1994, *Prisoners of the Japanese: POWs of World War II in the Pacific*, William Morrow, New York.

Denoon D., Hudson, M., McCormack, G. and Morris-Suzuki, T. (eds.), 1996, *Multicultural Japan: Palaeolithic to Postmodern*, Cambridge University Press.

Dodo, Y., 1986, "Metrical and Nonmetrical Analyses of Jōmon Crania from Eastern Japan", in Akazawa and Aikens 86, q.v., pp. 137–61.

Doi, T., 1971/73, *The Anatomy of Dependence* (trans. J. Bester), Kōdansha International, Tōkyō (Japanese orig. 1971).

Dore, R., 1959, *Land Reform in Japan*, Oxford University Press.

Dore, R, 1984, "The 'Learn from Japan' Boom", *Speaking of Japan*, 5/47, November 1984, pp. 16–25.

Dower, J., 1979, *Empire and Aftermath: Yoshida Shigeru and the Japanese Experience, 1878–1954*, Harvard University Press.

Dower, J., 1986, *War without Mercy: Race and Power in the Pacific War*, Faber and Faber, London and Boston.

Dower, J., 1992, "The Useful War", in Gluck and Graubard 92, q.v., pp. 49–70.

Dower, J., 1993a, *Japan in War and Peace: Selected Essays*, New Press, New York.

Dower, J., 1993b, "Occupied Japan and the Cold War in Asia", in Dower 93a, q.v., pp. 155–207.

Dower, J., 1993c, "'NI and F': Japan's Wartime Atomic Bomb Research", in Dower 93a, q.v., pp. 55–100.

Duus, P., 1983, "Taishō and Early Shōwa History (1912–1945)", *KEJ*, vol. 3, pp. 197–203.

Duus, P., 1988, "Introduction", *CHJ*, vol. 6, pp. 1–52.

Edwards, W., 1983, "Event and Perspective in the Founding of Japan: The Horserider Theory in Archeological Perspective", *JJS*, 9/2, pp. 265–95.

Edwards, W., 1996, "In Pursuit of Himiko: Postwar Archeology and the Location of Yamatai", *MN*, 51/1, pp. 53–79.

Elison, G. (a.k.a. Elisonas, J.), 1983a, "Oda Nobunaga (1534–1582)", *KEJ*, vol. 6, pp. 61–5.

Elison, G. (a.k.a. Elisonas, J.), 1983b, "Shimabara Uprising", *KEJ*, vol. 7, p. 98.

Elisonas, J. (a.k.a. Elison, G.), 1991, "Christianity and the *Daimyō*", *CHJ*, vol. 2, pp. 301–72.

Farris, W., 1985, *Population, Disease, and Land in Early Japan, 645–900*, Harvard University Press.

Flynn, J., 1944, "The Truth about Pearl Harbor", *Chicago Tribune*, 22 October 1944.

Flynn, J., 1945, "The Final Secret of Pearl Harbor", *Chicago Tribune*, 2 September 1945, and given as appendix in Bartlett 78, q.v.

Forster, C., 1981, "Australian and Japanese Economic Development", in Drysdale, P. and Kitaoji, H. (eds.), 1981, *Japan and Australia: Two Societies and Their Interaction*, Australian National University Press, pp. 49–76.

Francks, P., 1992, *Japanese Economic Development: Theory and Practice*, Routledge, London.

Frei, H., 1991, *Japan's Southward Advance and Australia: From the Sixteenth Century to World War Two*, Melbourne University Press.

Frost, P., 1983, "Occupation", *KEJ*, vol. 6, pp. 51–5.

Fukuzawa, Y., 1872/1969, *Gakumon no Susume*, translated by David Dilworth and Umeyo Hirano as *An Encouragement of Learning*, Sophia University Press, Tōkyō, 1969.

Futabatei Shimei, 1887–9/1967, *Ukigumo* (Drifting Clouds), translated with introduction by Marleigh Ryan in *Japan's First Modern Novel: Ukigumo*, Columbia University Press, 1967.

Gay, S., 1985, "Muromachi *Bakufu* Rule in Kyōto: Administrative and Judicial Aspects", in Mass, J. and Hauser, W. (eds.), 1985, *The Bakufu in Japanese History*, Stanford University Press, pp. 49–65.

Gibney, F., 1992, *The Pacific Century: America and Asia in a Changing World*, Scribners/Macmillan, New York.

Gluck, C., 1985, *Japan's Modern Myths: Ideology in the Late Meiji Period*, Princeton University Press.

Gluck, C., 1992, "The Idea of Shōwa", in Gluck and Graubard 92, q.v., pp. 1–26.

Gluck, C. and Graubard, S. (eds.), 1992, *Shōwa: The Japan of Hirohito*, Norton, New York.

"Goodbye Japan Corporation", 1996, video produced by Film Australia and NHK Japan.

Gordon, H., 1994, *Voyage from Shame: The Cowra Outbreak and Afterwards*, Queensland University Press.

Hadley, E., 1983, "Zaibatsu Dissolution", *KEJ*, vol. 8, pp. 363–6.

Haley, J., 1991, *Authority Without Power: Law and the Japanese Paradox*, Oxford University Press.

Haley, J., 1992, "Consensual Governance: A Study of Law, Culture, and the Political Economy of Postwar Japan", in Kumon, S. and Rosovski, H. (eds.),

1992, *The Political Economy of Japan, Volume 3: Cultural and Social Dynamics*, Stanford University Press, pp. 32–62.

Hall, J. W., 1968, "Feudalism in Japan—A Reassessment", in Hall and Jansen 68, q.v., pp. 15–51.

Hall, J. and Jansen, M. (eds.), 1968, *Studies in the Institutional History of Early Modern Japan*, Princeton University Press.

Hall, J. and Mass, J. (eds.), 1974, *Medieval Japan: Essays in Institutional History*, Yale University Press.

Hall, R., 1949/74, Introduction to *Kokutai no Hongi: Cardinal Principles of the National Entity of Japan*, q.v., pp. 1–47.

Hane, M., 1986, *Modern Japan: A Historical Survey*, Westview Press, Boulder and London.

Hanihara, K., 1991, "Dual Structure Model for the Population History of the Japanese", *Japan Review*, No. 2, pp. 1–33.

Hanley, S. and Yamamura, K., 1977, *Economic and Demographic Change in Preindustrial Japan, 1600–1868*, Princeton University Press.

Hashizume, B., 1996, "Four Poems and an Essay by Hashizume Bun, Poet and Atomic Bomb Survivor" (trans. S. Bouterey), *NZJEAS*, 4/2 (December 1996), pp. 76–90.

Hata, I., 1988, "Continental Expansion, 1905–1941" (trans. A. Coox), *CHJ*, vol. 6, pp. 271–314.

Hearn, L., 1904, *Japan: An Attempt at Interpretation*, Macmillan, London.

Heinrichs, W., 1983, "World War II", *KEJ*, vol. 8, pp. 271–7.

Henshall, K., 1989, "From Sedan Chair to Aeroplane: The Meiji Period Tōkyōite Transported Through Time and Place", *Journal of the Oriental Society of Australia*, 20/21, pp. 70–80.

Henshall, K., 1994, "In Search of the Pioneering Hoyt Brothers: Yankee–New Zealand Entrepreneurs in the 'Frontierland' of Early Meiji Japan", *NZJEAS*, 2/1, pp. 66–86.

Herzog, P., 1993, *Japan's Pseudo-Democracy*, New York University Press.

Hidaka, R., 1980/84, *The Price of Affluence: Dilemmas of Contemporary Japan* (trans. R. Mouer), Kōdansha International, Tōkyō (Japanese orig. 1980).

Higuchi, T., 1986, "Relationships Between Japan and Asia in Ancient Times: Introductory Comments" (trans. K. Pearson), in Pearson 86, q.v., pp. 121–4.

Hirakawa, S., 1989, "Japan's Turn to the West" (trans. B. Wakabayashi), *CHJ*, vol. 5, pp. 432–98.

Hong, W., 1994, *Paekche of Korea and the Origin of Yamato Japan*, Kudara International, Seoul.

Hori, K., 1983, "Mongol Invasions of Japan", *KEJ*, vol. 5, pp. 243–5.

Howard, A. and Newman, E., 1943, *The Menacing Rise of Japan*, Harrap, London.

Hunter, J., 1989, *The Emergence of Modern Japan: An Introductory History Since 1853*, Longman, London.

Hurst, G. C. III, 1976, *Insei: Abdicated Sovereigns in the Politics of Late Heian Japan, 1086–1185*, Columbia University Press.

Hurst, G. C. III, 1983, "Minamoto Family", *KEJ*, vol. 5, pp. 176–8.

Ibuse, Masuji, 1966/9, *Black Rain* (*Kuroi Ame* 1966, trans. J. Bester 1969), Kōdansha International, Tōkyō.

"Inside Japan Inc.", 1992, in the *Pacific Century* video series, q.v.

Iriye, A., 1983, "Sino-Japanese War of 1894–1895", *KEJ*, vol. 7, pp. 197–8.

Ishihara, S., 1976, "A Nation without Morality", in Japan Centre for International Exchange (ed.), 1976, *The Silent Power: Japan's Identity and World Role*, Simul Press, Tōkyō, pp. 75–96.

Ishihara, S., 1989/91, *The Japan That Can Say 'No': Why Japan Will Be First Among Equals* (trans. F. Baldwin), Simon and Schuster, New York and London (orig. *'No' to Ieru Nihon*, with A. Morita, 1989).

Iwao, S., 1993, *The Japanese Woman: Traditional Image and Changing Reality*, Free Press, New York.

Jansen, M, 1983, "Meiji History (1868–1912)", *KEJ*, vol. 3, pp. 192–7.

Jansen, M., 1989, "The Meiji Restoration", *CHJ*, vol. 5, pp. 308–66.

Jansen, M. and Rozman, G. (eds.), 1986, *Japan in Transition from Tokugawa to Meiji*, Princeton University Press.

Japan 1995: An International Comparison, Keizai Kōhō Center (Japan Institute for Social and Economic Affairs), Tōkyō, annually.

Johnson, C., 1982, *MITI and the Japanese Miracle: The Growth of Industrial Policy, 1925–1975*, Stanford University Press.

Kahn, H., 1971, *The Emerging Japanese Superstate*, André Deutsch, London.

Katayama, K., 1996, "The Japanese as an Asia-Pacific Population", in Denoon et al. 96, q.v., pp. 19–30.

Katō, S., 1981, *A History of Japanese Literature: The First Thousand Years* (trans. D. Chibbett), Kōdansha International, Tōkyō.

Kawai, T., 1938, *The Goal of Japanese Expansion*, Hokuseidō, Tōkyō.

Keene, D. (compiler), 1968, *Anthology of Japanese Literature to the Nineteenth Century*, Penguin, Harmondsworth.

Kidder, J. E., 1977, *Ancient Japan*, Elsevier-Phaidon, Oxford.

Kidder, J. E., 1983, "Jōmon Culture", *KEJ*, vol. 4, pp. 72–4.

Kidder, J. E., 1993, "The Earliest Societies in Japan", *CHJ*, vol. 1, pp. 48–107.

Kiley, C., 1974, "Estate and Property in the Late Heian Period", in Hall and Mass 74, q.v., pp. 109–24.

Kiley, C., 1983, "*Ritsuryō* System", *KEJ*, vol. 6, pp. 322–32.

Kimmel, H., 1955, *Admiral Kimmel's Story*, Henry Regnery Co., Chicago.

Kitahara, M, 1989, *Children of the Sun: The Japanese and the Outside World*, Paul Norbury Publications, Kent.

Kitaoka, S., 1992, "Diplomacy and the Military in Shōwa Japan", in Gluck and Graubard 92, q.v., pp. 155–76.

Kojiki—see Philippi 68.

Kokutai no Hongi: Cardinal Principles of the National Entity of Japan, trans. J. Gauntlett, 1949, Harvard University Press, and (this edition) 1974, Crofton Publishing, Massachusetts.

Kosaka, M., 1992, "The Shōwa Era", in Gluck and Graubard 92, q.v., pp. 27–47.

Krauss, E., Rohlen, T., and Steinhoff, P. (eds.), 1984, *Conflict in Japan*, University of Hawaii Press.

Kumagai, F. (with D. Keyser), 1996, *Unmasking Japan Today: The Impact of Traditional Values on Modern Japanese Society*, Praeger Press, Westport and London.

La Fleur, W., 1978, *Mirror for the Moon: A Selection of Poems by Saigyō*, New Directions, New York.

Large, S., 1992, *Emperor Hirohito and Shōwa Japan: A Political Biography*, Routledge, London.

Ledyard, G., 1975, "Galloping along With the Horseriders: Looking for the Founders of Japan", *JJS*, 1/2, pp. 217–54.

Ledyard, G. 1983a, "Yamatai", *KEJ*, vol. 8, pp. 305–7.

Ledyard, G. 1983b, "Horse-Rider Theory", *KEJ*, vol. 3, pp. 229–31.

Leupp, G., 1995, *Male Colors: The Construction of Homosexuality in Tokugawa Japan*, University of California Press.

Li, L., 1992, "The Pan-Asian Ideas of Tachibana Shiraki and Ishiwara Kanji", in Henshall, K. and Bing, D. (eds.), 1992, *Japanese Perceptions of Nature and Natural Order*, New Zealand Asian Studies Association, Hamilton, pp. 63–84.

Low, M., 1990, "Japan's Secret War? 'Instant' Scientific Manpower and Japan's World War II Atomic Bomb Project", *Annals of Science*, vol. 47, pp. 347–60.

MacArthur, D., 1964, *Reminiscences*, McGraw-Hill, New York.

Mason, R. and Caiger, G., 1972, *A History of Japan*, Cassel Australia, Melbourne.

Massarella, D., 1990, *A World Elsewhere: Europe's Encounter with Japan in the Sixteenth and Seventeenth Centuries*, Yale University Press.

Mathews' Chinese–English Dictionary, Harvard University Press (this edition 1966).

Mayo, M., 1974, "Late Tokugawa and Early Meiji Japan", in Tiedemann, A. (ed.), 1974, *An Introduction to Japanese Civilization*, Columbia University Press, pp. 131–80.

McClellan, E., 1969, *Two Japanese Novelists: Sōseki and Tōson*, University of Chicago Press.

McCormack, G., 1996, *The Emptiness of Japanese Affluence*, M. E. Sharpe, New York/Allen & Unwin, Sydney.

McCormack, G. and Sugimoto, Y. (eds.), 1986, *Democracy in Contemporary Japan*, Hale and Ironmonger, Sydney.

McCullough, H., 1959, *The Taiheiki: A Chronicle of Medieval Japan*, Columbia University Press.

McCullough, H., 1971, *Yoshitsune: A Fifteenth Century Japanese Chronicle* (trans. of *Gikeiki*), Stanford University Press.

McCullough, H., 1988, *The Tale of the Heike* (trans. of *Heike Monogatari*), Stanford University Press.

McCullough, W. and McCullough, H., 1980, *A Tale of Flowering Fortunes: Annals of Japanese Aristocratic Life in the Heian Period* (trans. and study of *Eiga Monogatari*), 2 vols., Stanford University Press.

McKean, M., 1981, *Environmental Protest and Citizen Politics in Japan*, University of California Press.

McNelly, T., 1987, "'Induced Revolution': The Policy and Process of Constitutional Reform in Occupied Japan", in Ward and Sakamoto 87, q.v., pp. 76–106.

"Meiji Revolution", 1992, in the *Pacific Century* video series, q.v.

Meiroku Zasshi: Journal of the Japanese Enlightenment (trans. and intro. by W. Braisted), 1874–5/1976, University of Tōkyō Press.

Minear, R., 1971, *Victors' Justice: The Tokyo War Crimes Trial*, Princeton University Press.

Minear, R., 1983, "War Crimes Trials", *KEJ*, vol. 8, pp. 223–5.

Mita, M., 1992, *Social Psychology of Modern Japan* (trans. S. Suloway), Kegan Paul International, London.

Morgenstern, G., 1947, *Pearl Harbor: The Story of the Secret War*, Devin-Adair, New York.

Morishima, M., 1982, *Why Has Japan Succeeded? Western Technology and the Japanese Ethos*, Cambridge University Press.

Morison, S., 1953, *By Land and Sea*, Knopf, New York.

Morita, A. (with E. Reingold and M. Shimomura), 1987, *Made in Japan*, Collins, London.

Morris, I., 1975, *The Nobility of Failure: Tragic Heroes in the History of Japan*, Holt, Rinehart and Winston, New York.

Morris, I., 1979, *The World of the Shining Prince: Court Life in Ancient Japan*, Penguin, Harmondsworth.

Morris-Suzuki, T., 1989, *A History of Japanese Economic Thought*, Routledge, London.

Morris-Suzuki, T., 1994, *The Technological Transformation of Japan from the Seventeenth to the Twenty-First Century*, Cambridge University Press.

Morris-Suzuki, T., 1996, "A Descent into the Past: The Frontier in the Construction of Japanese Identity", in Denoon et al. 96, q.v., pp. 81–94.

Mosley, L., 1966, *Hirohito: Emperor of Japan*, Prentice-Hall, New Jersey.

Murakami, H. and Harper, T. (eds.), 1978, *Great Historical Figures of Japan*, Japan Culture Institute, Tōkyō.

Mushakōji, K., 1976, "The Cultural Premises of Japanese Diplomacy", in Japan Center for Educational Exchange (ed.), 1976, *The Silent Power: Japan's Identity and World Role*, Simul Press, Tōkyō, pp. 35–50.

Nakai, N. and McClain, J., 1991, "Commercial Change and Urban Growth in Early Modern Japan", *CHJ*, vol. 4, pp. 519–95.

Nakamura, M., 1968, *Modern Japanese Fiction 1868–1926*, Kokusai Bunka Shinkōkai, Tōkyō.

Nakamura, T., 1981, *The Postwar Japanese Economy: Its Development and Structure*, University of Tōkyō Press.

Nakamura, T., 1988, "Depression, Recovery, and War, 1920–1945" (trans. J. Kaminsky), *CHJ*, vol. 6, pp. 451–93.

Nakane, C., 1967/70, *Japanese Society*, Weidenfeld & Nicolson, London (Japanese orig. 1967).

Nakane, C. and Oishi, S. (eds.), 1990, *Tokugawa Japan: The Social and Economic Antecedents of Modern Japan*, University of Tōkyō Press.

Nihon Shoki/Nihongi—see Aston 1896/1972.

Nippon video series, BBC, London, 1991.

Nishi, T., 1982, *Unconditional Democracy: Education and Politics in Occupied Japan 1945–1952*, Hoover Institution Press, Stanford.

Nitobe, I., 1905/69, *Bushidō: The Soul of Japan: An Exposition of Japanese Thought*, Tuttle, Tōkyō (1969 edition).

NLSSTSS (National League for Support of the School Textbook Screening Suit), 1995, *Truth in Textbooks, Freedom in Education, and Peace for Children: The Struggle against the Censorship of School Textbooks in Japan*, Tōkyō.

Oda, H., 1992, *Japanese Law*, Butterworth, London.

Okamoto, S., 1983, "Russo-Japanese War", *KEJ*, vol. 6, pp. 345–7.

Okamura, M., 1992, "Babadan A", contribution to Pearson 92, q.v., pp. 49–50.

Okazaki, T., 1993, "Japan and the Continent" (trans. J. Goodwin), *CHJ*, vol. 1, pp. 268–316.

Ossenberger, N., 1986, "Isolate Conservatism and Hybridization in the Population History of Japan: The Evidence of Nonmetric Cranial Traits", in Akazawa and Aikens 86, q.v., pp. 199–215.

"Out of a Firestorm", 1991, in the *Nippon* video series, q.v.

Pacific Century video series, project director Frank Gibney, executive producer Alex Gibney, Jigsaw/Pacific Basin Institute, Santa Barbara, 1992.

Pascale, R. and Athos, A., 1982, *The Art of Japanese Management*, Penguin, Harmondsworth.

Paulson, J., 1976, "Evolution of the Feminine Ideal", in Lebra, J., Paulson, J. and Powers, E. (eds.), 1976, *Women in Changing Japan*, Stanford University Press, pp. 1–23.

Pearson, R. (ed.), 1986, *Windows on the Japanese Past: Studies in Archaeology and Prehistory*, Centre for Japanese Studies, University of Michigan.

Pearson, R., 1992, *Ancient Japan*, George Braziller/Smithsonian Institute, New York.

Peattie, M., 1983, "Ishiwara Kanji (1889–1949)", *KEJ*, vol. 3, pp. 345–6.

Philippi, D., 1968, *Kojiki* (translation and introduction), University of Tōkyō Press.

Piggott, J., 1989, "Sacral Kingship and Confederacy in Early Izumo", *MN*, 44/1, pp. 45–74.

Pineau, R. (ed.), 1968, *The Japan Expedition 1852–1854: The Personal Journal of Commodore Matthew C. Perry*, Smithsonian Institute Press, Washington.

Prange, G. (with D. Goldstein and K. Dillon), 1986, *Pearl Harbor: The Verdict of History*, McGraw-Hill, New York.

"Reinventing Japan", 1992, in the *Pacific Century* video series, q.v.

Reischauer, E., 1964, *Japan: Past and Present*, Duckworth, London.

Reischauer, E., 1988, *The Japanese Today: Change and Continuity*, Harvard University Press.

Reischauer, E. and Craig, A., 1979, *Japan: Tradition and Transformation*, George Allen & Unwin, London, Boston, and Sydney.

Rusbridger, J. and Nave, T. E., 1991/2, *Betrayal at Pearl Harbor: How Churchill Lured Roosevelt into World War II*, Michael O'Mara Books, London/Simon & Schuster, New York (expanded edition 1992).

Russell, J., 1991, "Narratives of Denial: Racial Chauvinism and the Black Other in Japan", *JQ*, 38/4 (Oct.–Dec. 91), pp. 416–28.

"Sacrifice at Pearl Harbor", video produced by Roy Davies, screened on *Timewatch*, BBC2, 5 April 1992.

Sadler, A., 1970, *The Ten Foot Square Hut and Tales of the Heike*, Greenwood Press, Westport.

Sahara, M., 1992, "Yoshinogari: The World of the Wei Dynasty Annals", contribution to Pearson 92, q.v., pp. 154–7.

Sakai, S., 1994, interview with M. Nakazawa, *Tōkyō Journal*, Dec. 1994, pp. 18–21.

Sakudō, Y., 1990, "The Management Practices of Family Business" (trans. W. Hauser), in Nakane and Oishi 90, q.v., pp. 147–66.

Satō, E., 1974, "The Early Development of the *Shōen*", in Hall and Mass 74, q.v., pp. 91–108.

Satō, T., 1990, "Tokugawa Villages and Agriculture" (trans. M. Hane), in Nakane and Oishi 90, q.v., pp. 37–80.

Sayle, M., 1995, "Did the Bomb End the War?", *The New Yorker*, 31 July 1995, pp. 40–64.

Schoppa, L., 1991, *Education Reform in Japan: A Case of Immobilist Politics*, Routledge, London.

Schultz, D., 1987, *The Maverick War: Chennault and the Flying Tigers*, St. Martin's Press, New York.

Seidensticker, E., 1981, *The Tale of Genji* (trans. of *Genji Monogatari*), Penguin, Harmondsworth.

Seigle, C., 1993, *Yoshiwara: the Glittering World of the Japanese Courtesan*, University of Hawaii Press.

Sethi, S., Namiki, N., and Swanson, C., 1984, *The False Promise of the Japanese Miracle: Illusions and Realities of the Japanese Management System*, Pitman, Massachusetts.

Shibusawa, K. (ed.), 1958, *Japanese Culture in the Meiji Period*, vol. 5 (trans. C. Terry), Tōyō Bunko, Tōkyō.

Shillony, B.-A., 1973, *Revolt in Japan: The Young Officers and the February 26 1936 Incident*, Princeton University Press.

Shinoda, M., 1978, "Victory in Battle and Family Tragedy: Minamoto no Yoritomo and Yoshitsune", in Murakami and Harper 78, q.v., pp. 79–90.

Shinoda, M., 1983, "Kamakura History (1185–1333)", *KEJ*, vol. 3, pp. 169–72.

Stanley, T., 1983, "Tōkyō Earthquake of 1923", *KEJ*, vol. 8, p. 66.

Steinhoff, P., 1984, "Student Conflict", in Krauss, Rohlen and Steinhoff 84, q.v., pp. 174–213.

Stockwin, A., 1992, translator's introduction to Banno 1971/92, q.v., pp. xi–xv.

Storry, R., 1963, *A History of Modern Japan*, Penguin, Harmondsworth.

Suzuki, H., 1969, "Micro-Evolutional Changes in the Japanese Population from the Prehistoric Age to the Present Day", *Journal of the Faculty of Science, University of Tōkyō*, s. 5, vol. 3, pt. 4, pp. 279–308.

Suzuki, M., 1992, "As Long As I Don't Fight, I'll Make It Home", in H. and T. Cook 92, q.v., pp. 127–35.

Suzuki, N., 1983, "Eschatology", *KEJ*, vol. 2, p. 231.

Tada, M., 1996, "After the Bubble", *Japan Times*, Weekly International Edition, 29 July–4 August 1996, p. 4.

Takeuchi, R., 1983, "Nara History", *KEJ*, vol. 3, pp. 163–5.

Tayama Katai, 1907/81, "The Girl-Watcher" (*Shōjobyō*, 1907), in *"The Quilt" and Other Stories by Tayama Katai*, translated and introduced by K. Henshall, 1981, University of Tōkyō Press.

Tayama Katai, 1917/87, *Thirty Years in Tōkyō* (*Tōkyō no Sanjūnen*, 1917), translated and introduced by K. Henshall, 1987, in *Literary Life in Tōkyō 1885–1915*, Brill, Leiden.

Taylor, J., 1985, *Shadows of the Rising Sun: A Critical View of the 'Japanese Miracle'*, Tuttle, Tōkyō.

Theobald, R., 1954, *The Final Secret of Pearl Harbor*, Devin-Adair, New York.

Thompson, E., 1945, *Prisoner of War Preliminary Interrogation Report*, submitted 7 July 1945 to HQ First Australian Army Allied Translator and Interpreter Service, Advanced Echelon.

Torao, T., 1993, "Nara Economic and Social Institutions" (trans. W. Farris), *CHJ*, vol. 1, pp. 415–52.

Totman, C., 1980, *The Collapse of the Tokugawa Bakufu, 1862–68*, University of Hawaii Press.

Trefalt, B., 1995, "Living Dead: Japanese Prisoners-of-War in the Southwest Pacific", *NZJEAS*, 3/2 (Dec. 1995), pp. 113–25.

Tsuchihashi, P., 1952, *Japanese Chronological Tables*, Sophia University Press.

Tsukada, M., 1986, "Vegetation in Prehistoric Japan: The Last 20,000 Years", in Pearson 86, q.v., pp. 11–56.

Tsunoda, R., de Bary, W. T., and Keene, D. (compilers), 1964, *Sources of Japanese Tradition*, 2 vols., Columbia University Press.

Tsurumi, S., 1987, *A Cultural History of Postwar Japan 1945–1980*, Kegan Paul International, London and New York.

Turnbull, S., 1987, *Battles of the Samurai*, Arms and Armour Press, London.

Ueda, K., 1983, "Pollution-Related Diseases", *KEJ*, vol. 6, pp. 217–20.

Ui, J. (ed.), 1992, *Industrial Pollution in Japan*, United Nations University Press, Tōkyō.

Umegaki, M. 1986, "From Domain to Prefecture", in Jansen and Rozman 86, q.v., pp. 91–110.

Uno, S., 1992, "Spies and Bandits", in H. and T. Cook 92, q.v., pp. 151–8.

Upham, F., 1987, *Law and Social Change in Postwar Japan*, Harvard University Press.

Utsumi, A., 1996, "Japanese Army Internment Policies for Enemy Civilians during the Asia-Pacific War", in Denoon et al. 96, q.v., pp. 174–209.

Van Wolferen, K., 1989, *The Enigma of Japanese Power: People and Politics in a Stateless Nation*, Macmillan, London.

Vansittart, Lord, 1943, foreword to Howard, A. and Newman, E., *The Menacing Rise of Japan*, Harrap, London.

Varley, H. P., 1983, "Kemmu Restoration", *KEJ*, vol. 4, pp. 191–2.

Vlastos, S., 1989, "Opposition Movements in Early Meiji, 1868–1885", *CHJ*, vol. 5, pp. 367–431.

Vogel, E., 1979, *Japan As Number One: Lessons for America*, Harvard University Press.

Ward, R., 1987a, "Presurrender Planning: Treatment of the Emperor and Constitutional Changes", in Ward and Sakamoto 87, q.v., pp. 1–41.

Ward, R., 1987b, "Conclusion", in Ward and Sakamoto 87, q.v., pp. 392–433.

Ward, R. and Sakamoto, Y. (eds.), 1987, *Democratizing Japan: The Allied Occupation*, University of Hawaii Press.

Weinstein, D., 1995, "Evaluating Administrative Guidance and Cartels in Japan (1957–1988)", *Journal of Japanese and International Economies*, 9, pp. 200–23.

Whitehill, A., 1991, *Japanese Management: Tradition and Transition*, Routledge, London.

Wilcox, R., 1985, *Japan's Secret War: Japan's Race against Time to Build its Own Atomic Bomb*, William Morrow, New York.

Wilkinson, E., 1981, *Misunderstanding: Europe vs Japan*, Chūōkōronsha, Tōkyō.

Williams, H., 1972, *Foreigners in Mikadoland*, Tuttle, Tōkyō.

Williams, P. and Wallace, D., 1989, *Unit 731: The Japanese Army's Secret of Secrets*, Hodder and Stoughton, London.

Wohlstetter, R., 1962, *Pearl Harbor: Warning and Decision*, Stanford University Press.

Wolf, M., 1983, *The Japanese Conspiracy: A Stunning Analysis of the International Trade War*, Empire Books, New York.

Wood, C., 1993, *The Bubble Economy: The Japanese Economic Collapse*, Tuttle, Tōkyō.

Woronoff, J., 1985, *Japan: The Coming Economic Crisis*, Lotus Press, Tōkyō.

Woronoff, J., 1990, *Japan As—Anything But—Number One*, Yohan Publications, Tōkyō.

Yamaguchi, K., 1983, "Early Modern Economy (1868–1945)", *KEJ*, vol. 2, pp. 151–4.

Yamamura, K., 1986, "The Meiji Land Tax Reform and Its Effects", in Jansen and Rozman 86, q.v., pp. 382–9.

Yanai, S., 1992, "The Case for a Coup", *Japan Views*, December 1992, pp. 3–6 (Japanese orig. in *Shūkan Bunshun*, 22 Oct. 92).

Yokota, Y., 1992, "Volunteer", in H. and T. Cook 92, q.v., pp. 306–13.

Yoshida, S., 1961, *The Yoshida Memoirs: The Story of Japan in Crisis*, Heinemann, London.

Glossary of Japanese Terms

ama: nun

amae: childlike dependence on others

aware: = *mono no aware*

bakufu: military government, shōgunate

bunraku: puppet drama

burakumin: 'hamlet people', social outcasts

bushi: warrior, often = *samurai*

bushidō: way of warrior/*samurai*

butōnetsu: 'dance fever', applied to early Meiji cabinet

chōnin: townspeople

chōninmono: tales of merchant success in Tokugawa period

chōzen naikaku: 'transcendental cabinets' of Meiji government

daimyō: feudal lord, esp. in Tokugawa period

endaka: 'high yen' of late 1980s

eta: 'great filth', nowadays *burakumin*

fudai: *daimyō* traditionally loyal to Tokugawa house

fukoku kyōhei: 'rich nation, strong army', slogan popular in early Meiji period

geisha: 'artistic person', originally male but now exclusively female, who entertains clients and at times also functions as a prostitute

genrō: 'original elder', oligarchs of early Meiji government

gunki monogatari: medieval warrior tales

gyōsei shidō: administrative guidance, esp. of economy by government

haiku: form of seventeen-syllable poetry popular since Tokugawa period

han: feudal domain

haniwa: ancient burial object of hollow clay

harakiri: 'stomach cutting', a method of honourable suicide for samurai, often in lieu of execution

heimin: commoners

hinin: 'non-person', nowadays *burakumin*

honne: true inner feelings

ichioku gyokusai: 'self-destruction of the jewel-like hundred million', belief that the entire Japanese nation in World War Two might commit mass suicide rather than surrender

insei: 'cloister government' by retired emperors esp. of late Heian period

jinrikisha: rickshaw

jitō: medieval steward (of land)

jiyū minken undō: 'freedom and people's rights' movement of early–mid-Meiji

jōmon: cord pattern on ancient pottery, and period name

jū-kō-chō-dai: 'heavy-thick-long-big', catchphrase for economic focus of early postwar period

junshi: 'following one's lord in death'

kabuki: colourful form of drama esp. favoured by Tokugawa period merchants

kamikaze: 'divine wind', originally used of storms that helped save Japan from Mongol invasion in the thirteenth century, later used of World War Two suicide-pilots trying to protect nation

kana: Japanese phonetic script

kanri shakai: 'controlled society', used of complacent society of 1960s and 1970s that meekly accepted government control in return for material benefits

kare: aesthetic value of severity and naturalness

kazoku: nobles, from early Meiji period

kegare: impurity

kei-haku-tan-shō: 'light-thin-short-small', catchphrase for economic focus of postwar period after *jū-kō- chō-dai*

keiretsu kigyō: 'aligned company', postwar *zaibatsu*

ko: child or junior in relationship

kofun: ancient burial mound, and period name

koku: measure of rice and land, equivalent to yield sufficient for one person for one year

kokugaku: 'national learning', Tokugawa period nationalism

kokusaika: 'internationalisation', buzz-word of 1980s

kōshokubon: = *ukiyo-zōshi*

kōzoku: imperial family

mappō: Buddhist belief in final decline of humankind, esp. in late Heian period

mono no aware: aesthetic value of the 'sadness of things'

mōretsu-gata: 'fiercely determined type', used of hard workers of postwar period committed to rebuilding nation *musubi*:   bonding with nature, natural purity

Nihonjinron: 'theories about the Japanese', type of self-congratulating and usually simplistic literature of 1970s and 1980s seeking to explain Japan's success, often stressing uniqueness and superiority

nō: restrained form of high-class drama

oitsuke, oikose: 'catch up (the west), overtake', slogan popular in early Meiji period

okashi: aesthetic value of the unusual and diverting

omote: front or surface appearance

oya: parent or senior in relationship

rangaku: 'Dutch learning', usually western learning in general

risshishugi: successism, achievement-orientation, self- help

ritsuryō: ancient law code, *ritsu* being penal sanctions and *ryō* instructions for officials

rōnin: masterless samurai

sabi: aesthetic value of elegant simplicity

sakoku jidai: 'closed country period', later applied to Tokugawa period

samurai: retainer, later warrior

sankin kōtai: 'alternate attendance' of *daimyō* at Edo in Tokugawa period

senryū: humorous form of seventeen-syllable poetry popular in Tokugawa period

seppuku: = *harakiri*

shamisen: three-stringed lute-like instrument

shi-nō-kō-shō: 'warrior-peasant-artisan-merchant', hierarchical social structure in Tokugawa period

shinpan: *daimyō* related to Tokugawa house

shinpū: = *kamikaze*

shizoku: former samurai, from early Meiji period

shōen: medieval estate

shōgun: military ruler

shugo: medieval protector or constable (of land)

shunga: sexually explicit prints of Tokugawa period

sonnō jōi: 'revere the emperor, expel the barbarians', slogan popular in late Tokugawa period

soto: outside

tameshigiri: 'trial cut' of samurai sword on corpses or sometimes live criminals

tatemae: front or pretext, often 'lip service'

tennōsei: emperor-system, used especially of emperor-centred nationalistic indoctrination of mid-Meiji to World War Two

terakoya: schools for commoners in Tokugawa period, originally in temples

tokuju: special procurements for Japanese products from US forces fighting in Korean War

tōyō no dōtoku, seiyō no gakugei: 'eastern ethics, western science', slogan popular in late Tokugawa period

tozama: 'outer' *daimyō* not traditionally loyal to Tokugawa house

uchi: home or inside

ukiyo: 'floating world', originally a reference to transience of life but from Tokugawa period a reference to human relations, including sexual

ukiyo-e: prints of life and people of Tokugawa period, often sexually explicit

ukiyo-zōshi: sexually titillating books of Tokugawa period

ura: rear or that below surface

wabi: aesthetic value of subdued taste

wakon yōsai: 'Japanese spirit, western learning', slogan popular in early Meiji period

yōgaku: western learning

yomihon: popular tales of romance in Tokugawa period

yūgen: aesthetic value of elegant and tranquil otherworldliness

zaibatsu: large financial combine or company

Index

233